AMERICAN RAINBOW

AMERICAN RAINBOW

Early Reminiscences

Francis Hackett

Liveright
New York

Copyright © 1971 by Liveright Publishing Corporation. All rights reserved. No part of this book may be reproduced in any form without permission in writing from the publisher.
1.987654321

Standard Book Number: 87140-514-8
Library of Congress Catalog
Card Number: 72-131269
Designed by Madelaine Caldiero
Manufactured in the United States
of America

CONTENTS

Foreword	vii
Introduction	ix
Arrival	3
Kilkenny	11
The Fallow Year	22
I Go to Work	28
Mrs. Pomeroy	46
Mrs. Hatch's	55
The Tree of Knowledge	65
New Job	77
Book Cloth	83
Christian Brinton	92
Mooney and Medbury	100

George and Mabel	105
John Quinn	112
The Ship	124
Chicago	145
Florida	154
Bobbs-Merrill	161
Marshall Field's	166
Hearst	170
Chicago Evening Post	182
Hull House	187
North Side	212
The Erskines	233
More Chicagoans	236
Joe Patterson	240
The Rebel	250
"Dear"	253
Getting Away	262
Politics	273
The New Republic	286

Foreword

Robert Frost wrote poetry about his people—I write prose. But it is people whom an artist feels, and if he brings in group or political life, it is for its inescapable effect on people. I have admitted politics in my story for the sake of the story. Not for the political program or will-to-power.

This book covers youth. It has structure. The motives that compelled me to emigrate are in my bones. No celebrities are in the book except as they are part of the structure. The story happens to deal partly with Ireland, but it might as well be Poland, Spain, or Russia. It disentangles a boy from the Victorian conventions and shows how he grows up. It shows how the youngest of six sons, deep in a political crisis in childhood, struggles to adapt himself in the usual laconic, pleasure-seeking, amused and amusing life of the provincial, middle-class gentry. And how he emigrates without shedding this convention, but comes, underneath, to work out a relation to people of every kind. He has to, because he has to work with them. He has no tricks. He is working out a relationship. Step by step this brought people into focus, and this means hundreds of people, those I worked with, those I worked for, not having any other purpose than to know and elucidate them.

The essence of the book is its revelation of a life—a young Irishman exploring equalitarian and inequalitarian America. Luckily I wrote home every week, and I have those letters. They were all buttoned up, but I know how and where I *learned* America.

The rainbow does not vanish, but it recedes.

Francis Hackett

Introduction

Off and on, between about 1922 and 1955, Francis Hackett wrote his reminiscences, or at them, rather. He could not quite decide whether he would do them in the third person, or "soothed into a novel," or in the first person. As was his habit, he made many versions and did not finish them, but that was usually because some other pressing task had to be attended to. Between those years, being freelances, we moved about a great deal, both in Europe and in the United States, and our "papers" would get still a little more scrambled. But he did write long sequences, and fragments as well that could be arranged in such sequence as he, I know, would have fixed on himself.

He did not continue them after he joined the original staff of *The New Republic* in the year of its preparation, 1913. He meant them to close in 1914, at least that part of them, because that marked the end of an era for the world and also for his own life. Of course he continued to comment in writing on what he was experiencing—he couldn't not do it. As he wrote once: "I was born to express myself"—but he reminisced in letters or in diaries. ("I have the largest collection of diaries for January of anyone.") That was not in a form he would necessarily have used for publication.

Very few proper names have been omitted or changed by him. It would have been contrary to his respect for privacy, for me to have restored them. In any case, Francis Hackett did not describe people and his experience of them for the sake of news, scandalous or otherwise, but because it fitted into his attempt to convey his point of view about life, not only his own life. That in describing people he also gives the best possible picture of what he himself was like is something I am sure did not occur to him.

He had a fabulous memory, whether it was for an elevator boy or an unhappy millionaire.

When in the novel *That Nice Young Couple* he used his notes from the 1912 Democratic Baltimore Convention, he changed some of the names of the politicians, and as I haven't found all of those notes I'm not sure I've restored all the names. In general, except for a few connecting sentences I've added nothing.

Signe Toksvig

AMERICAN RAINBOW

Arrival

The first man I saw on the New York pier was a black-skinned human being. He was out in front of the shed, waiting to catch a hawser from the *Furnessia*. The friendly sunlight dwelt on him—it was October 6, 1901—as he stood by the bollard in his faded light blue overalls, gazing up for the rope that was to be cast to him. America was his fate. It was going to be mine, so we would be having the country in common.

That was a big surprise to me—a colored man. I knew of them, since one had come with a circus to Kilkenny. But here was this one, easy and free, giving a hand to us to land in his country. That was something new. It was all going to be new and different.

My spirits were high. For the moment I was in charge of an extraordinarily leaky baby, Tilly Hackett's baby, while the mother, with the blackest hair and dark sweeping eyes that went with her impetuosity, was feverish with anxiety about her grips. Funny word, grips. Madge, her much younger, red-haired sister, to my eyes, seemed to be amused and self-possessed.

For Madge and Tilly it was a homecoming. They lived in Bay Ridge, and two Hacketts, my brother Eddie (later to call himself Byrne) and my cousin Ned, were on the pier to meet them. Ned was married to Tilly, and my brother was to marry Madge. I was free to unite with America in surreptitious excitement. If you ever see a family reunion with rather a chubby young man on its outskirts, wearing pince-nez and a pair of black gloves, his eyes twinkling and snapping at all around him, be sure that "suppression of the truth" (the word is five hundred years old) is imposed on him by his unimportance in the tribe. The unimportant are surreptitious.

Ned Hackett giggled when he saw my pince-nez. They were the kind that connected the lenses with a straight bar. The poet Yeats used to wear them, for the reason that both of us bought our glasses at the same place, Prescott's in Merrion Row. "We'll have to get you American glasses instead of those," he said genially. I grinned. Luckily I had not copied Yeats by wearing a black ribbon out of my glasses.

My heart had risen at the sight of land that morning. October had brushed the dying leaves with old gold, and the dry earth was astonishingly seared after a long summer. It must have been on Staten Island I saw the frame houses. I was used to stone houses and brick houses, or to thatched cabins with mud walls. It was marvelous to see such differences. The sky over New York was flawless, and it seemed much further away than the vaporous Irish sky. The warmth of the air was too much for a youth wearing a thick Irish tweed suit, but it was part of the novelty. Everything was like a vacation; it was all so gay and foreign. Yet under the excitement, the contrast that refreshes the imagination, I was aware, while grinning my way into a new family, that Ireland was forsaken. It was ten years to the day since Parnell died. Now I was entering into fraternity with another people, the white man and the black man.

It was in four-wheel cabs, as I remember, that we drove out to Bay Ridge, but I could not leave the Furnessia without a word, just saying goodbye to Captain Black at the foot of 23rd St. and the North River.

To tell the truth, it had been hellish on the *Furnessia*, or rather on the big ocean by which our little Anchor Liner had been so contemptuously pounded. Except for the serene crossing from Dublin (North Wall) to Greenock, I had never been on broad water in my life. The ocean had frightened me. At eighteen I should not have been scared. Those September gales were just equinoctial gales, nothing to be excited about. But when I lay in my dark bunk, when the doleful oil lamp creaked and the ship's timbers crunched as the waves smashed into her, I could only hold my breath until the shuddering vessel started to right itself, only to be jolted by another blow, for all I knew the decisive one. All that dirty weather was in the past, if anything is ever in the past, and after the first horrible week or ten days we had graduated from ragged skies to the good American weather. It was such bountiful good weather, warming our bones, and nearly all the haggard, seasick women came on deck. Mr. Neumeyer and myself stood in the prow, and he said like a fond proprietor, "It's what we call the Indian summer, it's always like this in October." Wonderful country, America! I had gone to Clongowes. I was a little superior, a Jesuit boy, inclined to be sniffy. But after the terrifying storms I was less ready to dispute any talk that collided with my Clongownian presumptions. An angry ocean puts a budding intellectual in his place, for a week or two.

In any event the air was no longer raw and clammy. As we came nearer the October continent, the heaving seas and slobbering clouds off Newfoundland changed to a cleaner light; at first flashes of sun and then warmth, and in the western sky the little clouds gold at the edges. The land seemed to reach out for us to welcome us. All those steamship folders that had wooed me in Dick Callanan's ticket office, with their sumptuous harvests and their blue heavens, were a fraud when we labored in the murk, but now it was blue, the *Furnessia* sheered through it, and we gazed to the horizon beyond which lay the sunning land. These last evenings were a promise. They picked me up as a fat warm nurse picks up a bambino. My young heart lifted to America.

It was just as well, for already it was sore. During those

gruesome days at the beginning, I had endured agony. An American Indian who has gone through puberty rites, standing up to the pains inflicted on the young ones who have to pass from childhood into manhood, might smile at my lack of toughness. A youngster in fox-hunting Ireland whose face has been daubed by the bloody stump of a fox's tail, he has had a puberty rite. But I had no Indian training, and I had not followed in my father's hoofprints by learning to hunt. My soreness was no less primitive than an Indian's, but it was puberty worked out surreptitiously and in private.

At eighteen I had a thin education and six governing passions that might lead me to thicken it. The first was a passion for Ireland as against the British Empire. The second was for Parnell's Ireland as against the Catholic Church. The third was a passion against the British Empire as such. The fourth was against the Catholic Church as such. The fifth was a passion for literature as such, and the last was a passion for a red-haired girl.

The girl had let me fall in love with her, while she was visiting in Ireland, because she was lonely for the man she was to marry, and then when she knew I would turn up in America she said it was all a mistake, she was soon to be married.

These are puberty rites, if you choose to look at them that way. I writhed on the floor of my small cabin, dragging that arrow out of my entrails, and it was agony. Between that injury to lust and pride and the terror of the storm, I was Catholic enough to think of praying. That too was an agony. I refused to pray. I was extricating myself from the girl, from Ireland, and from the Church. Terror-striken as I was, with that dim oil lamp whinging above me, the stench of the ship inescapable, and the cold in my marrow, I still throttled those violent feelings. The power of not-praying is a considerable one. I was scared almost to death, but if I was ever to face the future I had to do it free from fear, and the religion I had been taught made me afraid of the wrong things and for the wrong reasons. It made me dependent, especially on priests and their exploitation of dependence. In the midst of my turmoil, I believed that my only hope was to go it alone, since my fears were feebleness of spirit which I could only increase by invoking Heaven. For ten years I had been going to confession and making acts of contrition without ever reaching any sense of moral security, and at this point I was aware that I had either to defer forever to this futile routine or I had to break with it. It was essentially, as I felt it, a surrender of the will to an institution that I no longer respected. In the throes of that long, dark, turbulent voyage, I succeeded in deciding to leave the Catholic Church. I have never regretted it.

It was after the Boer War and the world was at peace. All was serene, except for McKinley who had just been assassinated. But even in that golden age we were homesick, heartsick, seasick. We did not leave our native countries out of sheer exuberance.

While still at the foot of 23rd Street and the Hudson but before we left the *Furnessia* I wanted to bid Captain Black goodbye. Very different the women looked, dressed for going ashore from those forlorn figures who had crumpled into themselves with each thud of the sea until we were over the worst of it, and they had dared to come to the rail, one hand clasping a shawl, a Scottish plaid; and here they were flocking around the burly Captain Black, just as keen for entrancement as if they had never wilted. He wore a short beard, and he had a warm paternal manner than went well with his double-breasted coat. He joked with them. They sparkled. They felt he was somebody. He was a captain. The best place on the ship was the bridge, and once he left the captain's table he went up a few steps to authority. It never occurred to me to curry favor to worm up that ladder. Up there, his back turned, his eye on the ocean or scanning the stars, he had to be master or the sea would be master. It was no reflection on owner, or shipper, or crew, or passenger that he turned his back on us. It was strange that his tangible mastery, like a surgeon's or a scientist's, meant something I respected, as if he were remote as a priest at the altar. While for an actual priest, in spite of awestruck experiences when I had tried to serve Mass at Clongowes, I had lost my respect. And I was never to lose respect for the man with a master's certificate. I never lost sight of Captain Black. It was no secret in the merchant marine during the First World War that captains could be frayed to shreds, and by that time he was wearing out in the grim fight with submarines. But there was no dog-eat-dog about his officers. They did his stint as well as their own, true to a hierarchy that had meaning for them. The bridge was theirs, inviolate as far as I was concerned, and justified in making one man captain and the rest subordinate.

Were these the Scots who one wi'Wallace bled? If so, they had bled dry. They were clattering facts into one another like coal chuting into cellars. No sound is more dreary if you are independent of housekeeping, though none more like music if you've frozen. My imagination could be caught by a sea captain, but I could make nothing of implacable anecdotes about machines, about real estate transactions, about one man's hernia and another man's gall bladder. Had these Scots sprung from the jocund earth of Robert Burns? Or even from Carlyle's hand tillage? I put down my Carlyle, not that I was making head or tail of it, and asked myself what kind of life these grubbers were leading, with their relentless monologues about families, diseases, hotel bills, travels; one talking as the other sucked his pipe, or twisting his neck to look at me like a credit man inspecting a poor risk. I wasn't having any. There were no

It was not that way in the smokeroom. This was a squat saloon on the upper deck, blown by winds every time a passenger opened the door; yet for all this gustiness smelling of stale tobacco and lemons. It was pure freshness, however, after the vile air that bullied us between decks, and once the heaving had subsided, I curled into a corner near the door and tried to bury myself in a book, half-listening to the Scots on their way back

to an America that had macadamized them for business.
invaluable facts to be gleaned from my ignorant head, nothing about drainage, turnips, mangel wurzels, freight rates, or bog turf.

Then a rugged Scot spoke to me. "Young man," he said, "ye must never do that. Ye were never brought up to put a book face downward when it was open."

He had me there, the old Tartan.

He closed the book, which belonged to the Anchor Line. "By Thomas Carlyle, 'Sartor Resartus!' " He looked at me. It was as good as a Masonic Grip.

"He was readin' another buke yesterday," a wee man said. "I believe he's read about everything."

The statement, though shockingly loose for a Scot, was meant to soothe my feelings, and it gave me intense pleasure. The other Scots, cormorants for a bit of novelty, began to go silent and look me over.

"Ye're not Scotch?" said one.

"Oh, no!"

"From the North of Ireland, maybe?"

"God help me, no. From the South."

It trembled on the older man's tongue to ask the covenanter's hard question, "Are ye Catholic?" But he skirted it. "What have ye in mind to do in the States?"

I lifted my eyebrows. I didn't know. God would provide. "It's got to be either a priest or a policeman," said a younger man, and they chuckled one and all. "Or a saloonkeeper," said a wit. That covered the subject.

They were not as stereotyped as they sounded. In a smoke-room where ideas have to be glib to pass current promptly, men resort to stock jokes and standard teasing. But the set shapes into which the immigrant would be stuffed left me at a loss. It was easy to see these were stale ideas, but I could detect and reject them. But it was one thing to be critical. It was another to know what I'd fit into. And that was what had puzzled the two American women I had traveled with. They were bringing me to their home in Bay Ridge, but what was I to do? They hoped Ned could guide me.

"Do you know what you want to be, Francis?"

"Happy, naturally. Very happy. And wealthy."

And then Ned would say, "We'll educate you yet. Just a moment, I have to stoke the furnace."

How does one stoke a furnace? I didn't know. Aren't the Americans practical! I felt like an imbecile Robinson Crusoe, R. Crusoe in a stiff collar. Down below I could hear the raucous furnace.

Our street was like the dry bed of a yellow river, still grooved and gutted by rains that had raced downhill. Ours was a rather gaunt frame house, perched on a green bank above this unimproved street. Vacant lots surrounded the house, most of them tangled with briars and long grasses and sumac. The crickets and the bullfrogs were still audible in October, and it breathed of freedom from the city to be so far away from it, to hear these sounds at night, the cadence of the new continent. I drank in those sounds. The fireflies were magical. And frost bit with sharp teeth in a few weeks, the bracing weather that was rare in Ireland.

We lived out near Fort Hamilton for economy. Ned Hackett, gallant in his desire to make a go of it, took rather a wary attitude toward this newcomer from Ireland. Was he to be a barnacle? Would he take hold? I didn't even make my own bed or learn to tend the furnace. In Kilkenny it was Big Nellie who made the beds and Paddy McGrath who looked after the coal and the ashpit. It always astonished me to arrive at Bay Ridge after job-hunting all day and find my bed dishevelled and yawning at me. "Home was never like this."

Kilkenny

Now let me say something very serious. To my mind Freud was not a genius, but one idea of his, not original with him, but intelligently developed and exploited by him with great thoroughness, is the idea that our earliest impressions are indelible. I don't suppose that many educators or psychiatrists quarrel with this. It does not imply, to my mind at least, that we are incorrigibly determined by our early impressions. We are not machines. But our prejudices are indelible because we take them to be normal, and if we accept our first impressions as establishing the normal, we hold on to them with the tenacity of crabs. Most people do not grow into the new country they are transplanted to. The Dane who is searching for sago flour in New York is no different from the American who hunts for Jello in Florence, and if you take this as a crude symbol of urgencies on a shopper's plane, what of the deep urgencies of a child's loves and hates in the immigrant? They imported loves and hates, in terms of their own native lands, and for many years every soul of them went on living in relation, not to the new patria, but to the old one. On the surface and for practical purposes it may make little difference. A Greek can up-and-down an elevator at $34 a week, and his psyche is independent of it. But his psyche, still indelibly Greek, must give and take with the American psyche, which has either to nourish that side of life or become a dustbowl. That is why I must revert to what I came from and what remained so long dominant within me, in the long process of American impatriation. We are accustomed, oddly enough, to see the process with great clarity when we think of American expatriates, Erza Pound, Henry James, T. S. Eliot. But the word immigrant, seldom applied to them, includes the word expatriate, which never applied to those of us who came to America in exactly the same spirit of adventure that sent such Americans abroad. True, we came to earn our living, to be clerks or laborers. But so did T. S. Eliot go to earn his living as a bank clerk. We who came here as expatriates brought Europe with us, whether we were huddled to Ellis Island or came down the gangplank to 23rd Street without a passport. We were first-class passengers who were expatriating ourselves. We had paid $45 for a first-class ticket.

My father had a strong feeling about Ireland and a passion for the welfare of its people. He became a doctor in Ballyragget, a village in Kilkenny, because his mother was a Byrne from Kilkenny, and he had a rich cousin—James Sullivan, the brewer. He was a spirited young man, even if encumbered with dependents. He planted his mother and sister in Callan, not far distant, where they had lean years, with Sheffield plate on the sideboard to remind them of departed prosperity. My mother would often pause in cleaning the family silver and say with her unsparing candor, "That was the tray that Grannie used when she fed the chickens." She could be a crashing realist, my mother. She saw no romance in the genteel Hacketts.

From the beginning I think I grasped why my mother felt aggrieved; I sided with her. I saw with her eyes as children do. I took not the slightest interest in our family tree. I pruned it of all its exotic buds and blossoms, scoffed at its tapering branches and the magic lanterns that bobbed at the thin end, not that a few Spanish marquises and a grandee or two could fail to tickle anthropological inquisitiveness, but all titles were suspect. It was only through my father, so innately delicate and agreeable, yet so free of snobbery, that we sidled over to amenity.

He had no flippancy, yet he was gay as a lark, an enchanting father, and a man of principle. You can't beat the Irish when they come through. He fought his corner, but he combined felicity of human intercourse with undeviating vision of his goals. When he dined at the Barracks in Kilkenny, and they drank a toast to the Queen, it was accepted that he didn't join them. They laughed and said, "You old Fenian!"

From the day I was born, January 21, 1883, to the day Parnell died, he was the hero of our saga. Those who follow "the party line" have tried, in the scant pages they devote to Irish history, to belittle the political leadership of Parnell for the sake of a neater emphasis on the class struggle. It is Michael Davitt who wanted state ownership of the land, as opposed to the tenants' proprietorship, and the Communists think of Parnell as a whistle stop. But if these victims of a bad system of tenure, crushed by famine in the forties and menaced by famine in the seventies, were as a class given a fresh start, with land under their feet, by this leader Parnell, the merits of state ownership related to another chapter. If you live at an economic whistle stop, you take the train that stops there. Parnell was our man, and Davitt, the economic radical, stood with the Church in casting the first stone at Parnell taken in adultery. In all the work of James Joyce—*Dubliners, The Portrait of the Artist, Ulysses,* and *Finnegan's Wake*—the travail of Joyce's spirit turned on something much more radical than land tenure. It turned on Parnell's clash with the Church in politics. It was Ireland's Dreyfus case, and nothing in our lives, before or since, was of such consequence.

"Your father, God bless him," said a man to me several years ago, "he was a caution. He knew every voter in the borough, down to the last man. If any anti-Parnellite was in the poorhouse hospital, when the election was due, he was sure to be at death's door. But if he was a Parnellite, barely able to drag one foot after the other, 'Get up, you blackguard,' your father would say, 'aren't you blooming?' "

"Did they die of it?"

"Not a bit of it. They saved the election."

It was Parnell's campaign in 1890 that was life and death for us. I was then "a bright boy of seven summers," and at seven life is black and white, the age of heroes and dragons. What could I know of Parnell? Only that my father was his right-hand man in Kilkenny. I dogged my father's heels, but there was plenty of action to excite loyalty. The priests spared no punches. Our parish priest denounced my father from the altar: "He feeds the poor of Kilkenny on dug, skin, and bone." He denounced my mother: "The women of that committee should be tied to an ass's back and driven from the city with their face toward the ass's tail." Hot shot! Hackett père, Hackett mère and all the little Hacketts rose from their pew and left the house of God. The same priest incited the miners of Castlecomer to throw lime in Parnell's eyes. My father was with Parnell when they succeeded in doing it. How fat a lime it was, he could not know, and there was no time to lose, so he opened Parnell's eyes, and in lieu of any other means, he ran his tongue over the eyeballs, until water was available. I once met a man who said to me, "It was to my house in Gowran that your father came for warm water."

In Carlow, as they sat in a brake at a later meeting, a sharp stone was thrown at Parnell. It missed him, but struck my father in the eyes, smashing his glasses. The broken glass ruined his left eye. He was in a Dublin hospital for five or six weeks. Parnell coming to visit him whenever he was in Dublin.

It may be imagined how a child feels when a valiant leader under attack becomes the "Captain, My Captain," of his endangered father. It might have been Hitler, or Stalin, Robert E. Lee, or Napoleon. Loyalty is stirred to the depths in a child by the graphic and tragic episodes of partisanship, not by the laying of ice bags on a hot head. At the age of six, Walter

Lippmann once told me, he was ardent for William Jennings Bryan.

The words that my father's committee put on a poster, "No Dictation from Any Source Whatsoever," summed up the issue at that moment. A friar denounced the Workingmen's Club in a lively phrase. He called it "the synagogue of Hell." It was the first club I ever joined. A card was given to me, and I went up to Walkin Street one Saturday evening to find out about an excursion to Maryborough. Because of scarlatina I had never seen Parnell in Kilkenny. I wanted to go with the club to Maryborough.

The small club room upstairs was massed with members. There was no room to move, but pints of porter were handed from upstretched hands to the thirsty mob out of reach of the bar. The clamor was wild. The heat was furious. The excitement was appalling. And those acrid words, "the synagogue of Hell," gripped me with fear. I ran home, burrowing my way out of the uproar.

But I had never seen Parnell, I must see him. Someone would be on the Excursion that I knew. I stole out of our house before breakfast and ran to the station. The train was ready to leave, and my cronies had been swallowed up in the mob. On the verge of tears I appealed to a man with a familiar face. He was annoyed. "We'll miss it. Lep in here." We bruised into a crowded box-carriage. "Have ye a ticket?" I had no ticket. "Begob, ye'll be put off. We're stopping for the ticket checker." "Ah, put him under the seat." So I bundled myself under the low wooden seat, trouser legs in front of me. The tickets were collected, they told me to come out after a long time, and I sat clumped like a fowl. The meeting had started by the time we dragged into Maryborough.

He was far away on a wagonette, standing up slim and erect, a bearded man, wearing a tweed deerstalker's cap, a peak to the front and a peak behind. His words were wafted over the silent crowd in a landlord's accent. I caught a syllable here and there, I could not follow him. But, the sight and sound of him were what I wished for. They were to live with me, to feed the flame of imagination, the flame of a free Ireland.

I had one step to mount into the Tholsel, a few months later, but before I could set my foot on it, hurrying from school, Dr. Russell stood tall in my path. "Hello, young man, I have sad news for you. Your friend Parnell is dead." I fell back. I brushed past him, not believing his words. At Coyle's, the stationer's, a pink telegram was pasted on the window. My flesh winced. I read it. "W.H. Smith died today." A wave of scornful glee swept through me, the doctor was wrong. I rounded the corner. On the other window was another pasted telegram, and then I was afraid. "Charles Stewart Parnell . . ."

At eight years of age pain can be absolute. Not until the executions of 1916, when the twenty leading men in the Easter Rebellion were sent to the firing squad did I feel pain like it. A nation is a selfishness, but inside it selflessness can be won for the nation's destiny. The day Franklin Roosevelt died it was evoked in Americans.

And Parnell, deserted by so many of his lieutenants, disowned by the Church, rejected by Gladstone and the Low Church English, wasting in his bitter consuming of spirit and vainly rallying the people, was at the same time no hero whose cause was merely personal. On that journey back from having seen him, we stopped at Abbeyleix, and a huddling group in dark frieze coats began to boo us out of the twilight. One man in our small carriage, the son of a schoolteacher named Donleavy, stormed to the window to demolish them. He could not open it. He smashed it, then with a harsh yelp of fury he shouted, "Ye'd be eating sods of turf, if it wasn't for Parnell!" Such was the core of it. He had won the land for them. He had set no limits to their dream. A half-American, whose grandfather had commanded Old Ironsides, Parnell had in him the seeds of the American Revolution and a tameless defiance of the island pharisees. His was a death and a resurrection, and he could love. That pale star is not extinguished.

But compromise, my dears! Should he not have compromised? Bah, bah, white sheep who end as mutton.

This half-American went with my father to Fennessy's Mills to look at the River Nore. Could it be electrified? He knew that the English who sold coal to Ireland did not want electric power developed there. It was not the English who harnessed the Shannon for electric power. It was a home government who hired Germans. The English "experts" said it could not be done. Parnell knew the English expertise. He also knew his Irish banking clique, his Irish police who looked on the Irish flame as fire extinguishers, his magistrates who were recruited from the landlord class, and he knew his landlords. He was a landlord. He lived in a country of Catholics that had no Catholic university. If Guinnesses wanted a good man, he had to be an Oxford or Cambridge man. If the Bank of Ireland or the police inspectors wanted a good man, he had to be the same. Parnell knew the Oxford and Cambridge touch. He was a Cambridge man. How could a nation of peasants come up if there were no ladders? They could not go to Oxford, or Cambridge, or to Trinity in Dublin to learn how to climb ladders.

They left for America, these peasants—nearly five million of them. Triumph of statesmanship. They broke out on the body politic in America, Charley Murphy, Boss Croker, Honey Fitz, Tom Taggart, James Curly, Boss Hague. Triumph of survival. My father, after all, was born in the year of the famine. And in the year 2049 some Jew will be saying, "My father was born in the year of Dachau." These are the stuffs from which ruling classes weave sackcloth, in cities that are in ashes. But who except the Ben Hechts suppose that there is wisdom in vindictiveness. There are Jews who suffer injury. There are also Jews who inflict injury.

To get such things in line, we were fortunate in having a father who had no vindictiveness. He lost an eye. Did he say "an eye for an eye?" Not he. Though the ease into which he was born so soon became distress, he was really a squire at heart, and this gave him comprehension of the class he was fighting. Turgeniev's *Sportsman's Sketches*, published in 1852, was a new testament of its kind, a cry of awakening, and it spoke for men like my father. To hunt, to fish, to shoot, to gamble, to make love—this was the acme of experience. With his Havana cigars, his delight in a bottle of Mumm, his love of hunting, my father had still the zest of bachelordom in him—the savor of sport, its flashing zip in the nerves, and yet its crisp code and fastidiousness. It was so insane, however, that my mother could never be sure. As she went around the house, her face flushed, whistling as she dusted, the truth that plodded through her mind was that if John didn't save his money, we'd be RUINED. And in the hall he hung a series of engravings which pointed the moral with ungloved hands, "The Road to Ruin." It prettified Hogarth. I took it seriously.

Yet my father was disciplined. He drank very little. He was an extraordinarily busy doctor—Poor Law doctor, sanitary officer, Infirmary doctor, coroner for South of the County, and so on. Also he hunted two days a week. Off he trotted, with a monocle in the rim of his hat, the big brute of a horse ready for anything. And when he came home, as I had the joy of pulling off his muddy boots, and as he sat to his beefsteak and stout, Mr. Keane of *The People* or the man from *The Moderator* would ask him about the run. Pappy knew every fox and every covert in the country.

Up to the Kilkenny election of 1890, where the priests grappled with Parnell to overthrow him, my father was the blithe Irishman of the seventeenth century. My mother was boldly handsome, but she was predictable; my father was quicker than the eye, off in the middle of the night to "cases." Notified of a sudden death by a constable with a telegram, dressed for dinner at the Barracks in his evening clothes, singing Irish songs off-key with beguiling smiles, elated by visitors as if they were wine, his life swinging in an orbit at which I blinked in vain, his perfection as a father was as certain as the sun unless a sudden shadow fell on us. Brisk and sparkling, brief and fastidious, he wore his beard as if a ruff should frame it. To watch him depart for a shoot on a sidecar, Harvey Duff and the other setters leaping up on the well and on the seats, with a tarpaulin over his knees to keep himself and his gun from the merciless rain—that was the father we partook of. Our little legs ran for him; we attended on his wishes; his was the whip-hand without a whip. He never swung us off our feet or tossed us in the air or got down on the floor to play with us. But he was a sunbeam beyond our reach, even the dust dancing in his rays. He was never gross, never tipsy, never unkind. Yet he was rich in mood and unpredictable.

But this was the Ardilaun side of him, the Irish squire, with no steel mills or chain stores or steamships or nitrate works behind him. His "means of production" were all in a bottom drawer in the study to be put in a black bag when Nurse Kavanagh alerted him. They and the little box he had for autopsies were barred from the children, as well as his cigars, his Rhine wine, his Zola and Ouida. But what he never barred were the periodicals he bought at auction from the Club. He bought the *Ladies' World*, edited by Oscar Wilde, and *The Academy*, the first intellectual weekly I knew, *Truth*, *The Spectator* and *The Strand* for Sherlock Holmes. This was the other side of squirearchy, not so much the Graphic and Black and White as the news of books and the scintillation of mind. We were ravenous for it.

Politics is the life of the will—a tug of England's will against Ireland's, and of the Church's against the Parnellites. I have dwelt on it for its bearing on a boy's character. Except for a few countries, the children of the present epoch have been torn by partisanship more lacerating than ours. The Irish once bore the label "pugnacious." They'd fight at the drop of a hat. "Is this a private fight, or can anybody get into it?" "Who'll step on the tail of my coat?" We were deplored, especially by the Germans, for lack of civic discipline. We would be at each other's throats if England did not police us. Ah, wait! Just wait! Superficial and supercilious observers said embittering words. The Irish said them of the Irish. Only few took the trouble that Lecky did to inquire into the cause and consequence of conquest and an army of occupation. The tribal Irish had been conquered, occupied, deported, dispersed, dispossessed, pauperized, disfranchised. They had been disarmed to make sure that Britain was protected on the flank. Their very name as Irishman was taken from them. If a man was a scoundrel, he was listed in the *Encyclopedia Britanica* as an Irish scoundrel. If he was a man of good repute, he'd be listed as "English author," born in that famous English county, Tipperary.

As a small boy, avid for sweets, I discovered that the Parnellite shopboys would give me raisins and currants, biscuits and raspberry vinegar, if only I would sit on the counter to talk politics and then at the end stand on it to sing:

> We are the boys of Wexford
> Who fought with heart and hand
> To burst in twain the galling chain
> And free our native land.

My friends were behind the counters, in the Brewery, in the railway yard, and in the workshops. My mother's family had many blood relations in the town without my knowing it, and I had gone to the Christian Brothers' School, threepence a week. The resistance years were to draw on those young men with whom I had this bond and the bond of Parnellism. I had kindness from these lithe young men, whose minds were quivering with the issues concerning Ireland. They had life on a hidden level—Frank O'Connor and Sean O'Faolain have put it in stories—like the river in Lady Gregory's park at Coole, which drew from buried sources, running lost to sight, and then returning to daylight. These inanimate faces, deferential and quiescent in the shops, concealed a sparkle, a striving and yearning, a primitive thrust and demand, in the national current they were hiding. These were to make the Flying Columns. Or, if you please, the Murder Gangs. When I tried to explain to Jewish intellectuals in 1916 what it was all about, they couldn't absorb it. They could not afford to absorb Ireland because they had hopes vested in England. Politics is the life of the will, of self-interest, of blinkered self-interest, and of self-righteousness, even if it must lead to murder. And one thing my father did surprisingly inculcate on this account, "Never join an oath-bound secret society." You are no longer your own man.

When I came to the New World, I came with an Irish mortgage on me, a psychological black knot in my feelings. The knot was made when I was seven, but it became black when the Church drew it tight. The Church had its own self-interests, and they were not national. The Church sold Parnell down river, since in their prudence they held by Gladstone. They erred. Life is imprudential. Only by imprudence could the U.S.A. have set out on its own freedom, and Ireland had to obey the same imperative to know itself. In leaving Ireland, its unfinished struggle was under my skin. I was on with the new love before I was off with the old. Theodore Roosevelt called it a hyphen, the commitment binding most immigrants who were caught in politics young. I had it badly, but being self-curious I was promptly alive to the workings of the new loyalty. The expatriate must, as I see it, be honest as an American, but he may seek to invigorate America so that for its own sake it can conceive of the nationalism he brought with him. I came in the belief that this could be the case, and the belief was well founded. Without American comprehension, entirely distinct from power politics, there could never have been an end to the Irish complex.

The Fallow Year

When a boy in his eighteenth year emerges from school discipline into the world at large, he loves to feel that his life is at last his own. I was free to go on long solitary walks, to cycle to Carlow and back, to smoke, and read, and play tennis, and swim, to ponder the future. My life was at last my own, but what was I to do with it? I had to admit what was implied by my father having debts—no balance at the bank. I would have to support myself. That bewildered me, as I left the school prison.

Deep down I knew what I wanted. I wanted to write. But we had absolutely no connections with the writing world. There were local and national newspapers, Catholic magazines, and rebel Dublin weeklies that gave their editors bare bread without butter. There was a brisk new paper, *The Leader*, but no publishing house to speak of, and about as much chance to live by writing as to live by playing the harp. Besides, had I any talent?

The result of the final examinations gave a hint that I could write, but on what terms and for what market? My parents were completely at sea. My mother's vigorous character made her say, "It's dogged that does it," but under many admirable phrases she concealed a nagging fear that I might dawdle forever, like another of the local molluscs, whose talents would be unemployable.

To make it worse, I would not look to the Jesuits for help. I might try to matriculate at the Royal University, an institution that gave courses and held examinations, but had no existence below the neck. Still, a degree from the Royal could lead to nothing in particular; and as even my brother Bat, nine years older than myself, had not yet poked out of the economic woods, my parents thought of my prolonged dependence with a shiver. I shivered myself. A fog descended on the immediate prospect, and I could only fumble ahead. My mother found me sulky and depressed. I got up late. I was no real help in the house. I was argumentative and cantankerous. Had I been really preparing for a career, the disorder inside me might have been tolerable. Any house under construction looks disorderly. But where was the blueprint if I was in revolt against the Church? Its tenets about sex were particularly confusing, but, in addition, it blocked the avenue that Ireland must travel; it demanded unconditional political obedience outside faith and morals; it had set itself to break my father's will or to punish stubbornness by depriving him of income. At such a period in a boy's life when he feels aspirations that would be embarrassing to put into words, unable to bring his powers under control and craving supports he wishes to reject, when he is intimidated and self-distrusting, yet obliged to rely on himself, then there is nothing for him to do inside but crawl on all fours till he can toddle.

He knows he is a maverick. As my father could not help, he wisely kept his counsel. The dignity of private conscience was safe with him. He was incapable of intrusion, and he held my mother to noninterference. Hence, we stayed completely on the surface of things, and I was rather like a girl in her first pregnancy. What a pity that a boy pregnant with ideas cannot actually make it visible he is gravid!

It was utterly impossible for any of us to put our violent craving for affection into words. We had been groomed at Clongowes by the Jesuits and by our fellows to consume our smoke, an exercise of discipline that at its best resulted in so-called Irish wit—the compressed spirit spurting up in a geyser, or else in playfulness of another kind, or in grim acrimonies. The girls as well as the boys were surcharged with chaotic feelings that roiled the stream of life; they were so unruly and ugly. And what was to be the refuge? Saying the Rosary? Writing? Singing? Fornicating? Hunting? Or going to America?

My mother could stand the strain no longer, whether it was of my or her making. What mattered to me as a son, or I might better say, an Irish son, was if possible to find a method or rhythm by which the daily contact with my mother could rub along without fraying nerves. To say she was difficult would be saying too little. It would leave out of account her son's mounting irascibility under the strain that her tight or even rigid infelicity of disposition so promptly created. Much is made in the divorce courts of the incompatible temperament and the hard shock and jar that this implies in an association that men and women come to regard as voluntary. But between a mother and her children, the simple notion that the incompatible permits dissolution is only tenable if it can be achieved with a degree of consent that incompatibility in its very nature refuses. If it is the son who speaks, he cannot disguise from himself the fact that the incompatibilities on which he is tempted to touch in self-justification may spring from a source on which he has drawn not only for his biological existence, but also for his nervous constitution, his basic complexity of likes and dislikes, his whole being. He surprises in himself betimes the thing to which he objects violently and from which he so vigorously divorces himself. Not that I had analyzed our situation at that time. I only know that I gave a jump when my mother said to me in a certain tone of voice, "Francis, come here, I want to speak to you."

I sat down next to her. She was mending socks. It was the same window in which she had tried to explain Hell to me. On that occasion she had been equally serious. "If you die in sin, Francis," she had then explained, "and you die before you can make an act of perfect contrition, you go straight to Hell."

"Is that bad, Mud?" I inquired.

"It is terrible," said my mother. "The sinners are plunged in fire."

That sounded bad, certainly. "How deep are they plunged?" I ventured to ask.

"Enough to burn them," she said, compressing her lips.

"Up to their knees?"

"Oh, higher up than that."

"Up to their middle?"

"Yes, about up to their middle."

"But what kind of fire is it?"

"Fire and brimstone," my mother answered. "It never goes out. It goes on for eternity."

I began to be sorry for sinners, but their plight puzzled me. "Why don't they burn up?" I asked. Everything else did, especially chops.

"They can't," she said decisively. "They burn and burn and they can't burn up."

I was silenced. I was searching for a constructive hypothesis, and then it came to me. "Are they made of asbestos?"

Here we were again, back to Hell. Her eyes were on her needle and the sock, and I dreaded her concentration. Yet I had done nothing, but that was precisely it.

"What do you mean to do with yourself?" she demanded.

"I? I'm matriculating."

"What can that lead to, Francis? Pappy could not see you through the University."

"I don't suppose so. But without a degree, what is there to do?"

"What could you be?"

"I might be a solicitor."

"It would take £200 or £300 to be apprenticed to a solicitor."

"What would you suggest?" I inquired feebly. I did not dare to say, "I want to be a writer." A jockey, possibly. A circus acrobat, a horse coper, a high sheriff, anything utterly unreasonable, but not a writer.

My mother bent down her eyes. "I'm afraid there's nothing but a bank."

"A bank!" I said incredulously. A grey limestone prospect, bordered with road metal waiting to be pounded into fragments and stretching to infinity was worse than an asbestos doom. Yet she gazed at me without flinching. "I am afraid that is all."

"I don't think I want to be a bank clerk, Mud."

"Maybe not, but beggars can't be choosers."

How little she knew! It's because we're choosers we're beggars.

"Hadn't you better speak to Pappy?"

"There's no future in the world for our kind of people, boy," my father said dolefully. "Paddy O'Brien will give you a letter to Mr. Mergenthaler. You should become a typographer. Work with your hands."

"But shouldn't I matriculate?"

"If you like. It can do no harm. But we can't send you to college."

So I matriculated. But the question of making a living remained. A typographer—I felt no mad urge for that. My father used vague terms, "Would you like to break stones with your hands in your pocket?" That indicated the fallen estate of ex-gentlemen. They had to break stones. It looked awfully like America.

Will you dive in or wade in?

America was the place the red apples came from. It was the place the barrel of oysters came from with Edward F. Hackett's name inside. It was the place the gay circus came from. That lady who visited the Castle, by the name of Gould—she wore a shirtwaist that had stars on top and was striped all around. She came from there! "I guess, pard."

You should go to Chick-cago, they said. My father was fond of telling a story of it, "That's where the bandit said to the doctor, 'Your money or your life,' and the doctor answered, 'In my business we take both.' "

One day my father said, "Darby White wants you to look in on him, up at the dispensary." It was a somber day. He was a formidable man, with that hard hat of his, and his trim beard. He talked into his beard. "I'd like you to have something, Master Francis, since your good father tells me you are thinking of voyaging across the ocean, and there will be little things you'll want."

He pulled out a drawer, and scooped up a number of coins. These he placed on his desk in two little pillars.

"Times are hard, Master Francis, and I can't be of as much help as I would wish. But it is yours, my dear boy, with my blessing." An involuntary sigh came from him as he wheeled to me. "Now, hold out your hand." And he put the heavy gold coins into it.

"Goodbye, Master Francis," and he gave me his big hand. He was tender for my father and passed this tenderness to my mother and to all of us. In that somber room I felt the depth of undying friendship.

It was the money I had with me when I landed at 23rd Street.

I Go to Work

It was a very immature young man who arrived at the foot of 23rd Street, and at the foot of the ladder, in the New York of 1901. In January I was to be nineteen, and it was the turn of the year before I got a job. The difficulties were many.

Some of them were inside me. Eagerly as I had left home and willing as I felt myself to face the dragon, I was a rash-timid youth in an unfamiliar setting. Though I had a brother and cousins and a roof over my head in Bay Ridge, it was a moral imperative that I must look out for myself, hustle, and get busy. The pressure was not unfriendly, but it was unremitting.

My predicament at the start was highly complicated. Unless I ascribed guilt to England, I could not excuse the Irish for all those failings that made the English feel superior. And the "Superior," what about them? Was I to take them as my natural enemies?

The worst blow to inflict on any people is to strip it of captaincy. My nation had been stripped of captaincy so that captaincy's burden, its function, and its valor were not identified with ourselves but with our enemy. I came to America to seek equal justice in these matters, but did I retain an animosity to the strong as such? Would I ascribe guilt in especial to those who had the colonial English touch, the natural air and bearing of superiority?

I did not know. I'd heard the kettledrums of cavalry and the March Past of the Enniskillens, but the best music I ever heard, the stealthy thief of my heart, was on awaking in convalescence to a vagrant's "Men of Harlech" down in a showery Kilkenny street and floating up. Yet martial airs that catch a young gudgeon can't hide the red traffic he's bait for.

But for a brief moment the idea of the uniform had enticed me—though my bad eyesight would have prohibited it—when a friend in Ireland had taken an amiable look at me after a hockey match: "Now there's the right height for a soldier," he said, "not too tall, not too short. About five feet eight and a half." It was five feet nine before he knew it.

In that first year, piping down as an expatriate—you can't swagger at $3.50 a week, less 60 cents for carfare—I fed on my heart. How lonely one can be among strangers is unfathomable. I wrote some articles to send to Irish editors. You've seen an empty orange box cast over the side that seems to go the other way of its own volition. My articles were written for Standish O'Grady's *All Ireland Review* and for Arthur Griffith's *United Irishmen*. No vulgar money was paid for them, but in due time they appeared in print to disclose bitter yearning for Ireland. I began writing for *The Gael*, a little monthly that Samuel Richardson—then circulation manager of the *New York World*—was editing for his pure inner satisfaction. And in his office I saw a wraith, old O'Donovan Rassa, a Fenian with sunk cheeks and a smouldering eye, disreputable as a tattered flag. He had once been under Imperial lock and key, and he was having the sense to make a book of it. Books are the rebels' mausoleums. He was a "ham"; even his rakish hat betokening rebellion. But so was Yeats a "ham," with his Parisian flow of knotted necktie. And Oscar Wilde was the panjandrum of "hams": "carnation, lily, lily rose, darnation silly, silly pose"—the clash between bourgeois and artist. Myself I bought a soft black hat; the kind all respectable young men wore for $3.00—deeply depressing.

With little brawn and brass to speak of, no ordered brain, not wearing broadcloth to serve notice of a status, what had I come with? No one had asked me, "what's in your imagination, immigrant?" Homespun and juvenile as it was, it was really all I had with me.

But Ned Hackett wanted to find out. He picked me up for a walk downtown. We sloped down to the Bowery. He was not averse, I think, to having me see New York's object lesson in debris, its open sewer.

In Kilkenny we had derelicts, perhaps our best known public figures. Every child knew them. They had names and histories. The niche they vacated was still theirs. "Ah, isn't it a shame? Ah, his poor mother!" Some were rogues, just the same. The Wrecker had a hard, mean face. It was his copyright to wave at horses during hunts, and if there was a spill he rushed to the rescue.

"Sure I knew you when you could hardly walk," he once said to me, extending a hand as firm as wood. "It's like yesterday."

"And I knew you when you could hardly walk," I retorted, and it *was* yesterday."

He didn't crack a smile. His gimlet eye could see half a crown through a stone wall, and he was thinking, "It's a Yank. Three bob, maybe." And still he was part of the community.

The Bowery huddled such men together, and their identity was churned into ooze like green sod into muck.

They knew you were looking at them, but it had no community in it, and they bleared into flophouses. They were not members of the same body but in an inferno they wanted marked as theirs, sludge in their blood. You might try to stir their blood, eat with them, chat with them, but it would be bravado. Not even if you were Tolstoy could you disarm their suspicion and animosity. Tolstoy had failed in Moscow's Bowery. Yet as we walked in that Stuyvesant garden, now a sink, I felt painfully the isolation they made of it in thick and indiscriminate swarm, dumped are the rebels' mausoleums. He was a "ham"; even his rakish hat betokening rebellion. Jacob Riis, had tried to redeem it.

Ned heard me say "they" instead of "we," and at last, taking my arm with friendly warmth, he said, "I think I have a job that's made for you, Francis." hat; the kind all respectable young men wore for $3.00—deeply depressing.

He gave a short laugh. "No, not exactly. It's in North Dakota."

Why not the Fiji Islands? But so far—and it seemed far—so good. "And what is it?"

"It's secretarial. You could do it with the back of your hand."

Fine. I looked at his dry, Iberian face, with its ardor and narrowness.

"It's secretary to a society for the conversion of Red Indians to Catholicism."

I stopped. "You're serious?"

"What do you think?"

I laughed. Here was I, busy unconverting myself, and he proposed I should say, "wo, wo," with a bridle behind my back to the Navajo or whatever they were.

"Think it over, son." Though earnest and sallow, he could force himself to be lenient. "You don't want to let go of the 'ould Faith.'"

I said nothing, but I could imagine myself at some far post in Dakota as a lard-faced indoor worker going through a card index while Indians, wearing shawls like my ancestors in Ireland, sat graven on their bench waiting to embrace the faith of Cortez.

So we went our ways, he to Hanover Square and the business built up by a Kilkenny man, W.R. Grace, and I to Bay Ridge. What a remarkable Church, though, to be picking up those unconsidered Indians before it got around to the wigwam of Tammany and the Bowery. Maybe without this prehensile Church I could find a job. Willy Marum, a cousin of ours, the son of an M.P., owed his job to the Jesuits over at 16th Street. He was their doorman. If one was sinking unbefriended in the lightless ooze, the sloblands of the Bowery, one might regret not having clung to a plank shot along the mud. But America, land of the free, need not be a quagmire. There was always Help Wanted.

My own expatriation was not from Ireland but from Catholicism. Had it been the Catholicism of the Jansenists, Ireland might still have been a country with a backbone. But Ireland's brand of religion was tribal, not spiritual, and you were periodically examined for it as doctors inspect immigrants for smallpox. How recently have you been vaccinated? Since last Easter? The forms were rigid: baptism, confirmation, confession, communion, extreme unction. "He died a beautiful death," leaving a beautiful memory of Gradgrind and Scrooge. My fellow Clongownian, James Joyce, had become a maverick, and the branding in his flesh he had scratched, probed, licked, picked, gouged and chiselled. It never quite came off. But Irish Catholicism gained by this. It has two monuments to it, *Ulysses* and *Finnegan's Wake*. And once Joyce got off the reservation with the ineradicable brand on him, he was never rounded up. Whether to take him into camp remains the quandary of the faithful. If you take him in, what about the purity of Irish womanhood, "Faith of our Father Holy Faith, We Will Be Trew?" If you kick him out you lose a genius.

James Joyce could be accepted as a cathedral cat, washing his face during the Elevation and pouncing on mice during the Benediction. If you expel him, you expel one of God's creatures. And you cannot change him; he is invincibly cat. But if accepted as a recalcitrant, he is certainly the most expressive Irish Catholic that ever gave the Knights of Columbus a minority report. It was safe for the late Cardinal Hayes to say that Bourke Cochran was Christlike, but there was enough tiger in James Joyce to make his cat-laugh at such effusions an unforgettable one at any policemen's cathedral breakfast. The Church he knew was the going concern he grew up with. It did not woo him as a convert, cocking its bonnet at him. It devoured him as a conscript. His extrication from its claws left him in livid shreds. The mangled heart and the suppurating intellect exposed with fidelity in mocking pages, no fit reading for recent converts sitting in the lap of the Church, cuddled and nuzzled, without a thought for either Ulysses or Finnegan.

How sublimated it all is, with Rouault designing the windows, and Huysmans forgotten, with the censer swinging and the censor forgotten, and delicious subtleties of some confectioner turned theologian taking the place once conceded to Ernest Renan. Any port in a storm, even Port-Royal. It isn't lost on candy makers anywhere, not on the Book-of-the-Month Club, nor on Hollywood. But in the false antithesis of any dialictic, or, in nursery words, the swindle that says, "If you are not Black you must be Red," the whole point of America is blunted. I was born Black, for my part, as many a Russian is born Red. But we are not obliged to swap. If I give up heart disease, must I take pneumonia? I don't like the machine age. I don't like machine-made religions. The virtue I see in America is that it permits convictions to be personal, and the hoax of the "masses" is no better than the blind affirmations of the mass. Why must the faithful be sheep? Why not men and women? It was for this that democracy was invented.

※

"Now," said Ned, handing me a list, "you have three good openings. Call on these firms. They're the best."

"And which ought I to take first, Ned?"

"Mr. Platt's. Uncle Ed has written for you from the Fort Orange Club. Platt is a Republican boss."

"And then?"

"Let's see. It's a tossup. Knauth on Broad Street, Philbin, Beekman, and Menken at 111 Broadway. You'll be shot with luck, my bucko, if they take you. A greenhorn, a spalpeen like you, straight from the 'ould sod.'"

"And what'll they pay? What should I take?"

"Take what you get and be dum glad to get it. It'll be around three or four dollars."

Ned believed in keeping me from dangerously high hopes, lest I fall hard. It was his form for affection.

I went to the Platt office, I dimly recollect, and in a big carpeted room, with a fire smiling in it, I was pleasantly greeted but the job seemed to spiral up the chimney. At the one with the German name there were other applicants. We sat in outer darkness until a man of extreme definiteness—the spike on their helmet—gave me the wrathful answer that turns away the soft. He implied that even I should have known better than to apply. And though 111 Broadway was in full view of a graveyard, it was cosy by comparison. I liked the law offices of Philbin, Beekman, and Menken. A Mr. O'Brien told me that I might be allowed to see Mr. Menken. It went splendidly. $3.50 a week. Report on Monday, 8:30.

No boy who shipped before the mast ever ran into a quicker gale than I did.

It all seemed so easy to start with. Mr. Menken had let Mr. O'Brien do the introduction. Being a smallish, but self-confident little cockatoo of a man, I had adjusted my full respect to him, until I saw him diminished by Mr. Menken's rather summary manner. Mr. Menken nodded him out and took over.

Then I adjusted respect to Mr. Menken. He was the junior partner, just turned thirty, with an irrepressible vitality that showed in his sanguine color, his bright eyes behind thick lenses, and a certain springy, bouncy exuberance that made me think of President Theodore Roosevelt and his patent medicine, the Strenuous Life. Mr. Menken was kind, informal, and warm. He asked me by what name I was addressed.

"Francis," I said. "I have a cousin Frank, so I'm called Francis."

He looked at a letter I'd presented. "How do you sign yourself?"

"F. Byrne Hackett."

S. Stanwood Menken looked at F. Byrne Hackett. "You don't have to sign yourself that way. Why do you do it? It's not my business, but I should think you'd find it better to sign yourself Francis Hackett."

I liked this man. Not only did he treat me like a sentient and intelligent being, but within a day or two he halted in one of his rushes. "I hear good things of you, Francis." That warmed my spine.

It was then we changed course.

An office clerk, John Heep, who had a rictus that looked like a set smile and with it a wrinkled forehead, evidently tense with responsibility, becked to me with his head.

"I want to show you this," he said. "Sit down."

I had never observed it before. It was a big box. There were lots of little holes in its face, and short reddish plugs at the end of rubber tubing could be picked up from a ledge on which it stood and pegged into these holes.

"Ever operate a switchboard?"

"Never looked at one before."

His wrinkles deepened though he still smiled. He had crinkly dusty-gold hair. I gave it my attention too.

"Have you used a telephone?"

"Oh, yes. Three times."

"Holy gee!" He stopped smiling. At that moment a little metal flap fell down from in front of a hole and began trembling. "That's an incoming call," he said. "Here's what you do." He pulled up a plug and jabbed it into the hole. "You plug in. Now you're connected. 'Hello,' " he said into the mouthpiece, " 'PhilbinBeekmanMenken, I'll see if he's in.' " He made a few lightning passes; a plug was flipped in, another flopped out, and snapped back surprisingly to where it had come from. It was dazzling and mystifying.

"You see how it's done," he said, standing up. "You understand everything?"

"Oh, everything," I said. There were twenty connections on the switchboard.

"Well, try it." And I sat in the electric chair.

Some things exceed one's expectations. The switchboard did. Anyone could have seen it. The Irish suit I wore was thick tweed, and the office was heated with the usual American anticipation of death by frostbite. I steamed like a bullock. My new glasses clouded with it. I was putting the intensity into connecting and disconnecting people that the occasion obviously warranted. This was a law firm.

I thought I could count on English, my dearest asset as an immigrant, but strange and startling voices would demand wholly unfamiliar names over this system of rapid communication, and as I sought to connect the unconnectable, a new little flap would drizzle down and begin its dribble. The voice "at the other end" was a silhouette in a long tunnel. "You Philbin-Beekman? Isn't Mr. Glubbub in the office? I've called three times." "Hold on," I'd say, because a fresh little jigger would have begun jiggering. "The connection is bad." I knew. I had made it bad.

Voices differed. Some were frankly unintelligible, others unintelligible less frankly. A few rang out like Gabriel's trumpet. But even then, generous though they were, I was often baulked in recompensing them. As I went about extracting the person in demand, connecting outside to inside, some other party would demand to be connected, inside to outside. This was not all. Three might be seized of the idea at the same time to speak from the outside to the same party, who, lacking extrasensory perception, would choose that precise instant to call his golf club, where frantic legal confederates might be waiting on his pleasure.

I said to myself, "Fortitude." I was sleeping badly and had indigestion, but each day found me gallant. Then it happened. Influx and efflux came to a peak simultaneously. It created what in geographic circles is known as a bore. I lost my head.

Three of the staff rushed at the glass door that gave me flimsy protection, lunged into the outer office where I sat, and burst toward me as though I were Louis XVI instead of an office boy, and they the rude rabble, instead of the Constituent Assembly. I had wrought upheaval with a telephone plug.

Mr. Menken brandished his fist. "What the devil possesses you, Francis? I don't want to speak to HIM. I told you distinctly to turn him over to Mr. Rathbone."

Mr. Rathbone, deceptively chubby, writhed his lips as if he had sipped distasteful poison. But before he could rebuke me, Mr. Charles Kellar Beekman, straight from the arcana of the Social Register, one hair of his head out of place, his features acidly sharpened, penetrated whitefaced from his room. Mr. Anderton oozed slowly toward me, menacing. They hung over me. The coils of the plugs were like Medusa's locks. The switchboard began blinking with six eyes, and all the flaps chattering.

"Oh, Miss Benton. Miss Benton, please!"

Miss Benton, her brown eyes soft and even her movement that of a Quaker, came noiselessly from her desk. With a few demure gestures the plugs, contorted like a generation of vipers, were returned passive to their nests. She gently nodded to one infuriated lawyer after the other, but as they receded to their dens they showed their teeth at me.

Luckily Judge Philbin had not been in the office. He only appeared when his job as District Attorney was done. He was rather a stately figure, with a pale skin and a black beard and formal clothes, a morning coat it was called. There had been an Irish member of Parliament whom they nicknamed Melancholy John, or the Melancholy Humbug, and Judge Philbin, not in the least a humbug, or perhaps only very slightly, had a suggestion of John Dillon. Because Eugene A. Philbin was Irish, I wished to attach myself to him. But ivy cannot cling to a glazed surface, and he shed me before I had sent out a shoot. He was a monolith in black tiles, a kind of cenotaph. I mean, I was scared of Judge Philbin. He offered no foothold. He did not use condescension, but he rose in a sort of bleak rectitude. I am sure he was good, but no warmth leaked from him. How he and Mr. Beekman ever generated a partnership between them belongs to legal genetics.

Sometimes it was delightful work. For some traditional reason I had to keep a book called the Register, a summary of office history put down by hand in pen and ink. Scriveners did it on parchment, and I was doing it in the neighborhood of Trinity Church, as old as Queen Anne, both of them brownstone, trying to feel that it was professional. There is a voluptuousness in penmanship, with flourishes that are virtuoso, but I wrote a fair schoolboy hand. At the same time Miss Benton's fingers were flying, a little bell telling her when she'd better stop, and bzz, a new line at the gallop. If I struck a snag and had to appeal to her, I hesitated. Mr. Menken had snubbed me for trying to be a Paul Revere. "Francis," he had snapped, "you're a prize interrupter!" But in spite of the snowdrop bend of her head, Miss Benton could see me turn toward her. With mild resignation, her eyes on her dictation book, she'd ask, "What is it, Francis?" She used only the top of her lungs to breathe a question. Her meek voice had no resonance. But in the midst of this exacting and impeccable work on her typewriter, she could desire to help. She was a Queen Anne piece too, a brown angel.

At this time the firm of Philbin, Beekman & Menken were paying me $3.50 a week, with 50 cents supper money when I had to work overtime. This was poverty. How honorable it could be I once demonstrated when I stayed late to help out McIlvaine and Parsons, a firm on the floor above. After some hours' work producing law books for the Parsons firm, the young lawyer I was serving offered me 75 cents. I said, "No, thank you. Our firm is always very happy to be of service to you."

He gaped at me. But I still thought in terms of human decency.

At the same time, decency has to be clad. I did not wear an overcoat, but we then wore wollen mittens, and my soft black hat had cost three dollars. My boardinghouse was taking six dollars a week, laundry was 60 to 80 cents a week, and I was still a burden to my father. I received twenty or twenty-five dollars a month from home, and it was too much. I did not like to accept it.

To go to law school was far in the distance. I could not be admitted until I was five years in the country and a citizen. Five years seemed like eternity.

It galled me to be working so hard and to have nothing for it. Every time Mr. A. came to our outer office, went to the basin, washed his hands, then cleared his throat and spat into the basin, I reflected on the subordination to such oafs that was included in the $3.50 remuneration

Another office boy had just come, Chester or Grover, named after some president. He had a reddish blond head, a clean-cut, impertinent nose, and a short, curling upper lip. Like me, he was often sent to the bank to deposit checks and cash. But one day, obeying those laws of economic determinism that hadn't so far determined me, he took $68 in cash to the bank and didn't come back. Chester had yielded to a base and regrettable impulse, overcome by the inelasticity of $3.50 a week. O'Brien, the cashier, became very intent and fussy. But we were told that they weren't going to prosecute. We were much relieved, but we were staggered by it. We condemned Chester. As a matter of fact he was unpunctual, careless, and distinctly averse to hard work. And of course he had a widowed mother. He was a Brooklyn boy. With his grasp on $68 in bills, he passed from history.

It occurred to me that this was a good moment in which to bring up my own financial plight, so I asked if I could speak with Judge Philbin. He gave me an appointment. I told him that

I needed a raise. He looked out the window, on lower Broadway, and then fixed his melancholy gaze on me.

That was a bad moment.

Nobody is ever going to eliminate competition from the world without substituting some sort of escalator for it, I suppose. But, when two wills meet over the question of wages, one the will of a youth who is nerving himself to make a demand and the other the will of an employer who has to resist what he takes to be encroachment, you do have a painful wrench, a breach of the peace, a naked grapple for advantage. I felt I was at fault to press my claim on the inapproachable man, but a mob of my own deeds and desires was shoving me forward, so I tried it on, being desperate.

"How much do you want?" he asked me. It was in a voice as dry as an alkali desert.

"Five dollars a week," I quaked.

He was silent.

"I cannot go on asking my father for money, Judge Philbin. I can't live on $3.50."

"All right," said the judge. "But this sort of thing must never happen again, Francis."

"No, Judge Philbin."

By God, no. I began to read the little ads in the *New York Times* to see who wanted an office boy. How much would it take to live on? $8, at least. I would quit the law if I could find anyone who would offer me $8. We were in the classic idiom of the Law. Every Monday morning I washed seventeen ink bottles. The fountain pen was not in use, and only in ink were legal documentation and endorsement as sacramental as they should be. Yet a breach with high ethics though a typist might be, Miss Benton had found foothold in the Law among the scrolls of John Heep, the authentic inkwells, the noble old copying press and the shining spittoons. It was lulling to sit there doing the Register, and odd that we said miles when we might have said parasangs. Behind my back was the switchboard.

Years afterwards, associating with men of brains, playing a game of rather uncoordinated golf with them, it would occur to me that for those who so easily tell others how to manipulate the ship of state, it might be well if they some time tried a bout with a mere switchboard. They could master it. They are not inept. But when the intellect rides high, when on its chessboard of abstraction the moves are so thinkable, a sobering memory of a switchboard might give a point of reference to the thinker. Anything so loaded with actuality as a switchboard can make one feel clumsy and humble, no more than that.

I would have dodged it with pleasure. But I was an economic conscript. And this, by the way, gave me a consuming interest in the Command. Yesterday's conscript—Lev Bronstein, let us say—stores away such impressions for the Day of Reckoning. I didn't think of that; I just dreamt now and then of an Emancipation Proclamation.

My intellect was not engaged so far. Here I was in a big law office, ostensibly with some idea of where I was going, but remaining virgin soil, raw and wild. I had no map of life. Lawyers I was to know—Justices like Robert Jackson, Felix Frankfurter, William O. Douglas—saw the legal map from the start. To me it was a short word, like God—one I used but had never tried to map for myself.

When you leave school at seventeen, as I did, the hinterland can remain extremely vague. And our Irish education system had its own blank spaces. In later years I was to ask my Jesuit brother what he thought of William James and pragmatism. It was his business to study and know philosophy, but in 1913 he had never heard of the American. When I was at Clongowes, science was an alley cat we did not admit, and European history a tiger that raged about religion during 1500 to 1800. Catholics and Protestants had agreed to a deal on the Education Board. European history in the period of the Inquisition, the Renaissance, the Reformation, the Wars of Religion, the Enlightenment, and all the way to the French Revolution was deleted from the Intermediate Curriculum in Ireland. Not until I found English six-penny classics could I begin to comprehend our times.

Being Irish, I lived in relationships, the more human the better, and I take it that this kind of vivid reciprocation with associates and neighbors may be what the supposed natural gift of the Irish for politics actually rests on. Anyhow, I was personal and infra-intellectual. I had not much power to generalize.

But it was bewildering. This whole office was built around the Law, and while I saw the action, I did not grasp the motives behind it. Contracts were being shaped, franchises devised. An intricate society was being elaborated for the future and without subtle attention to law, its strains and stresses could not have been borne. Had my family been on the spot and the Law a part of our daily experience, rooted in the familiar pulling and hauling, I could have taken it in. But this wasn't Rugby, this was American football. I could not see how to do it.

I could see the clients' part in it. A burly Mr. Jaffray with moustachios and a stiff leg would come in on his cane. He brought a cheerful breeze with him. A Mr. Sloane ambled in, looking like an English sheepdog. A Mr. S. Levy Lawson was as neat as a little black spider. When such men arrived, bustle began; Mr. Rathbone the competent interne, Mr. Roelker stalked like a Durer figure to the Library, Mr. Anderton shuffled morosely, taking a bunch of typewritten material from the hearty, perky, tousled blond, Miss Marsh. She was a receptacle for Whereas and Therefore, chewing gum, furrowing her forehead when I addressed her, as if I were foreign. And indeed I was, especially foreign to the Law.

Had an interpreter appeared, had someone said, "Behind this glib legal facade is an organism," I might have caught fire. Had I even read Abraham Lincoln's *Notes for a Law Lecture*, I might have put two and two together. Most of our business, after all, was not likely to be litigated, "ordinary collection cases, foreclosures, partitions and the like." Universities and law schools exist to entice and feed this curiosity, and curiosity was latent in me. But it was for the legal elite to come out gloved and smart, and for me to run ahead to wheel up their ladder. The upper reaches were theirs. How could I fly?

Our human trash basket of trial and error is crammed with more than rubbish. There are selves in it we no longer care to exhume, selves we have discarded. But it should be said, if it is any comfort to beginners, that most of us have been through nightmares, and that these spasms, conjured by apprehension out of the unknown, come from a double ignorance. We don't know the jump we have to make or the self that has to jump it. Ignorance holds the novice back. He has often to be kicked before he will parachute, and the most awful plunges are actually undertaken by a beginner who believes them to be impossible. We have no easy means of reconciling this contradiction between the thing to be attempted and the self in revulsion. Women, too, have these revulsions to overcome, the desire to go into reverse, of all feelings the most human. But where mature men, having once broken through this pain, seem to prefer to forget and let the novice suffer on his own, women behave better. That is, kind women. Marie de Medicis did indeed have her son birched every morning on principle, assuming he was sure to have misbehaved the day before.

No discipline blighted our law office. There was no clock to punch, no fines to be paid. But while no one was trying to break me, neither was anyone trying to break me in. The flattering assumption that youth is enormously versatile and that adaptation is his pride was ignored for a cool pretense that underpayment was in return for an apprenticeship which, in fact, did not exist. At best I was a paper-server and bottle-washer, in the office but not of it.

But it wasn't wasted, not by a long shot. I wasn't an apprentice to the Law. I was an apprentice to America. And here was America, all alive O!, kicking me to make me jump.

I jumped every time I took a message into Mr. Beekman. Mr. Beekman had in his own way parachuted, but he had landed in a family tree, and he hung there, suspended from the Beekman branch, excessively genealogical. I did not know then that he partly owned the Social Register, but such was, or came to be, the fact. That organization fits polite punishment to the crime. You transgress and you are dropped, and I imagine that Mr. Beekman separated the quick from the dead with nimble conscientiousness. He was a man, however, whose teeth were easily set on edge. He rather resembled a polished actor in a drawing-room comedy, a pale Charles Cherry. He was meticulous with glossed hair, and fine linen, and finely cut clothes. But he was I thought, icy and disdainful. "Leave it there," he would say with the accent of faint boredom or, "What is it?" with the intimidation that it probably shouldn't be. Obviously I was not drawn to him, and it was reciprocal.

At the same time, as I improved at the switchboard, I could nearly always tell by the first note of inquiry that the call would be for Mr. Beekman. It would be a fluted note, a gentle sussuration, a murmur. No one ever called Judge Philbin in these tones. And Mr. Menken's tree did not have exactly the right seeds, or the proper suet, to excite these blue flutters and rapid darts. So, mingled with my revulsion, was a propulsion. I had just bought some books, and two of them were translations from d'Annunzio. *The Child of Pleasure* was the name of one, published by George Richmond in a startling yellow cover, and somehow there was something in New York, especially about the Plaza in the amethyst twilight, but elsewhere too, tangled in the trees, caught in the vistas, twanged in the lighted windows of Martin's or Delmonico's, that an office boy could catch in these tuned voices. They were just heard at the first dull, "Is that you?" or, "Is *That* you?" or, "Is that *You*?" The lamination of voice to voice says a great deal. Even my own voice laminated now and then.

Not that Mr. Beekman did not work. Apparently the birth-pangs of corporations, particularly of railroads, have something about them which, since corporations are persons, calls for a man-midwife. Mr. Beekman delivered these babies. He never asked for hot water, though he often made me feel I was in it, but he labored manfully. These creative deeds transacted in inner offices with mystery increased by unfamiliarity, both bewildered and intimidated me. I stood at a distance and wondered if corporate persons were ever girls.

I also wondered how, if there was no caste system in America, Mr. Beekman could so shrink from the vulgar. The notion of pedigreed stock was not alien to this American. His Social Register was confined to Blue Ribbon Stock, who married, if possible, as their fathers had married. "A Boston blueblood and a Brahmin," could be said with perfect simplicity by those who ostensibly took pride in Abraham Lincoln.

Yet Mr. Beekman's condescension or tepidity only repelled me because I had so little clue to him. Was he really meager? Was he a lightweight? Or was he a good sort at his club, a shrewd New Yorker, at least on the East Side. I wasn't a Dead End kid who had to hate him because he brushed his teeth. But as he sat wrinkling his brow over a document while I waited to snap the thread of thought, it was not Mr. Beekman, in reality, who turned on me impatiently and ungraciously. It was a member of a similar class in Ireland, whose wounding manners I could not but hate. I saw him through the twisted windowpane that looks back on conquest. He was a little like the snobs in Ireland.

But the adamantine elegance of Mr. Beekman did not close my mind. By chance I was meeting other descendants of patroons less oblivious that the once-proud estate of the Stuyvesants was now the Bowery. Estates do fluctuate.

Mrs. Pomeroy

I was now living in my brother Eddie's boardinghouse in New York. Through him I met Mrs. Pomeroy, born a Skeel. She was a neighbor of the Van Ziles on West End Avenue, and this was a glimpse into New Amsterdam. Her massive bearded brother could have walked out of Rembrandt, brooding and imperturbable, beautifully Dutch.

Laura Pomeroy was quite the contrary. She was Whistler's mother in exterior, but tremulously tentative. She longed that one, for example, should "see" her brother. She was an American of a vintage that was already rare. This I could not know. She was an extraordinarily gentle human being. I was going to say "old lady" because she had a little dog called Gyp, and she wore a Persian shawl draped fondly over her thin shoulders, and looked at one with great, pale, filmed eyes, while her voice groped for its pitch almost as falteringly as her gait when she came to greet one. But that tentative voice, that feeble gait, and that long, bony, veined hand, so feverish in its clutch, could reveal little of the ardent, sensitive, and amused artist, who could still laugh at folly and reverence the jewel in the toadhead of culture. She had been a sculptor in Rome. Without much money, a widow, rather ailing and exhausted, she could have settled into a lonely old age, shrinking into herself from the growing New York that bounced all around her, but she was too strong for that. She had the vitality to draw the young to her tea table on Sundays and during the week, a band of the tamed and untried, most of them fledglings, who came to sup on the fine arts as well as cookies. She was not afraid to be heterogeneous, though she had been reared in the transcendental America and moved in the classic orbit. In spite of that tightness, she could be receptive, and she created a haven for us.

At first I took her to be Byrne's affair. (Eddie had become Byrne in America). I never doubted that he had a taste for the Real Things, except perhaps in myself, but I watched him in this milieu with some misgivings. Where my father could become endearingly florid when visitors excited him, Byrne was quickly bent on bestowing his charm, which was enhanced by good looks that sometimes attained physical beauty. But as he spread himself boldly, paying lush compliments with teriffic liberality and audacity and soaring on bold flights of cultural fancy, I waited as one waits at the circus to see if the diver would hit the tank of the obituary column. As a rule he enchanted his group. They gazed into his big, brown, bog-water eyes with answering sincerity. They loved him as a typical Irishman. In Mrs. Pomeroy's cordiality, however, there was a shade of indulgence, and this did not estrange me. She was one of those easily-hurt mortals who are not simply tender for themselves and born to shiver and shrink. Mrs. Pomeroy, as I came to know her, was no such sensitive plant. Rome had emboldened her. It dwelt in her as a rich, adventurous presence, a city that loves those who have loved her, and she had lived into it. Her partner in it was gone, but when she spoke of Edward Pomeroy, a clergyman who had tutored as well, she did it with gentle deference. I was wary of this deference, and when it extended to Lyman Abbott and Moses Coit Tyler, who was Abbott's literary editor on the weekly that was to become the *Outlook*, I reserved my judgment. But the clue to her husband's taste was on her bookshelves, and on our own, since she willed many of his books to be divided between Montrose J. Moses and myself. The tendril of her friendship was extremely clinging but longer than life, and holding to a shared devotion to letters.

I could well understand Noel Coward's later remark to his mother in her nook of a hotel, "You do have a lot of musty old bags here!" But these frumpy dowagers may guard a refined tradition, as distinct from a genteel one, and the relation of the refined to the civilized was Laura Pomeroy's sole preoccupation, mellowed by her years in Rome. Whenever she mentioned it, she would give me a second for response, and when W.W. Story left me blank, she would say a gliding word or two, not perhaps of rhapsody but of reverie.

The people who came to her—Hilda Belcher, Henry Holden Huss, Blanche Ostertag, William Jordan, Effie Holden—had yet to make their way or were in that peculiar stress of climbing the descending escalator, which means you have an infernal time of it. All the more reason why Mrs. Pomeroy's company was a boom. In this brassy city as elsewhere, in Rome, in Paris, Chelsea, or Bloomsbury, or even Dublin, the exiles from expedient upheaval seek a windbreak.

Jordan was a gray-haired, almost furtive man, who at times would bring a whimsical ditty. He designed colophons for McClure, Phillips, exquisite Aldine anchors, and in his slim mournfulness you had a sense of native defeat from the beginning. A tree on a foreland may not yield, but it is warped from exposure; and you could hear the wind whistling through this parched, tenacious Puritan. His work was good, but McClure's was doomed. Doubleday soon swallowed it with a gulp. Yet at Mrs. Pomeroy's Jordan thawed out.

Hilda Belcher was black-browed and strong, a young etcher, firmly braced by her sense of tradition and a vigor that seemed dauntless. Yet she, too, had sustenance from Mrs. Pomeroy. Montrose Moses was small, mild, and erudite with a Southern urbanity that had alertness in it. He could almost purr when he was amused, and he was as immaculate in spirit as in decorum. He administered a reproof like an affronted dove. When he married he chose a woman of the same perfect gentleness, a sister of the actress Chrystal Herne.

Sometimes we left in a crowd together, and the compression of her apartment, where we had been subdued by her authority, gave way in a gush, a torrent a talk, a gayer and wilder mood, a descent to a less attentive, more familiar and teasing level. On these evenings we separated with utter reluctance. We were at the age when fellow students kept on till dawn, or young artists said goodbye to time, but we were in harness; we had jobs, and we had to face Monday morning. Laura Pomeroy, after all, had not been without some money of her own.

As for myself, I haunted Mrs. Pomeroy's once or twice a week. Her meals were not exactly ruddy. But the frailty she sometimes simulated, as if a weeping willow were about to whimper a bit, was entirely misleading. While she deftly skirted any harsh collision with immovable fact, she did not refuse to chart it. This was an immense satisfaction after the evasions of Bay Ridge, which shrouded naked fact in platitude. I often talked to her five hours at a stretch; she had robust critical sense and the power to vivisect without maiming her victim. (Imagine Bernard Shaw being against vivisection, when he has made his fortune by it!) I would stagger from her house after these debauches, but we would have traversed books, art, music, her guests, and the story of our lives. Or excerpts.

As I was parting from her one evening, she said at the door, "Do please come on Sunday. A young woman I scarcely know, but very nice, I think, has asked to bring a friend. You'll be of great help." Her flattery was liberal, and, of course, I came. The couple entered with flowers, flowers of speech anyway, but candy and flowers were at that time signs of amiability. He was by no means young, but spruce, with exceptionally yellow gloves. She was very much his junior, quietly dressed in a soft beige, or some such warm neutral color. He rather took the floor. He had an easy, practiced flow of talk, and while it was on several floors lower than was usual at Mrs. Pomeroy's, out in the big broad plaza of newspaper topics and facile effects, it still was animated. I remember I'd spoken of lunching after two.

And why so late? Well, why? "Because after two one could have a 15 cents lunch for ten cents."

He laughed, "When I was your age," he said genially, "I used to lunch at a wagon, coffee and sinkers for 10 cents. Or was it 5? And, do you know, I passed it the other day, and I said to myself, 'I bet it's wonderful.' But it was terrible, terrible!"

He had a name that must have been invented by Dickens. I'd heard it. The newspapers spoke of him a good deal. He was a lobbyist at Albany, and the profession paid well. His young companion, her attention straying from the lobbyist, came to rest on me, and in a few minutes I was conscious of a most pleasant rapport. She wasn't American, but she spoke with very little accent. The thing I liked was an equable and serene openness of mind that still did not rule out an impression that hers might be a heart which would dispose of itself more primitively. I picked this up, and then, in a way, she picked me up. On the following Sunday she'd be at home, if I were free.

That Sunday found me a little ahead of time. This was not Mrs. Pomeroy's. It was around the corner from the expected, and I was at once elated and troubled. My trouble came from the line of verse, "big fleas have little fleas and so ad infinitum." I hoped and yet I feared. Was it in my heart, that fluttering organ, to be little flea, a Sunday flea? I went up to her nest in this quandary.

She was in those tones of café au lait that seem to tinge the clear skin with a light memory of sunburn and that rest in light hair as glint and radiance. Her nest was well feathered, with a window on the Hudson. In spite of my confused feeling, I had a hope that I might find favor with her, though at what point and in what manner I could hardly imagine. And then a slight accident occurred. She had been idly fingering a book. It slipped. I stooped for it.

"You're reading Dickens?" I said.

"Yes. Isn't he the best in the world?"

Not in my world, at that time. "You think so?"

"Don't you?"

It might have been begonias, but I was an incipient critic, and I began on Little Dorrit. I ran on. I turned to Little Nell. At first she was amused, and exclaimed, "Oh, but surely!" Then she was less amused. At last she said to me, narrowing her eyes, "He means a lot to you, Dickens?"

"No," I said, "he's too gross a sentimentalist."

"I see," she said. "Now I'll put him away. Which would you like, tea or coffee and sinkers?"

As she put on the kettle, I felt like Napoleon on the way to Elba. She said, from the alcove, "You're quite a student, aren't you? I hadn't realized it."

It was still quite light when I went back to the boardinghouse.

I was nineteen and still completely without experience of sex outside myself. My power of impure thought was frantically active. Did I have anything else? A young man like myself was sure to be divided in his heart. He craved the female of his kind with feverish desire, yet he was impelled to love no less imperiously, and in this meaning of the word love was not another name for lust. A woman's grace and beauty incited him but could not be narrowed to her bodily response. Within him there was a single wellspring of generous fervor, the uncontaminated source of aspiration, whether he drew on it as a soldier, an artist, a worshipper, or an adventurer. It was in the woman's power, if she possessed this generous fire, to stir in him an unremitting ardor and rapture, never to be fully requited unless she loved him physically, but fed from an exaltation that drew on everything that either could imagine or experience as pure and tender delight. This exquisite solicitude for the woman sought no recompense beyond access to her inexhaustible heart, so easily conceived as a divinity's. And a poet like Yeats, at the beginning of the century, gave new words to this divine rapture, which shared with male and female exigence the simple name of love.

On my walks I'd see the streetwalkers prowling; I knew a number of them by sight, and so did the cop, bracing himself on point against the biting wind, and the news vendor cowering in his shelter. A few stragglers who only had pennies for the "smutoscopes," machines in an arcade that gave a motion picture if you turned a handle, glued their eyes on the antics of fat-bodied, flouncy chorus girls, a substitute for action that disgusted me as aggravating and barren. All along Broadway the shop windows prodded and the lights blazed demands. One's appetite for company, for excitement and sensation, was whetted by offers of delight, a sharp pressure that spurred and goaded the flesh. The city rolled by, lavish, prodigious, indifferent spreading a feast and refusing it if one had no money. I was irritated and thwarted. The bars, the restaurants, the theatres kept clamoring and selling opportunity, and I was a novice, roiled and inopportune.

There was a salesman living at the boardinghouse who ignored Broadway. He sold brushes or some such household article from door to door, a surprising occupation for a Southern gentleman, but he did not conceal its attraction. He was an eel, if ever there was one, slippery, sinuous, oblique, with a lulling indolence that would beguile a bodyguard, even though his eyes were hot and beady, his nose long and inquisitive, his lips thin and red. He had one intense object, the study of wild life in city flats, and if he made a hundred calls in a week, he was perfectly satisfied if he could ensnare one of his clients. He spared no pains, this naturalist. Nonviolence was his method, and he so proceeded with the frustrated and cheated, the lonely and unhappy, that their desire to resist him dissolved in his arms, his lechery sweet as music and magnolias. "I'm bad, aren't I?" He said this with a leer, a cigarette smoker's cough, his whole aspect lean and feverish. He wanted to boast but also to propitiate. He was lascivious, not lewd.

This was a lesson. I pondered it. And I pondered other New York lessons.

One of them was quite apart from this Broadway I so drearily patrolled. Two girls who were great friends brought me to see an aesthete, one a brusque brunette who found me droll and the other a flaxen girl with fanatic pale blue eyes, whose body was stiff and whose laugh creaked. She was a devoted artist. Our host gave us tea. He was in the thirties, a tall, rather stooping man with a sliding Adam's apple—bony and refined to his long fingertips. He dangled praise before the artistic visitor, but not within reach, though this acerbity he did not inflict on me. He asked me to come again, and on the evening I arrived he was emerging from his bath, his gawky frame in a monkish robe. He was eager to show me a folio, one of the treasures the girls had mentioned, and he sat me down face to face with him, this big book on our knees, his head inclined toward me so he could point out its exquisite effect, and very soon his knees touched mine; his bony hands slithering to and fro, touching mine as if by accident.

At this time the word "homosexual" was hardly known, unless to those who had followed the Oscar Wilde trial, and I was ignorant of it. At school we had not heard it, though our friendships might have sex in them. But here was a stranger making an approach such as I might have made to a girl, if I followed the brush salesman's fashion. It stirred no feelings in me except to get out, without hurting his feelings. It was as if one's home had been broken into. My throat went dry, I mumbled words and tucked my knees back. In a few minutes he stood up, and replaced his folio, whatever it was, and I beat a retreat. What had made him think he could pursue me?

This same astonishing assault was repeated by a younger man a little later. He was a beginner in the magazine field and earning so little that he had to add to it by tutoring some children in Montclair. We talked of magazine writing, on the occasion we met, and he suggested I come to Montclair to go into it further. After a pleasant, insipid evening, interminably long, this timid, mouse-colored, neat young man, who had the temperament of a bookkeeper, pulled out his watch and said I'd better spend the night as it was so late. I agreed. He brought me to a room with a great double bed. We had to share this; there was no other room, the house was semiclosed for the summer. I didn't like it, but I agreed. I wasn't used to such a consortium, but what to do? And then this poor devil poked his leg across in my direction. California was invading the State of Maine. Virgin, as I was, I sat up with State's Rights bristling.

"What's the matter?" he asked sleepily.

"I'm going to New York," I said.

"You can't. There are no trains."

"That makes no difference," I declared, "I'm going."

He was scared. He begged me not to. He offered to go back to the Pacific, leaving me on the cold Atlantic Coast. I accepted somberly. Breakfast the next morning was less pleasant than the dinner and even more insipid. It might be true that there was sex in schoolboy friendships, but this aggressiveness was nothing I had ever imagined; he might as well have proposed we smoke opium. What did he take me for? It was ugly.

Yet sex was not ugly, far from it. But how to approach it, if one was earning five dollars a week, nineteen years old, with no prospect of marrying?

Mrs. Hatch's

When I moved to Mrs. Hatch's boardinghouse, it was not into complete independence. I chose the one where my brother was living. But he was often absent "on the road" for Doubleday, Page, so I was for the first time much alone, taking a step in the direction of self-possession.

After life in a big family and the supervised existence at a public school, this was a bracing adventure. It was true that I had the classic "hall bedroom." It was a boxed-in space under a big skylight. I could lie on my couch and look straight up to heaven. Outside the thin box I could hear the swirls of casual talk and slop emptyings, the rush of top-floor boarders and the thuds of housecleaning. But I could wring no pathos out of this cabin. At Clongowes I had a cubicle in the dormitory that was much smaller, and there I was one of a mob. Here I was master of my little cell, of my own coming and going. I could read all night. I could smoke. I could write verses, letters, articles. The boon was priceless—to be free from collision with other wills, to have time clear and uninterrupted, and the proprietorship in my consciousness. That may not seem a big thing, but for me it was everything.

It was in that enclosure, under that skylight, that I came to know Turgeniev; I met Gorki there. I felt the enchantment of Bjørnstjerne Bjørnson. The texture of English literature was familiar, but here was another, a more limber emotion, a vastly expanded sense of human equality, and youth races for these, the novelty of spring, both a liberation and a torment.

And there was *The Sun*. I do not yet know how Mr. Haseltine filled its tight columns on Sunday with reviews into which I always penetrated with eagerness, then floundered and languished and perished. But James Huneker was a tantalizing acrobat. It was arid, yet glittering, that spangle of names and performances, with at times a pocket of rich appreciation, a human smile. Such journalism caught the mood of our common adventure, which came down to one's demand for signposts in the unknown territory of experience where certain propositions had already been assumed as valid. New York offered Huneker, as it offered Walter Damrosch to the neophyte, and the hunger for orientation was rabid, since there had been no preparation at college, no prearrangement in the name of tradition. It was a challenge to native powers of ascertaining and deciding. I brought a sharp appetite to the aesthetic feast, but no guide except the domestic one. The marvel of New York, after boyhood in a provincial town, was its multiplicity of invitation. Had I been cultivated in music, for example, it would have been easy to grasp helpful hands thrust out to me. At Mrs. Pomeroy's I met musicians. The Huss family was consecrated to music, and their house was radiant with it. They asked me to lunch there. I felt no obstacle to friendship except that I was too ignorant.

High up in Carnegie Hall I listened to orchestra for the first time. The clang of Walter Damrosch's chanticleer voice and his crisp touch when he picked out themes on the piano aroused in me a passionate longing to plunge into the flooding symphonies; but had the music been the Russian language, it could not have been stranger. I had learned the Blue Bells of Scotland under Mrs. Fallon's ferule. She slapped any finger that struck a wrong note, and thus made me drop music. Walter Damrosch had a better method for an ignoramus. He was inside music; I was outside, so he invited us in. In a few years I could have frequented in the Huss household; now when they said "Bach" I looked vague. I knew only Handel, because Handel had lived in Dublin.

The boardinghouse was at 45 West 25th Street. No one who designed a convict prison could fail to be impressed with the pattern of midtown Manhattan. The dullest turnkey could find my "block" between Fifth and Sixth Avenues. The whole gridiron, long avenues crossed by twenty short streets to the mile, was an engineer's triumph. Such a masterwork of monotony, however, with even the sunsets cut into segments like neapolitan ice cream, was not really crowned until Messrs. Belmont and Gould bethought themselves of pronging up railroads on iron pillars and running them lengthwise on four of the principal avenues, to thunder and clatter and bang, clouting the inhabitants of this gridded island into further submission to the machine. Belial spawned these elevated railroads, the most rawboned, rattlepated, unwashed and raucous contraptions that besotted money-grubbers had ever devised. On avenues that, for all their straight lines, were noble and spacious canals for traffic, the Els became angular monopolists, jabbing their legs like millipedes into clumps of cement, peering into bedrooms, and ripping sleep as well as privacy into ribbons. An immense power of capitalists, bankers, lawyers, lobbyists, pushed these Els through state and city legislatures, with Tammany aldermen and contractors to help on the spot. And a superb natural site for an empire city was transformed by these monstrosities into the remorseless shuttling of millions for long hours every day.

It was partly to avoid this shuttling that I had come into Mrs. Hatch's boardinghouse. This was a picture of shabby gentility. At one time the block was highly respectable and Dr. Hatch was no doubt proud of his brownstone mansion. But he left his widow without means. She was a small, harassed gentlewoman, well on in years, curbed under the weight of feeding and lodging a couple of dozen people with help that had no more expertness than herself. She could offer a few big rooms, pompously furnished, to splendiferous visitors, but those of us who climbed to the top floor had the old servants' quarters.

Through the thin wooden partitions I could hear the eddies

of boardinghouse life—two spinsters coming and going with their own lives guarded behind walls of platitude, while a virile newcomer rushed by and left them fluttering. The morning stretched the household on the dissecting table. Bedlinen and towels were tumbled into corners until Adam, the colored handyman, bundled them down to the laundry, while Stasia and Delia mopped and slopped, and scrubbed and rubbed with constant calls on them from the anxious Mrs. Hatch or some half-dressed boarder who was in desperate fix. Stasia, a jaundiced Irishwoman of about fifty, her thin mouth downcurved and her eyes burnt holes in the parchment mask. She was so exhausted by the demands that she could reduce to neither order nor reason that she met each new request with a querulous snarl. Delia lunged at her work as though she were still pitching hay in County Clare. She was extremely beautiful, as any Italian painter would have seen, with a brow swept free of her black locks, and her deep, soft eyes, and a fullness of her glance when it dwelt on you. But Stasia nipped her like an old sheep dog, and then Delia rushed to take an order or to remove plates. Before the end of the meal her damp hair would be slapped into place with an impatient hand, and her eyes would be wild and distracted. Mrs. Hatch, a small woman, gray in dress and with a tight bun of gray hair, would give an estimating glance over her shoulder and then resume her dishing out. The Irish girls were the only ones you could hope for.

My brother introduced me to his friends, or some of them. Immediately on my arrival he had taken me to see Billy Ivins, who worked at Doubleday. The first day I sat in his home, fresh from the boat, he was not unnaturally amused (as he told me years later) at Byrne's Irish brother, sporting a shock of black hair, wearing a stuffy suit, wearing new black gloves, thoughtfully flapping the long unoccupied fingertips of one glove against the other. As for myself I was cogitating. The talk was of rare books and prints—of Meryon's etchings—in which a startlingly clear view of Paris was cut across by flights of fantastic birds. Billy Ivins, lanky and curly-haired, twinkling with cordiality, was yet aloof, aloof as a lighthouse, signalling his own situation but holding his distance. I felt small under his critical lens, though he never suspected it. That he was remote from "The World's Work," from America's absorption in the machinery of survival, or its insistence on "progress," was of itself a solace; but his years at Harvard and his first visit to Europe had so developed his taste that my babblings were at best to be tolerated. As with most subtle and acute young men of 22 or 23, the gap he set between himself and a boy of 18 or 19 was too deep to be forded and too temporary to be bridged. But he had not a trace of snobbery. As Byrne's brother, he welcomed me.

Another young man from "The World's Work" came bounding into our lives. Isaac Marcosson was from Kentucky, and he was a young Alexander, nakedly avid for conquest. He was short, compact, the throbbing nerve of a dizzy powerhouse, and if a machine could have graphed his leaping ambition, Ike would have taxed its capacity. With his chin thrust out, adjusting his glasses to take in the mob in the boardinghouse, restively tapping them as he exhausted their sorry display, he would say to me, "Go on, go on, I am listening." He ought to have been listening. He had a way of squatting in the middle of your privacy, dipping into the bowl for your most succulent secrets, brushing your protective hand aside to pluck from you the apple of your eye, and then, as you at least expected a response, shifting his gaze to some object of superior interest, even as you approached a poignant death scene. He had a prompt laugh as you protested, for intimacy was his turkish bath; he elected for nudity; the world was his oyster, his nude oyster, and if he had proposed the most personal questions he would meet your own with extraordinary generosity. This air of profuse generosity was immensely tempting to me, yet the facilities of his nature seemed achieved by the omission of some element which his intelligence renounced yet which, while illusive, seemed indispensable to me. But he attracted me, this avid, vivid Alexander.

I felt he had put childishness behind him because he was a writer by profession. But that he could readily believe what he wished to believe, and what it feathered his nest to believe, was the comic trait I seized on. It was in doing that and in pretending not to know it, that he appeared to me droll. I relished him, but I could not envy him, though I envied his having this voluptuous present.

Youth seeks heroes; it respects patriotic heroes; it needs to worship. When I asked my "Uncle" Ed in Albany if he had fought in the Civil War—he was a round, rosy man with a neat white moustache and a carnation in his buttonhole—he took me to his Fort Orange Club where everybody liked him—but it appeared he had not fought, he had put up $300 and was exempted. His son, however, young Lieutenant Ed, home from the Philippines and still wearing his gray uniform, redeemed our tribal honor, and I was proud of him. He was also at our boardinghouse. He did not look well; he had, in fact, tuberculosis and the end of his days was not far off. But his very quietness, his melancholy acquiescence, and a certain look of honorable discharge won me to him from the first. He had the soldier's "dominion over self," grave and enviable.

But after a few weeks in New York, a friend from home asked me to meet a Rough Rider from Texas, and I was delighted. George, my Irish companion, had no iron dominion over self He had little or no sense of self, but an astonishing sense of life. Amusing, easy, roguish, he dispensed his time for me without a thought. He wanted me to meet Roy Sykes out of his joy in sharing.

Roy was a breeze. Carlyle once said that Daniel Webster was "a magnificent specimen." Roy was another. Tall and straight as a pine, he was bronzed, had laugh wrinkles around his keen eyes and a drawl that was pipelined from the Texan border. He wore a cream-colored hat, a gay tie, a thin light suit; he had cigars peeping from his pocket. He was a Mason. More than that, he was a Republican.

For a very simple reason we became fast friends. He had moved from the Rough Riders to a high stool in Washington, a modest billet that had to do with agriculture. And literacy, which till he sat on a stool, left him oblivious, suddenly took on importance—a ladder in his hands but few rungs on it. I was all rungs and no ladder. He had never met anyone so overflowing with literacy; he drank from me as from a spring. Because he was on probation as an inspector and obliged to write reports, he did not mind my alien behavior; for I as a ginger ale drinker, a youth under nineteen with glasses and green as an indigestible apple, was alien at sight. Yet every word I uttered held him and still the wonder grew. George purred. The three of us became inseparable.

Where could we be together? It had to be easy, friendly, and we'd like it lively and bright. It could not be the YMCA. It had to be the Tenderloin, about 29th Street. So there we met after dinner; we moved from one glaring joint to another till we found a congenial one. They drank freely, and, in a sense, they never wanted to go to bed. It was all one to me. Roy had ridden with Roosevelt, and he came from the Lone Star State. I did not know that a Republican in Texas stuck out like a poppy in a cornfield, but we exchanged our wares. I paid out geegaw words; he spread out Texas for me. He'd have given me Brooklyn Bridge for my baubles. He felt I "knew." He talked of his wives—he had only had two—and I gave him advice from the depths of my soul, for it touched him nearly. His second wife, she, too, was literate, and he mounted to her on a shaky ladder. I supplied him with rungs. In return, after seven or eight whiskies, he threw light into dark places for me. He gave meaning to the Iliad.

In his hotel lobby another Texan, a corpulent Elk, tossed his horns and gave a war whoop and hugged Roy. "You old son of a gun! Painting the town? Who are these boys?" He beamed on us like a cheery old sheriff. I was cut to the heart when Roy replied dryly, "My boon companions." But I realized he was being the respectable office holder. They sank their voices, pulled down their mouths, were somber, confidential, and terse.

"Say, he never told me!"

"I gave it to him straight, Joab."

"I'll tell the world!"

They matched tactics in office holding, the robust Joab urging Roy to take chances. "You're the man, Roy, why don't ye . . ."

"I would, quick as a whip, but if I do . . ." My hearing was sharp, but they talked too low. Why do people talk so low!

What a pity Roy was to fall ill in Washington! He had begged me to apply my literacy to a letter which would show his wife that George and I were positively ducal and friends of the Colonel and that we had learned that the Colonel thought the world of Roy. I did it. I was wrong to do it. It was low of me to do it. I did it. And what a pity his so literate wife had to open his letters for him. All his letters. When we next met his breeze had lulled, and the heat seemed to have wilted him.

"Sir, I was like to die. Yes, sir, like to die." He was mourning over his plight so hard that I studied him. He was a magnificent specimen still. But he would not be cheered.

"Roy, what's troubling you?"

"Son, you sure balled things up!"

"I did what you asked me to, on Waldorf Astoria notepaper. Wasn't it all right?"

"The one you wrote building me up? That was swell. But the funny one you wrote about your terrible hall bedroom where you really lived! What made you do it. You done me wrong!"

"But it was for fun!"

"Not for her, it wasn't. Only my double pneumonia saved me from divorce."

"But I wrote to your office."

"She took over the office."

I said, "Gosh!" That was all. And my verbal bankruptcy caused him surprise and cost me his respect. If I was dumb, I was zero to him.

"She'd found me out," he said dolefully. "I hadn't a word to say. It was only when the second lung was attacked that she come around. But there it is. She don't forget."

He sat stonily, sunk deep in the drab old lobby armchair. It was very different from San Juan and *la gloire*. It was more like ginger ale and green apples. Marriage had settled on him in its sobriety. He was thinking about crops in Texas and the scant crop of Republicans in Texas and with codfish eyes. He did not offer me a cigar.

But he was not permanently lamed. One day in the Sherman House in Chicago I thought I saw him flash by me. I gave a peace whoop, "Roy Sykes!"

A bronzed man in a cream-colored hat wheeled around. "No, I ain't Roy. I know him well."

"And how is he?"

"Roy? Going like a house afire."

You can kill these Roys, but you can't cure them, except very lightly.

One day my brother announced that a distant cousin of ours was coming for Sunday dinner to the boardinghouse. I should have been glad, but it depressed me.

This cousin was a young man, brisk and compact, with a hearty manner. He was fond of interjecting "that's bully" or "isn't that corking!" He had been trained to be a teacher, and he was a born scoutmaster. It was a raw and chilly day on which my cousin was with us, and I remember it because he said to me after our dinner, "I'd like to have a talk with you, young man." He was four or five years older.

So we walked up Fifth Avenue, a blustering wind ruffling the wet patches and then swiping the street with sunlight. That is the way spring begins, two weathers fighting it in, bracing and disorderly. I liked it, but I could feel that my good cousin was bourgeoning with a mission. "Francis," he said, "I have something serious to speak about. You were overheard in your boardinghouse boasting you'd been in a brothel."

As he blinked his light eyelashes at me, I felt a revulsion that made me incapable of speaking. We were on the opposite side to where the Public Library now stands. It was then the site of a small reservoir.

"What business is this of yours?" I asked him. "Did I come to you for advice?"

"I think you need it," he answered curtly.

"When I do, I'll ask for it."

That was a tense moment. It was in his mind to continue, I think, but I suppose I was jutting out my own chin, such as it was, and he decided it was hopeless to bring me to the paths of righteousness. I suggested that we wheel around and then did my damndest to find a new topic of conversation.

I did not believe an eavesdropper had heard me boasting. It was probably my cousin Ed who had told him, since he felt I was a young fool to be in the brothel, where we had met, and it would be Christian tact for him to lie rather than drag in Ed. And Ed did think me a fool. He was happily consoling the spinster in the boardinghouse, whose room was next to his, while I, walled away from all spinsters by my upbringing, could only believe that sex was sin, and sin had to be committed with wicked women, "bad" women. So I thought and cast down my eyes whenever I met ladies hurrying to the tin bathtub.

The thing that makes a smug missionary a revolting creature is his failure to find a common ground from which a start can be made, if it is a question of behavior. A smug Nazi is no better. Neither is a smug Communist. All three intrude their decision about behavior without finding out where one agrees and where one disagrees. The thing I resent is the intrusion. And this is made worse by preventing one's expression of partial agreement with a real criticism.

The Tree of Knowledge

A few days before the incident with the missionary, Bill K., a friend of my brother's, had said to me, "So you're the brother from Ireland? Come on. I'll show you the town."

Bill had a way of jerking his chin free from his collar and at the same time giving an aggressive tilt to this chin that went well with his slim, agile body. He walked with a paddleboat use of his elbows, and he cocked his hat to one side. He had a curt, pugnacious nose. He was as raw as a radish, but sparkling in a lively, almost combative fashion, like a boy on leave. Toward me he was perfectly friendly but inclined to laugh a little readily, as if the words I used, and my glasses with the straight bar, and my Irish clothes and a politeness that leaned toward formality had something comic in them.

"Have you a few dollars—you have? Fine and dandy! I'm out of a job. I'm going to work on Monday."

We got on all right. We strolled up Broadway to 42nd Street, passed by the nickelodeons, and amused ourselves by seeing others, just as the others saw us. Two boys on the town, Saturday night in New York.

"Ever been in the Red Light District?" Bill asked with a grin. He grinned easily. "Here we are."

A short block between Broadway and Sixth Avenue was brilliant with lights. The houses were exactly the same in style as my brownstone boardinghouse, but every window was alight, and the steps had iron railings instead of coping stone. Restaurant windows showed that the big rooms downstairs had been made over, as in the French restaurant on 25th Street.

"We'll have a glass of beer," said Bill. "What do you say?"

"Or ginger ale," said I. "I don't drink."

"Or sarsaparilla," said Bill. "They'll give you anything."

It was blindingly bright. Bill swaggered in, nodded to a girl in a white shirtwaist and black coat and skirt. Her hair was in a pompadour. We sat down at a small table. The room was at the back, looking out on the Catalpa tree. The house seemed meaner than the boardinghouse, but mirrors, white walls, bright raw lights, and advertising gave it a sharp gaiety. A piano was clanging from the front room.

Another girl joined the first, and they sat on the cheap chairs near our table. Then Bill invited them to sit with us and ordered beer for them. Others came in, and he jollied the girls. He was from Brooklyn, he said. At that they laughed, and he laughed. Very funny, Brooklyn.

They left for a moment, "for Brooklyn," they said. And then he said, "Want to go upstairs? Have you five dollars you can lend me? You can take the pretty one."

They were back in an instant. And after a little more conversation Bill stood up and jerked his chin. "Coming, Frank?" The girl in black and white looked at me. She was about twenty with an open Irish face and friendly eyes. I nodded to her and we went upstairs.

We had a big bedroom blatantly lighted, with an enormous, entirely white, bundly sort of bed. Bill took his girl to the backroom. It was a violently exciting moment, and my heart beat fast. But in bed the girl could not help laughing. "Not in there, dear. Here." And then she said softly, "Your first time?" She was gentle. "Gee, your face is red! Here, take your towel. There's water over there." I looked in the glass. My face was the color of a peony, and yet I looked immensely relieved, twinkling with relief. Something had happened to take me out of a damnable imprisonment in self, and I felt grateful to the girl, who was looking at me indulgently and wonderingly. "Go ahead, dear. I'll fix my pompadour."

And as I went to the room at the back, a young man in a U.S. lieutenant's gray uniform with red facings was sitting at the table by the bar. He was my cousin, Ed Hackett, from Albany. "Hello, Francis," he said in a warm, amiable, easy tone, so different from Bill's banter. "What are you doing here? Are you alone?"

"No, I was upstairs."

"With a girl?" His smile faded. "You have to be damn careful, Francis, you know that." He looked around. "I hope she was all right."

"Oh, I'm sure she was."

He shook his head. "I hope so." He had a glass in front of him, and had apparently no interest in the girls.

In an instant Bill and the girls came down, and I left my cousin. We sat at a long table, running from the bar to the window, with benches next to the wall and ordinary cane chairs on the outside. Others were already sitting there, especially two men who gave some support to the notion that we had descended from apes. They were squat, beady-eyed, and uncompromisingly ugly. With these rival customers before me, I began to feel not uncomfortable, but how degraded I must feel later on. I did not think sex was sin, but to share it with apes was horrible.

Bill was in high spirits. So were a company of boys and young prostitutes nearby. Whiskies and beers kept being ordered with winks from Bill, and in an hour or two the whole room began singing. The waiters stood around, glad of a let-up, while the chorus grew louder and louder. My cousin had vanished by the time the singing began, and a wild flow of spirits, a strong thrust of animal hilarity and geniality went into the idiotic rhythms:

> *We had to carry Carrie to the ferry,*
> *And the ferry carried Carrie to the shore,*
> *And the reason that we had to carry Carrie*
> *Was that Carrie couldn't carry any more.*
>   *O Annie Moore,*
>   *Sweet Annie Moore,*
> *For Carrie couldn't carry Annie Moore.*

"Just for that," cried Carrie saucily, "I'll have another rye."

Carrie was the center of attraction, fresh in her frilled blouse, and Bill, who had taken the tousled blonde, Louise, upstairs, was now dwelling entirely on the younger girl. So they sang the song again, Carrie repeating it, her eyes gleaming with fun. Bill took on a cockier air than ever. Louise was glum; she couldn't bear being ignored. "For Christ's sake," she muttered, "can't you quit it now?" "Oh, dry up," snapped Bill, and he leaned over the table, shouting the chorus into Louise's face. With her raddled cheeks quivering, her dyed hair mercilessly exposed under the lamps, the haggard blonde was so angry that Carrie intervened. "Don't be sore on the kid, Lou," she said, soothingly. "The boys are having a good time."

"A good time," snorted Louise, "you couldn't give it to them!" This reflection on her professional talent touched Carrie to the quick. It made her start and recoil from her colleague, but in an instant, lightly raising her voice so that the whole room could hear, she said lazily and clearly, "You can say what you like, but there's one thing you can't anybody say! I was never in the family way!"

Bill burst into a roar of laughter. Encouraged by this, the girl muttered some scathing remark to one of the gnomes, who scowled. Carrie was a little drunk and laughed, "I meant you to hear it, see? That's what you look like, too." "You know what *you* look like, don't you," the hairy man said angrily, "you look like what you are, a two-bit whore!"

At which Bill, clearing his throat, spat full in the face of the man.

Up till then my head had been spinning with a picture of that brilliantly lighted room upstairs, and the friendly voice of the girl, and the feeling, "I've done it." She was part of a wholly inhuman, grimly calculated machine, the Red Light machine, for extracting money from customers and, with light glaring and privacy impossible, from all the Saturday trade there was. I had no fear that the girl was diseased, and no other girl but one of her kind would have been willing to have me. A "good" girl wouldn't, not unless I could marry her. But the serenity which came with having acted, rightly or wrongly, was suddenly spilt by this eruption into savagery that the drunken girl had provoked and that Bill had no less drunkenly resented. Never before had I seen one human being spit in another's face. The vileness of this insult produced a revulsion in my veins, as if the blood curdled, and yet I could see why Bill had done it. He wanted this girl when he first saw her, and had allowed me to take her and was now feeling protective and her proprietor. The older men saw it with their own kind of sophistication, drinking their whiskies and chewing their cigars. She was a cheap whore, and the boy didn't see it, but until he spat, their condescension did not change to cold venom. They both stood up, and as the burly one mopped his face he growled, "Come outside." Bill staggered up, doubling his fists, and I stood up. The girl's face was shocked, and her drab companion said, "You've started something."

The four of us left the house in that apparent fraternity, which even a cop cannot discount, and we crossed Broadway toward Fifth Avenue. It was dark in this block and quite empty.

"We'll settle it here," said the burly fellow, while his companion said to me, "You want to fight too?"

"Why should I fight?" I said. "Can't you see my friend's drunk?"

"I'll keep out of it if you do," the man said. "If you butt in, I'll fix you."

By this time Bill's antagonist had set out to square the account. He was outraged at what had been done to him, and in his fury he was delighted that Bill was unsteady on his feet. He was angry enough to kill Bill, and his first onslaught was so successful that he knocked Bill down and fell on top of him. Bill was underneath, lashing out hard with hands and feet, but the man he'd insulted thrust one hand into Bill's mouth and began pounding his head in spite of the teeth that clenched on his hand. He hoped to batter Bill's skull against the pavement.

"He'll kill him," I said. "Stop it." And I grabbed the man on top. "Stop him!" I cried to the rival's second. We separated them. They were panting and gasping. Bill's face seemed to be in ribbons, and blood streamed down on his white shirt. He wore no waistcoat. I was holding his coat.

"The cop!" At that word we parted, the two squat men scuttling toward Fifth Avenue, North, while we took the other direction.

"You didn't hit the other fellow," Bill said bitterly.

"I was holding your coat," I said. But it was true, I had not joined in the brawl. For some reason—was it cowardice, I asked myself—the evening's companionship with this wild fellow had not ignited any real feeling of loyalty. At the beginning, yes, I had felt we were together, but when he spat into the other's face, it revolted me. It opened into a whole-souled barbarity that I did not share, and yet I was ashamed of holding back. Bill was, however, so chastened by the knockout he had suffered and the confused feeling in his head, that I led him back to my boardinghouse without his objecting. We crept upstairs, and I helped him wash his wounds, and I persuaded him to take my bed. He was like a crumpled pup, badly mauled and utterly exhausted. I lay on the floor, covered by a good heavy Irish rug, and looked up at the skylight. I had much to think about.

The youth of military age—18 to 21—who lives on a low wage in a big city cannot possibly afford to be married. Neither can a working girl of the same class. What are they to do for erotic experience? When I was young the girls knew nothing about birth control, and the ideal prescribed for them, as for the young men, was chastity. My nature was relatively fastidious. One of the reasons I was glad to be in America was to escape from Ireland's sex surveillance; but the Church does not originate sex tension, any more than capitalism originates cupidity. Wipe out the Church and the glands still secrete. It is not the Catholic Church which makes the Australian Bushman reprehend incest. The difficulties created by incest and by homosexuality are inseparable from the repercussion on social life of any practice that regards both one's own person and another person. Sex is a purposeful force that can only be diverted to delight by means that react on the character as a whole. Sex is a conscription, though there is room for a conscientious objector.

Chastity was never my goal. I resorted to prostitution for several years, but as I never took a drink until I was 42, I could not hide from myself the ugliness and disappointment of the subterfuge. Between 1901 and 1904 I accepted their mistreatments less than half a dozen times. They were known as "hustlers." They went through the motions of sex to earn their money, and they did it with an apathy that was at once stupid and callous. They behaved as the underpaid are prone to behave, with disgust for their job and for their customers; their existence so inherently repulsive to themselves that they diffuse its horror and mortify the man who degrades them. These were the very poorest of their class, not the strapping, bulky hustlers of Broadway that modelled themselves on the big chorus girls. Those hustlers had a higher tariff, and I did not aspire to them. I aspired to a mistress.

But in this quest for erotic happiness I went below the surface of the great city to find what I could, and it was a jungle swarming with misdirected passion, a tough, uncouth, immoderate anarchy of hot blood and cold vice, a storm of goaded instincts that the city whetted by its parade of immeasurable wealth, and, behind its ostentation, the glitter of its subtler beauty, the sinuous stream of its refinement.

When summer at last arrived in New York, it was a marvelous surprise. I roamed until dark on a rapturous June evening. The sky, festooned with stars, could not show itself unless there was an isle of darkness, but I could wander along quiet avenues that had city trees in leaf, which made me think of the country and its solace. Uncle Ed had given me a bicycle, but as I knew no other person who was using one and could not bring myself to do it alone, I plodded the sidewalks as a substitute, under the strangely tender sky, and in the gentle air, caressing and serene after the Manhattan winter. I avoided the Saturday crowds, to bring the evening nearer, but as it became tedious toward midnight, I turned down Sixth Avenue, preferring its crassness to Broadway, where I'd be solicited by streetwalkers. I did not want to go home. It was the end of the week. I was in the mood for company, but the increase of summer did not add to my wealth. I had paid for my board and had only two dollars left, plus a dime for *The Sunday Sun* and Mr. Huneker.

Sixth Avenue, burdened with the El, was a grove of metal trunks, a monstrous banyan tree that sucked up the sky, stars and all, and pushed the houses apart with iron branches. I saw no one in sight, once I passed Mouquin's, and neared my stuffy boardinghouse. It was unbearable to go in. I stood at the end of our street, and I said to myself, "I'll have a woman."

A woman came along. She stopped when she saw me. There was nothing to allure me. She was stumpy, in dark clothes, and approaching middle age. "Hello," she said in a drab voice, "waiting for somebody?"

"I was waiting for you," I said.

"Come on, then." And she led the way toward Seventh Avenue, along the clapboard houses on 25th Street. "You're young," she said, giving me a look. I could not respond in kind. Youth had vanished from her, leaving her without its faintest spark, a thickened, even dumpy figure, with her face rather heavy and inexpressive. "Here we are." She opened the door with a latchkey, and we mounted to the top floor. How the devil had I got into this?

The room was so tight under the roof that the sun's warmth was held in it behind small guillotine windows that looked as if they had never been opened. It was a rather large room, with a double bed in it, vast and white and billowy. The gas was burning low. "I guess we don't want a light," she said. It was rather brown, the whole room, except for the bed, with a cheap mantelpiece and a thin carpet on the floor. All the freshness of June was excluded from it, and I drew in a desperate breath. This attic smelt of dried sweat and shut-in dust, cooked under the day's sun, with a stealthy reminder of bad perfume, stale tobacco, and urine. A rickety washstand had a basin and jug on it, with a few pleasure towels lolling on the edge of it.

"I have only two dollars," I said in a shy voice. "If that's not enough . . ."

She was nearly stripped, her back turned. She grunted impatiently. "You about ready?" And she took her place in bed. "Don't worry."

I did worry. She was an object to me, this two-dollar woman, and I hated myself for using her, but it was two months since I had taken this course. A month before I had followed the lead of a colored girl, whose roost was in an unoccupied theatre; but just as we were climbing to the dressing rooms by a bold iron ladder, a colored gentleman in shirt sleeves had appeared on the top landing and had called down over the railing with a snarl that reverberated angrily. I was inclined to the pretty girl, but this black guardian was too much for me. I felt that both he and the step ladder were untoward; the girl wavered and I stood still. I lost my desire. He seemed to me to be drawing the color line.

Now there was no such violation of privacy, no hindrance to the act, except its terrible impersonality, its inhumanity. But if the woman felt it, she did not resign to it. When I had completed the brutal evacuation that was my purpose, she held me tight. "Wait," she said in a muffled voice. She pressed her hand on my back, and I could not deny that she intended to keep me with her. In that inarticulate pause I had an impulse to rise and to shove off her staying hand, out of caution if nothing else, but as we lay together in that two-dollar embrace, it penetrated my skull and my heart that she knew everything about me—my reluctance to seek a prostitute, my shrinking from the fetid room, my shame to have so little to offer her, my tremulous aloneness and inexperience. And as it dawned on me that she must understand, that she wished me to have the full bounty of her body and to reap whatever my youth could give her, the ice that my upbringing had packed into me began to crumble, and she could feel me thaw and seek to possess her. She was an old war horse. All I needed was to grip her tight, and the confidence she had willed and bestowed was rewarded by our coming together. Yet the warmth we engendered and the glow of happiness I felt to have had her disown and conquer my sour pride was still not complete for her. We spoke no words, but we grappled again, and at last she was satisfied.

When I came to leave her, I said, "I'll see you again?" We had lit our cigarettes. "Maybe," she answered, without a glint of enthusiasm. She had no illusions to feed. In that one deal she had chosen to play a hand, touched by some loneliness of her own, some dream or memory, and she had opened to me without reserve—prodigal and beyond shame, proud to do her job as a woman. She knew what she had given me: I needed to have a woman.

If humility is good, whether Christian or pagan, my heart was full of it as I walked east. That attic room, so thronged with fornicating, had been no place for love, and yet she had merged me in the ocean of its simple human impulse, the oldest in the world. She had not sold it to me. She had given it to me, common creature of the night, not in the South Sea Islands, on 25th Street.

I could hear the steamers on the Hudson River, as I lay awake at night in my windowless box, and the hollow boom of an ocean-going vessel that was on its way out to sea seemed to me the unbearably mournful, unbearably urgent voice of my own wish to be gone from where I was, so powerless and bewildered. Kipling was the vile poet of Empire against the Boers, but at the same time he was the enchanter whose light was swung on a horizon, the man who evoked distances and stars over Asia. He peopled us with men who had left their own world and its commonplaces—men who had "go fever," who knew the East, who had its remoteness and mystery. It was the sun and multitudes and camel's dust and names that were better forgotten, romantic love that drove lean-faced, broken-hearted, silent men into the night and left the right word unspoken. No writer was ever so deep in the opium traffic and at the same time the godfather of all boy scouts. And when the cargo boats went down the Hudson and their hoarse throats said goodbye, I heard them under the skylight with a wild heart. "Francis, take this to the Guaranty and Trust Company. Then you can get your lunch." Cup of coffee and a piece of pie. Was this to be the future?—So my thoughts roiled me.

It was not that I could confidently think. I was not trained early enough. I was one of those Irish who have great difficulty in sustaining a thought. Fidelity to feelings, the sole sovereignty of the poet, is perhaps the best such Irish can achieve, since deviation from a line of thought, abhorrent and confusing to a strict reasoner, may be a necessity of their vagrant feelings. An intuitive intercourse with reality seems to require indulgent space in which to move around and about delusive appearance. It exacts time for meditation, in which to brood on this deceptiveness, and all this an Irishman covers by the magic word "liberty." To catch what is truly felt, to transmute it in words not premeditated by the ductile, with music in them that has the tremor and the danger of flame, must not proceed from the will; for this ductility, this mobility, must not subserve a cold-blooded purpose. On brute matter a man may properly impose his will. On disorder he has to exercise his intellect. But the maze of his feelings has to be ordered as a free partner in a dance is ordered, by intimation, by intuition, by suasion.

When the capacity for rapture is fresh, feelings seek what is pleasing and lulling in a world obsessed by activities that ignore or violate feelings. The courage to open out the most hidden feelings is a proof of maturity. Yet a wholehearted poet who dares to deploy a legion of miscreant, dauntless guerillas must not be corrupt. Many poets are as dark as they are proud, and if they are not themselves manumitted from anger, greed, and ignorance, they can only reveal what is perverse, vengeful, and vicious.

Liberty has tollgates on its road, and the pure of heart alone can attain "the highest standard of living," that is sincere feeling, "in the world." Feeling is at the core of living.

New Job

I had been in America a year. I was still nineteen. In that time my parents had sent me about twenty pounds, but I wanted to become self-supporting. Under the surface I had no wish to be a lawyer.

I turned to Help Wanted, the biggest lottery there is. The *Cosmopolitan* magazine wanted an office boy at $8 a week. If I could have that, then I'd be able to tell my father not to send me any more money, and I'd be in some way connected with writing. I drew the ticket in the lottery, not in the icebox of the law, out in the climate of rude society. My wages doubled in a month, as compared with the law.

It was in the advertising office of the *Cosmopolitan* magazine. Two driving men ran it. One was a pale blond, a reserved and decorous German-American in a high stiff collar, complementing a black-haired Kentuckian, who was brisk as a freshet, a tremendous worker, who sparkled and rippled as he performed—Mr. Eisenwald and Frank Griffin. These men were alive. I was to fetch and carry between Park Row and Irvington-on-Hudson, our classic building to be seen from the N.Y. Central trains. My bag bulged with "cuts"—copper plates mounted on wood, then were transferred by the springheeled from magazine to magazine. I took to this strenuous, exacting, long-hour, train-hopping job, my bosses congenial. That is, my immediate bosses in the advertising department. The same could not be said for the Walkers.

Irvington, however, was a new experience. After the iron tightness of Manhattan, the space in this Hudson River town was a prisoner's release. The tender haze of the twilight, with the pungence of burning leaves in it, and October keen as a violin brought a promise of new life, a touch of beauty. The climbing vines were brilliant, but better still the hum of voices as neighbors heaped dead leaves for bonfires. It had more than the charm of a single, twilit town. It carried me away from avid enterprises to where women would tend vines for their blazing leaves and seek grace in the clean lines of white houses. It spoke to me of innumerable small communities in the states I was yet to see, of a light kinship that bound them across the continent.

I could feel it in the snug house where I was living as the only boarder with a married couple; Chichester I think the name was. The man was our accountant on the magazine, and when I inquired for a place to board he said, "I'll ask the wife." She was willing. It was a blessed change from New York. She was comparatively young, an excellent cook, a gentle, attentive woman of soft ways and deep layers of sentiment. He was sharp as a quill, and loving to talk. We sat by the oil lamp with its painted globe and tried not to trip among the rugs, the little tables, and the obtruding rocker. Pictures disputed with the patterns on the wallpaper, and everything in the room sought to look like something else—the wall brackets having a resemblance to rustic fences, the crockery from Atlantic City crisped into sponges, and dead grasses in a tall vase bringing back nature in its most fertile moment.

Mrs. Chichester was a hovering, curious presence. She sat apart from us when we talked after supper, and she often gazed at me. He was a nervous, harsh, disillusioned man with a crackling mind and a romp of ideas that poured out of him, ravenous for response. Whenever we got going, I was aware of his attentive wife, and I tried to keep pace while staying linked with her, not out of calculation but from thirst for affinity with a woman. She loved her husband, but he dragged her by sheer force of will over the verbal rocks and crags that excited his Yankee passion for savage exercise. He'd give cries of pleasure at our orgies. "Gee, I've been looking for this. This is great. This is wonderful."

Yes, until the night he said to me, "Say, Hackett, tell me something. Are you a Christian?"

"Well, what do you mean? Was I baptized, do you mean?"

"Of course you were baptized. You had nothing to say about it, young man. They took you to the font without asking your permission, didn't they? They grabbed you before you could say 'no.' I mean, do you believe in Christianity? No, I'll go further. Do you think it's proved that Christ ever really existed?"

It never entered my head to doubt it. But he was deadly serious. The little room was filled with it, and I stopped the smile I'd begun.

"You've never thought about that?"

"No," I said reluctantly. It was one thing I hadn't ever happened to think about, and I was ashamed. "How do we know he ever existed?"

That excited Mr. Chichester. "You see! They all believe in Christ, the pack of sheep, but they never stop to ask if the man ever existed."

"But people just believe what they're told."

"Yes, but you and me are not like that. Say, you have a mind, Hackett, Now, if he never existed . . ."

At that moment a sob broke in on us. We both turned toward Mrs. Chichester. We had entirely forgotten her; she was so quiet.

"Oh," she sobbed, "I can't bear to have you two talk of Christ like that."

Her tone sobered Mr. Chichester. "Say, I'm sorry, Mother," he said to her. "We oughtn't to have done it."

His voice was kind and full of compunction. It was too much for her. Streaming with tears, she rushed from the room.

She did not hold it against me, but somehow the zest went out of our talks.

Breakfast had to be very early in this household. It was part of my job to report at 7 A.M. And I had to report, not at the office, but in Mr. David Walker's bedroom. John Brisben Walker was one of the pioneer eagles, a keen, wide-visioned Yankee who everywhere saw empires inviting him and leaped after them with more avidity than patience. David Walker was the son whose anxious occupation it was to tidy up after his father. And I had to attend on this worried scion of a mad scramble for power at 7 A.M. before he stepped into his trousers.

David Walker wore a nightshirt. He had hairy legs, and in figure he was sturdily pugnacious like a bull terrier with a growling morning manner. As he extruded himself from his troubled couch, bare legs foremost, and then began to give me orders, still blinking from the night, I found myself out of sympathy with him. No doubt the empire was slipping, and he was tottering under its weight, but the orders he barked at me from his dressing table were no more ceremonious than his nightshirt.

"You know where Budd's is?"

"I do."

"Pick up three shirts for me. Tell them David Walker sent you."

"You'd like them here?"

"No, leave them at the office."

"May I go now?"

"You? No. I have to sign some checks. Meet me in the dining room."

More Walkers were in the dining room. There was one boy, a youngster, who was pleading for three dollars. The other brothers were hardhearted. Then David arrived, his sparse hair parted on his cranium and his face dark with preoccupation. A slice of bitten toast in one hand and his pen in the other, he signed checks in a huge checkbook, while the plump, ruddy youngster kept asking, "David, can't you let me have three dollars?" It was a dismal, tall-windowed room, the table dishevelled with half-finished meals, and the checkbook barely escaping the butter. I stood behind David Walker's chair, averse to the experience, while I meant no more to him than his napkin ring.

Then the cashier came in. He was, I remember, a thin, acid-bitten Southerner, and I vaguely recall something close to a brainstorm. Everybody's nerves were on edge at Irvington, trying to make more out of two plus two than was conventionally admitted. Nobody gave the baby brother his three dollars.

But it was entirely different in the advertising office. The manager was Mr. Eisenwald, and Frank Griffin was second in command. They had plenty to do, knew how to do it, were paid for doing it, and liked me because I went lickety-split to carry out any orders they gave me. It was a brisk confident office, and I soon gathered they were not overrawed by the Walkers.

"John Brisben is coming to the office, Francis," said Frank Griffin, whose keen profile and black hair gave him an almost Indian look. He was, I soon learned, half brother of Mary Anderson, the Southern actress.

"When, Mr. Griffin?"

"Before lunch. And, ah—if I were you I think I'd lock up the petty cash." With this he departed, whistling. And no one whistled more melodiously than Frank Griffin.

Before lunch the eagle flew in. He was affable, distinguished and very welcome. The calm, blond Eisenwald and the nervous, tall Griffin were on the trigger with their laugh and smile, and we had a merry ten minutes. Then as he walked out he said to me, "Ah, by the way, have you a little change? Is there anything in the petty cash?"

"I'm afraid it's locked, Mr. Walker."

"Never mind, never mind," he said amiably and left. I never saw him again.

It was really David Walker's crashing rudeness that made the *Cosmopolitan* unbearable. Legman I was, but no valet. The morning attendance in the bedroom bred little errands that found no favor with me. Had I liked him I'd have played. Instead I hated him. And I often said to myself, "Some day I'll hit him." I don't think I ever clenched my fists with more eagerness for *Der Tag,* but it was simpler to throw up the job than to brawl with so crass—and sturdy—an employer.

The Walkers jarred me, but even if they had been Lord Chesterfields, their enterprise jarred me. I was too young, too much an outsider to tussle with them on their own ground. Had I been born American, and able to find some backing, I might have nipped off a bit of their empire, as did young Ellery Sedgwick when he stood up to them and secured *Leslie's,* one of their magazines. But the game itself was like Harmsworth's in England, and I had not come to America for this.

My immediate bosses had won my loyalty. They offered me $10 a week, saying I was the best (most eager?) office boy they'd had. I hugged the praise, but after two most unpleasant days I refused the temptation. I could link with them but not for the Walker's frantic enterprises. What was the quality of this empire? Mr. Walker's *Cosmopolitan* was stuff I could not read, and I could read almost anything. Advertising was artificial manure, making two purchasers grow where one had grown before, but it did not trade with the purchasers; it traded on them.

The Kentuckian heard my decision, saying nothing, fumbling his tongue in his cheek. "So you'll leave. I'm sorry. I see why. We may not be here forever ourselves. We have an idea that may work out. Keep in touch with us. I'll send for you."

Book Cloth

Occasionally I had met Christian Brinton, to whom Frank Hackett had introduced me at Putnam. As I told him about the Walkers, he was amused at my resentment of their highhandedness, as Peter Dunne was by his New England innkeeper who stood wooden-faced after handing a Chicagoan his bill.

"What's this for?" boomed the Chicagoan, "This five dollars here? You don't put it down. You don't specify."

"It's for 'busin' me," said the innkeeper barely moving his lips.

The Walkers had 'bused me. In my prim Clongowes dialect, "They were very disposed to hector everybody, which was tiresome." And after Christian laughed, he said, "My boy, I know the very place for you. I'll tell Fred Clark."

Fred Clark was incapable of hectoring anybody. I went to see him in his office in the New York branch of the Holliston Mills, manufacturers of book cloth. As he perched on the edge of his desk, pouring Bull Durham into his cigarette paper, his eyes on it, his smile disarming, I found him as much amused as Christian. That he was the son of an eminent political economist, John Bates Clark, conveyed little to me, low organism that I was, but that Fred Clark had been a lumberjack in Minnesota brought back all the penny dreadfuls I had devoured at thirteen. He was never shot dead, of course, but he had seen shooting matches, several of them, and once when he broke a pane of glass, its owner drew a knife to kill him. Fred Clark, his Bull

Durham dribbling to the floor, allowed himself to talk of the "free life," where every man carried a "gun" a knife, wore a rude beard and a red shirt and high boots, played poker and faro, poured out his money and poured down his firewater. "You're your own master and lord of all you survey, which isn't much." They called him "the little fellow"; he was only 5' 11¾".

Eventually we talked of book cloth. If Mr. Borthwick approved, they'd take me on at $8. I ventured to say, "They offer me ten, the people I'm leaving," so he said he'd advise Mr. Borthwick to meet it. That was great news. At ten dollars I could pay my way. I hurried to write home. "The position is a peculiar one," I said. "It is one of typewriter, stenographer, stock clerk, shipping clerk, and salesman in the office of the Holliston Book Cloth concern. The peculiarity lies in the fact that I can't type, stenog, stock, ship, or sell. But it is a useful business and increasing rapidly. I hope to be a book-cloth millionaire soon. Then I'll wear a suit of my own book cloth. Salary $8 a week, with prospects."

Fred Clark had elated me, but all depended on his partner. I'd have to learn shorthand. I must, as Ned Hackett put it to me, "hump myself." I hankered for the woods after talking with Fred Clark. His heart was there. My heart was with him. But what alternative?

What was book cloth to me or I to book cloth? I wanted to possess my soul. A man can go into a monastery with bare boards to lie on, bare walls to look at, bare bread and water to live on. I could envy the Trappist, but if commercial compulsions seemed sickening to me, it was not human bondage that afflicted me, as it did the Trappist. I wanted above everything to gain a wider human range, and a sense of people better related to life as it is than to life as I imagined it. It was the bondage of circumstance that fretted me. How could I earn my living without losing the light at the end of the tunnel.

I went back to 63 Fifth Avenue to see Mr. Borthwick. The

elevator man seemed to differ from most Negroes. He had a small, finely modelled head and a throaty voice. His manners were dry and incisive, but he responded to courtesy. His name was Isaac. It was a freight elevator, but he ran it like a club elevator. "You'll find Mr. Borthwick in," he said.

Mr. Borthwick turned in his swivel chair and took a shrewd look at the visitor; then, when I gave him my name, he lighted up. He was a Scot, but not like those I remembered from the smoking room of the *Furnessia*. His was a glance of twinkling kindliness. He rose from his chair like a man of portly figure, but with fresh complexion, a gold chain across his middle to secure his watch. He had mutton chop whiskers. He must belong to some "warm" Masonic Lodge, I thought, and I could see him nursing a long Scotch and soda. As he studied "To Whom it May Concern," my letters of recommendation, I judged he was nobody's fool, however avuncular he looked. He was as prepossessing as an honest sheepdog. He pondered the unqualifications I had. I promised to learn shorthand, so he gave me the job at $10 a week.

At last the ground was under my feet, and at twice what the lawyers had paid. I was warmed by this genial man and the lack of penny-pinching. There was something to be said for commerce!

The Holliston Mills, whose small New York branch was in an old building, had a name famous in business enterprise, but Mr. Borthwick and I did our best to wed this enterprise to a more Gaelic tempo. Mr. Borthwick really was benign. When he had anything to disapprove of, he became short and chiding, but these splutters were like April showers. He could not bear to be at outs with anyone. But he was thoroughly conscientious, faithful and attentive to detail, with an innate shrewdness that went with a chuckle. Once he had worked for Harper's, the publishers. "How many books can you get into that packing case, Borthwick?" snapped a fussy, red-haired, junior Harper. "Weel, Mr. Harper, it depends on the size of the books." Mr. Borthwick's ramparts were smooth in contour, but they were still ramparts.

They had to be when it came to the Mill. The Mill made our book cloth, and Mr. Foss and Mr. Kendall had quite different adrenal glands from Mr. Borthwick. They were full of business enterprise, while unenterprise was much more our specialty. Luckily for us, they had the bright idea of enterprising in the decorative field. They argued that if book cloth could be pasted to cardboard for book covers, it could also be pasted to walls for wall covering, a New Field, and they kept goading us to develop it. "If walls can be covered with Japanese grass cloth and with burlap, why not with Holliston's basket weave?"

The Yankees rather enjoy getting your back up. They insist on results, and if they fray your temper, they savor it as they savor conflict with the elements. You can lead a Scot to water, but can you make him drink it? Mr. Borthwick did not like being hustled. For some reason flour paste that never oozed through book cloth was not able to reconcile itself to lime in the walls, or so we concluded. Unsightly blotches were complained of. Mr. Borthwick handed these to me, and I would go into the New Field to ask distressful young brides to show me the blotches. We could hardly hope to conquer the Field, if our cloth suppurated. I showed consternation, I bemoaned, I promised indemnity. With grunts and heaves Mr. Borthwick composed letters conveying our shame to the Mill. Ours was not the iniquity.

But though it rejoiced us to report blotches, giving us a holiday mood—our hearts skiffs on the blue and dancing waves—we had a return letter, signed Harry Kendall, that rushed up our serene sky like a thunderhead. Harry was Mr. Plimpton's nephew, the heir apparent. At college, wadded and gyved, he had bucked the line so hard that his reputation still ran round him like a light. Now he was bucking two lines, book cloth and wall cloth. To us his name was alarming. No gangster whose name forced Chicago to consider whether it would sleep on the bed or under it had more potency in it than Harry Kendall's for us. And one morning, his face betraying shock, Mr. Borthwick swivelled round. "He's coming."

"Who? Mr. Foss?"

"Not on your life. Harry Kendall."

I blinked. "When?"

"Would it be like him to tell?"

Football tactics, secret signals. We had to face the music. Our defenses were not in perfect order. The weak point was the stockroom. It held rolls of book cloth in two rows of open bins. You might suppose that a roll of book cloth, like a roll of wallpaper, would have just so many yards in it, and that if you counted the rolls on hand and multiplied them by the number of yards, inventory would be child's play, especially as we had a young man in charge of stock; John his name was, with a prominent Adam's apple and protruding eyes and a relaxed mouth. We liked him, but he was not very bright, and nervousness about not being bright led him into endless tangles. The rolls had a way of getting into the wrong bins, and the yardage suffered from incontinence that led to measurement and re-measurement. Our stockroom seemed to be the place where the objective and the subjective came to final blows. Objectively the yardage was indisputable, but after John lopped off five yards here and ten yards there, sometimes juggling rolls from one bin to another, or forgetting the bits he had sold, then an element of uncertainty was able to insinuate itself into the simple mathematics of the stockbins. And the sex element added to the drama. We cut samples for young women who did book covers. Many of them were fledglings, some trying to be hard and competent, others just balls of fluff, and all of them unwilling to decide before they had seen most of the stock in trade. John looked impervious to their chirping and fluttering, but by the time he had cut half a dozen samples, and rolled them up, and seen the girl or girls to the elevator, he vainly scratched his head with his black crayon in an effort to remember what the girls had bought. After months of such trial and error, our inventory and the Mill's inventory were scarcely on speaking terms.

Then Kendall came.

While Mr. Borthwick, weak at the knees, peered over his glasses at this eruption, I stood rigid with resistance, notebook in hand. In the cold gray eyes of Harry Kendall our totals were amiss because of foggy indolence, and he was the avenging deity from Norwood, Massachusetts, who knew how to tackle the job. Taut from the gridiron as he was and peeling off his coat to dive into the bins, he shot orders at us over his shoulders, reducing John to gibbering idiocy and stirring me to vague notions of murder. Business halted in its tracks, as it must for inventory. We shooed away the designers of book covers. Mr. Borthwick, a commuter, had to leave for home, but I was told to come back with John, so that the job could be wound up after supper. And the rolls of book cloth became unrolls.

This was the first time I had come across ruthless efficiency, and it gave me the creeps. Obviously we had to have a better stock clerk than poor John, but in the whirlwind demonstration of inventory-while-you-wait, the bullying of circumstances and of the human beings attached to them, I saw something else. I saw the love of power, as you see it in the faces of commissars. Kendall, as I recollect him on that dreadful evening, had lips as tight as a vise could make them, and a gray determination to achieve his results, no matter what. He was the first New Englander I had encountered of the type that really cares less for human beings than for foolproof gadgets, and later I was to find out that such men can be hellish even on vacation. Ruthlessness in matching their wills against some stubborn task can be carried out of the workshop into all relationships, until they either creak in their gambolling or have to be lubricated by vodka. It is men like this that make soldiering a crucifixion, and their abuse of power in management has produced antibodies in labor that exhibit callousness, primitiveness, and ferocity of a similar stripe. I was rather amused that night of the inventory to see train-time approaching with many bins still to be worked over. But the lesson was clear. We had to be on our toes and on everybody else's toes. Efficient. Working as if the whole world depended on it, gray sweat on his face, his lips clamped, Kendall had rooted out idle curiosity, playfulness, gambolling. He had no visible sensibility. He had trimmed off the immeasurable to conform to the inexorable, and he did it heroically.

I snatched a cab for him, and he piled into it, briefcase and all, intent on the next play, the five-yard gain, the goal ahead.

Of course we were slack. Poor John, even if we had given him a living wage, was clearly no match for this will-tightened, well-tempered cold chisel. John was doomed. But this child of fortune, did he have to be quite as harsh and unsparing? He is not in the least an American phenomenon. He is Prussian, Soviet, Swedish, French, British, Irish. He is a machine phenomenon. Hollywood is full of it. The while of New England's attempt to "measure" human nature is full of it in those incredible books on personality that are handbooks for its destruction—the kind of handbooks which want human beings to be foolproof gadgets. And bureaucracy everywhere attracts the men who have the same ideal. Creatures inhuman, all too inhuman, were not the only cure for slackness. I lit a cigarette and sloped up Fifth Avenue, half-laughing, half-despairing.

The new Flatiron Building was a monument I passed every day. It was freakish enough to attract me and to subdue my frivolity. The prodigies of structural steel were not to be scoffed at, and I watched this building's progress, its girders rivetted within sight and sound, with simple admiration. America was itself a surging workshop, displaying incredible marvels at world fairs with its spider web of electricity, its dynamos, its cranes, its transmission of power, leading to perpetual upheavals and revision, but promising amenity at the end of it to millions aspiring and deprived.

What lay at the root of an immigrant's inmost perplexities was his lack of preparation for all this. It was a sidewalk language known to all Americans, but inherently foreign to me. Mathematics was a trunk from which the sciences—or at least their methods—branched and at Clongowes we had never been grounded in it properly. Mr. McEachern did not drive it into our numbskulls by standing behind us and rapping with his iron knuckles. Nor had the fiery, irascible, drink-harassed McCloskey done better. We were left gaping at mathematics through a frosted window, the Jesuit window that made "natural science" impenetrable, shrouding biology, physiology, anatomy, as well as physics, in fact the entire concatenation of our material being, except for a certified class.

The Irish in New York could patrol the sidewalks, work on the railroads, put out the fires, carry the hod. Their hands and feet were adaptable, but there was this mind lag, and if they were uninitiated, it was not America's fault. Like the Spanish, the Arabs, the Russian, the Poles and other agricultural peoples, they were scientifically backward; England had crippled the Irish deliberately, just as it had practiced economic castration in Asia on a grand scale, and America had put the South at an economic disadvantage not dissimilarly. But if I admitted the Irish had to stop being backward, had to come forward, what about my strictures on Harry Kendall and his crew? We had to be "efficient," on the job. At what point would we draw the line. Why did I draw the line at all?

I wrote to my brother Willie to suggest books on political economy, but I was groping around, trying to educate myself, skipping here and there quite without method. I was taking eighty lessons in shorthand, at 50 cents a lesson, so my time was rather limited.

But I had a stroke of luck. To buy good books was out of the question at $10 a week. Mrs. Hatch had to charge me $7 for my dinky room, because of the coal strike, and it never occurred to me to leave the middle class. Then one day, near the office, I went into a basement book store. There I found a "library," bound in dark English cloth, the titles on printed labels glued to the back, the paper rather heavy and English, the leaves uncut. It was called the Camelot series. But the authors! The names ravished me—Goethe, Heine, Yeats, Pascal, Aristotle, Thomas Davis, Plato, Gogol,, Leopardi, Lessing, Maeterlinck, John Stuart Mill, Epictetus, William Morris, Renan, and Landor. They were as far above me as the stars, the eyes of Heaven, and I could have them, I could keep them. My heart beat violently. The bookdealer was a Jew, a perceptive man, and he quietly observed me.

"I have the two libraries," he said, "the Walter Scott and the Humboldt. I import them."

The Humboldt was for the scientific. It struck no spark. But I was aflame when he showed me the actual Camelot series, the Scott library. The smell of the books, new and fresh, was as good as the smell of fresh baked bread.

"If you want a number," he murmured, "I'll let you have them wholesale."

"You would!"

"Yes, at 37 cents. Help yourself."

An undergraduate would smile; he lived in the bread shop, but I was starved. The dealer understood. To satisfy a hunger he knew too well, he was willing to cut his own tiny profit. I took home an armful.

Christian Brinton

It was a happy day for me when Mr. Borthwick raised my dole to $12 a week. It meant I could move under the same roof as Brinton, that much nearer to my desired America. I did not see him often, but I knew he was my friend. He was a pagan, a Seneca, a man of delightful and springing spirit. In his lively forays against the enemies of his land, such enemies as were the allies of vulgarity, he had taken me as his natural ally. I longed to meet him oftener.

It was reprehensible of course to move to a dearer boarding-house. I had not the tenacity of those American heroes who secrete capital. Instead of saving a dollar a week, $52 a year, I wanted not only Brinton but an immediate pleasure, a gross solace in the region of the stomach, and I wanted a room with a window and the use of a sunny, immaculate bathroom. Would Russell Sage have lavished 8/12 of his intake on room and board, or John D. Rockefeller? But which would I rather be, John D. with money and no stomach, or Francis with stomach and no money? I was sick of my drooling skylight. I moved to Mrs. Meagher's, 73 Madison Avenue, and the relief was inexpressible.

Mrs. Meagher was a big, frizzy-haired, martial matron with vigilant eyes, and she had no more idle talk than a police lieutenant. The work she proposed for herself exacted her time, and it was never slighted. To keep her house shipshape, by the aid of colored help, and to run a dining room, where the food was honest in substance and the menu resourceful as well as sustaining, took the skill of a hotel proprietor. But she obeyed a personal principle—the principle of the true artist and the one which the French so well understand, that of *mesure*. She was not too proud to fight for her success in detail, but her desire to expand it at the risk of vitiating it, was held in check because the clients she aimed at had only just so much money. The little performance was staged with taste. Her maids in the morning wore those pleasant cotton dresses that were then so cheap. They were nimble and gentle, and the lodgers stayed on as faithful as the help. Was this help underpaid and exploited? Certainly they could not have taken home big wages, nor changed their family fortunes, but they had a share in a loyal venture, with its human leniencies and rewards, and they throve as persons. After four years at a Jesuit school, run by unimaginative males, I entered on a well-being that no digs in Dublin could have offered, and long years later when I used to meet English highbrows mooching down corridors to find their lugubrious hotel bathrooms in London, I marvelled at the ugliness that sour masculinity in medieval universities had ground into them. Those sodden bathtowels, those carpet slippers, those curious fibrous backscratchers. No doubt they made up for it at breakfast. They understood marmalade.

What did trouble me, having read the great Russian novels, apart from not saving money, was the aspect of self-indulgence. I was not breaking away from the tradition of Philistine comfort I was born to, and this was to prolong an ignorance of life, to cut me off from the millions who had no Philistine comfort. I was aware that the box under the dripping skylight at Mrs. Hatch's the greasy zinc tub, the three prunes at breakfast were not the acme of comfort, but they were inglorious deprivations, while the real proof of heroism would be to work with my hands. I had seen the cast-off people whom the incisor of New York was perpetually trimming off, with their worn and hounded faces. Ask any of these if they would like to move to a boardinghouse where, at any rate, there would be hot and cold water, and carpeted rooms, and bed linen. Dumped where the dignity of the individual has to be shared with vermin, they would have wept with relief to move into Mrs. Hatch's. And yet I moved out of it to Mrs. Meagher's, feeling I had passed from dark life to a place where the sun was shining.

The initiation in a boardinghouse is usually, or was usually, a genteel affair, and at Mrs. Meagher's we circled before we approached like good little inconspicuous birds. But there was one exception, Christian Brinton, my sponsor.

He was a small man, with compact little hands and feet, and two mischievous, brilliant eyes under a cornice of black eyebrows. His face was tanned, the nose a sharp beak, and the chin curved out, obviously the mask of a Punchinello. A more lively sense of the comic could not exist, but he was at pains to offset it. He dressed meticulously. He invariably entered the dining room with the gravest of mien, bowed as he met casual or amused glances, and then crossed to his table with such measured tread that it was impossible not to note him. He saw to that. He was a coxswain, every inch of him, prompt and assured, converting his size into a capital gain, steering with tact and daring. But at the slightest provocation of wit his mock gravity cracked. His whole face puckered, often so overwhelmed by laughter that he stamped his little feet and was forced to bury his face in his napkin when his fancy was thoroughly tickled. I shared his table and shared his comedy. I stimulated him because I took to him and looked up to him.

His intimates called him Dick, but to me he was Christian Brinton, the name under which he wrote. And he was the first writer I was really to know, the first saltlick that a craving novice had encountered. I was not yet twenty. At last I had a man with whom I could talk, one alive to the Sahara that spread around us, and to the meaning of a little word like "art" as a Philadelphian conceived it.

It was his pleasure to mock at New York. "These poor

people!" he'd exclaim after a trolley ride. "What's the matter with them? I tell them, 'For the lawd's sake, go home, lie down, take a nap!'" With this, a pocket titan in his singlet, he'd double his fists and prance around the room. It became part of our lives that I stayed in his room and continued with him in the bathroom while our talks went on. He would halt in his vigorous gargling to wave a toothbrush at me or to hold up a sponge, grooming himself as Paddy McGrath would groom a pony, with zest and flourish. I saw him through it all till he sallied out to dinner or theatre or opera, twitching his opera cloak with solemnity until the final wink said, "Exit."

I offered no repression. My gaze flooded him like footlights, urging him to keep it up. When he departed I supposed he'd shine, and when he returned with spangled names, Louise Homer or Schumann-Heink or David Bispham, I inferring he'd shed a dazzling light, and as he hung up his cloak, or unwound his high white muffler to open the shaped Beardsley coat that ran down to his heels, restoring his silver-knobbed black cane to its corner behind the white slop-pail and his Gibus hat to its box on top of the art books, throwing a favor on his table, a program, a scribbled card, a rose, he would hold forth as he undid his tie and took out the studs. My nose could tell me the evening had been good from its lingering fumes and fragrance.

"My boy, she was indescribable."

"But was she good-looking?"

"My boy, one look told me. Let an arm or a leg come out of the cab, and I'll tell you everything."

I think he was relieved that I liked him for himself and had no wish to push into his circle. The circle was of course his constant theme of conversation. Jeannette Gilder, Richard Watson Gilder, Robert Underwood Johnson, Gertrude Robinson Smith, Gari Melchers, Max Parrish, Ernest Haskell, Margaret Ayer, Otis Skinner—with these and for these he performed his harlequinade. I had no wish to gatecrash. But if he was hurried and I could pick up his clothes at the tailor's, I did it for him.

And one day he said to me, "My boy, you are to call up Miss Margaret Ayer. Tell her you are Mr. Brinton's new 'man.' Say that Mr. Brinton profoundly regrets that he cannot arrive at 7 as he promised, but begs Miss Ayer to let him come at 7:30." A commission like this appealed to Christian's roguish humor, and he beamed with pleasure when I reported every syllable of this communication, exactly how I had put it, exactly what Miss Ayer had responded, what sort of tone her voice had, and whether she was amused or disappointed or simply matter of fact. He had first explained that she was Miss Ayer had responded, what sort of tone her voice had, whether she was amused or disappointed or simply matter of fact. He had first explained that she was infinitely lovely and radiant.

Though I seldom missed Mrs. Pomeroy's, Brinton was nearer my own generation and more pointed in his mind than any of the Pomeranians, more saucy, more spicy. Besides that he was earning his living as a writer. He had disengaged himself from the treadmill. That I was a guileless young man, a Clongowes boy in pursuit of the Holy Grail, both touched and amused him, but my solemn regard for him as a writer was the real bond. He was serious about his discipline. When he as art editor of "The Critic" donned his eyeshade and sat down to work, he was as concentrated as if he were grinding lenses. The yellow sheets into which he packed his crabbed writing, his eraser at his hand, brimmed with his devoted elucidation. If he came into conflict with bourgeois discipline, it had nothing to do with laxity as a worker. He was robust and active, boasting of his prowess in the hayfield, but so far from ignoring the time clock for the sake of sport or diversion, he prided himself on doing his stint and respected nothing more than the gravity of the painters he knew, their integrity, their sacrifices, and their thoroughness.

One of the things that endeared him to me from the start was his enthusiasm for the new Ireland, though he was of English stock with many relatives in England of whom he was proud. He valued Ireland for real reasons—its poetry, its art, its drama, its historic past. He brought me to see Brandon Tynan in "Robert Emmett" at the Fourteenth Street Theatre, and he urged me to send home a notice of the play, which I did, not that *The Independent* ever acknowledged it.

He had a perfect tone with his disciple. He was so much more mature that he might have condescended, and he could not help being amused at times, but he was so little on his dignity, so fond of gambolling, so ready to entertain as to be entertained, that any strictures he had to make, or any chiding to risk, never went under the skin. Beyond this, he was, I think, somewhat touched that anyone could be so bright as I was and so transparently at sixes and sevens. Had I been his brother, he would infallibly have put up my guard, but ours was so voluntary and so unpurposely a fellowship, and my delight in his aesthetic activities so admiring and so abundant, that all it needed to keep it sound was his robust sense, his native salt, as well as his breeding and his kindness. Philadelphians, for some reason or other, have a happy touch in intimacy, though I base this on knowing perhaps twenty out of several millions. Anyway he had a happy touch, and France had developed it.

No writer in the course of a long life fails to come across all kinds of people, from royalty to the sons of blacksmiths who push royalty around, and the irritant in human intercourse can be injected by a disagreeable equalitarian just as much as by an inequalitarian with a pedigree as long as his arm. At his best, in any country, the well-bred man has one unfailing trait, he never affronts anyone's dignity, at least after his first cup of coffee in the morning. He does not use offensive categories in his own mind, such as "Irish" or "Papist" or "Proddy-Waddy" or "Limey."

What Christian had brought home from Paris was vivacity. This was of a quality that I had not known before, at least out of Ireland, and I took it for its prickle and its tang, with plain

Croton water as the alternative. But lively as it made my days and much as I revelled in this variant on other boardinghouse fare, the heart that Christian had taken abroad from Thornbury, Pennsylvania, was not in reality the sort of organ on which France best operates. "My heart," he once said to me, when I thought some judgment of his harsh, "my heart is the size of a mustard seed," and that was the Quaker in him revised by the Paris of "l'art pour l'art," of Murger, passed through the acid bath of Toulouse-Lautrec. He had learned to tolerate the whole conglomeration of inadmissible facts which France then relentlessly presented to the bourgeois, and this lent spice to his reunion with America's unsuspecting bourgeoisie. He was, as the bourgeois began to retort, a "sophisticate."

But sophistication in France, though a Toulouse-Lautrec can give it a wry twist, has never stopped short at this stage of illumination. I cannot believe that many foreigners, even the most tentative and sensitive, do easily grow so acclimatized in France that the Parisian emulsion can nourish them as it nourishes the native. The vivacity is contagious, but what the Seine mellows in the native along with piquancy is a peculiar French fidelity to an order of perception which at once sanctions the ego and inexorably judges it, but with a fineness that mingles commiseration and candor as the French hand can mix oil and vinegar. Brilliance can be imitated and candor can be found everywhere, but the flexibility which France has achieved for the sake of a completer experience of itself has a degree of understanding in it that, in its adepts, perfects human intimacy as in no other European elite.

My America, after all, was alien to his, and on my long tramps through New York that first year I came on hundreds of little scenes that pointed the difference. Over on Avenue A there was a Boys' Club where Frank Hackett was a volunteer worker. It had a smug air about it. The boys were prim little sycophants, I thought. But across from this Uriah Heep factory I watched a saloon in action, one Lincoln's birthday, as I chatted with a big breweryman who was rolling barrels toward the cellar.

"Where is the saloonkeeper from?" "Is it Smith? Sure he's from Cavan." Many Irish faces showed in the throng that flocked with jugs and cans, but I could hear French and German. Out of dirty, gloomy tenements they streamed to the saloon, past the empty barrels that blocked the sidewalk, where an immensely tall Hollander was trying to drag his tiny grandchild and enjoy his long pipe. "Good, let them drink," I said to myself. It's bad to live in this slum after hard work, without some consoler. They stopped to buy candy from an Italian, to bring home to the kids, and I did not envy their life. What good to waste time and skill on the Uriah Heeps when the root of poverty has to be treated. "Like consumption," I said to myself. And I wrote to my Jesuit brother when I got home: "Social reform lies deeper than mending sores or substituting for the home. So deep that the probing seems yet to be adoing."

But Gorki's *Twenty-six and One* fell into my hands, and I bought Tolstoy. New York was just as evocative of pain, just as ugly, as the Russia they brought into Mrs. Hatch's sour boardinghouse. They ravished me no less. On our street one night I saw a young man robbed; the two thieves running toward Broadway, one darting uptown, the other downtown, while their victim stumbled after them. He was dazed, half-drunk, helpless. I took him to his home. He lived on a top floor attic, much like my own at Hatch's, and he drooled to me about Dostoievsky after I put him to bed, while I countered with Tolstoy. I left after dawn, eager for his redemption, yet not so eager that I kept after it. What could I do if his self-pity was too sumptuous? He only asked to have a savior, but a savior who would do the listening. I thought a savior should be listened to.

Mooney and Medbury

I took more naturally to the broad swath of the middle classes, and most eagerly I turned to the Irish if I could find them. In Mooney and Medbury I found two heartwarming friends—Irishwomen from St. Louis.

They had been out of luck in their marriages. So far as I could judge, they had experienced what Victorians called "the brutality of man," but instead of sinking under their crosses, they had unloaded them and floated them down the Mississippi. Then they took to the dry goods business.

Any day in McCreery's fur department you could have seen Mrs. Mooney or, for that matter, Mrs. Medbury, who had a connection with Kilkenny. It was a sight to see Mooney as she breezed to and fro, her ample figure stretching black satin to its limit, obviously in command; she was head of the department. A plume of tawny red hair crowned her authority, which she dispensed like a sanguine bishop in his diocese, circling her "floor" full of helpfulness, judgment, brisk humor, and resources; her customers flocking at her high heels, her saleswomen trailing her. For hundreds of women the hierarchic word "furs" was indissolubly wedded to Mooney because she knew not only furs but also her fur-bearing clients, and so little niggard washer method, so quick her insight, so fertile her suggestions, that success beamed from her; she sported it like the lorgnette that either helped her to squint or dangled from her bosom, and in that era the bosom was high, wide, and handsome.

Mooney took me to it, though she had no Kilkenny bond with me. She was indulging her friend Angela Medbury who had a soft spot for the old town. Whether Mooney had in fact received a hard fate as a gift from God I was not sure, but certainly Angela had been bruised and injured. She leaned on Mooney, and as I came to see much of them in their small house on West 23rd Street, I often pondered on their living in common. Mooney's force of character, her indomitable spirit, and her inexhaustible vitality could easily attract a parasite, but while they were opposites, engineered together by circumstance, I was often struck by Mooney's contriving not to domineer and deferring to her more elegant and high-strung comrade. At times I would see her studying her housemate with a solicitous eye, whenever Angela seemed to be moody and nervous, but this vigilant care was not grudgingly rewarded. While Angela could not help being refined, and while she was at times amused by Mooney's brusqueness, she was so gladly and fondly admiring of her strong friend, and had such depths of confidence in her, that it surmounted their differences.

On the naked battlefield of the fur department, they were unequal. Mooney would brilliantly unhorse the brass hats who tried to lay down the law, and with a loyalty as gorgeous as the flame in her hair, she would bluff those chiefs for Angela's sake, but where she gathered roses Angela suffered thorns, being vulnerable and querulous and not sure of herself. The heads of big business are circus lions, responsive to firm management and proud on their directors' chairs, but instantly alive to timidity. In the end Angela had to part from McCreery's. She went from furs to a millinery shop. But they went on with their home, and made their sorties as Paris buyers together.

Business exacted so much from them that they had no time to keep up a social circle. High Mass on Sundays was part of routine, and they attended it in a style that did honor to the fur department. They lashed themselves into corsets that made Medbury strait and narrow at small cost but forced mighty effort on Mooney. I had soon slipped into their lives as a guest for Sunday dinner, and once they had come off parade, they lapped their contours in flowing gowns; Mooney giving the rocking chair the privilege of sustaining her, as she immersed herself in Hearst's Sunday paper, the discarded sheets lying around her and lapping her feet.

If I arrived early for dinner, Mary would be cooking it. She was Angela's sister, tall and angular, her domestic habits as rounded as old hills, and she stayed in their folds as dutiful and resigned as an old tree. She was happy in the background, concocting the stuffing, basting the turkey, mashing the potatoes, trimming the celery. She had the parrot to talk to. She ruled him by his maw, scolding him in a wheedling loving tone, and she took me very much as she took him, each of us green and loquacious. Some of Mary's teeth were missing. She wore specs and a black dress and had sparse hair, but in her soft voice, meek and trailing, she conveyed her patient mind, applying it to life as if she were stitching a sampler.

Then they'd arrive, and the joy of undoing those corsets would fill the house. We'd wait in the front parlor as delicious odors from the kitchen mingled with lewd scents exuded by plump cushions, for this chaste room, divided from the hall by a curtain of beads the color of boiled candy, gave off an entirely misleading voluptuousness. It was surfeited with furniture, and it swarmed with embellishments. Medbury preferred to sit on a straight chair, the picture of rectitude, at times folding her arms and smiling enigmatically. I suspect that she, like Mona Lisa, was paying a smile instead of paying attention.

Her mind ran on something else; she wanted to advance my fortunes. She and Mooney sometimes plied me with questions. They had plans for me. If the hard world so familiar to them was showing itself perverse, and I was always amusing them by my little encounters with it, they plotted to arrange another destiny—to marry me to money. They must have talked it over. The girl would naturally have to be a Catholic. It never entered their minds that this might cause a hitch. They were sure I was bright and fit to go on parade.

They had not left St. Louis behind them when they moved to New York. St. Louis followed them to McCreery's and with the warmest of feelings. Mooney was as much to them as the Statue of Liberty.

Toward the end of the year she and Medbury gave me some news. "Francis can you be on deck for us next Sunday?" asked Mooney. "We're having three girls to dinner. Maybe four if Fanny comes. We've known them from the cradle. They're just fine."

"Their father owns the biggest brewery in St. Louis," said Angela. "They're pretty as a picture."

"Are they well off?" I inquired, grinning.

"Well off!" Angela sniffed. "The youngest of them has a million dollars in her own right."

"Only a million," said I.

"You'll be joining us," said Mooney. "We'll get tickets for a show. You can't help liking them."

"If you do," said Angela, "we'll—I don't know what we won't do." She gave me a look. "Isn't he a pill, Mooney?"

Mooney laughed. "They're to be here ten days at the Holland House. You be on hand, Francis. We need a beau for them."

I must say they arrived at the little house in a whirl of magnificence. They might have been stepping out of a Rubens in their sables and diamonds, and they fell on Mooney's and Medbury's necks with the ardor of their young hearts completely open, and if they were more reserved with the young man, they were predisposed to him as part of a ménage that was "simply darling." Mary had cooked a marvelous dinner, and it did not take long to loosen every tongue, so that we overflowed with liveliness and laughter.

They could not help being dollar princesses, and it enabled them to enhance their physical splendor, but I could see them as "convent girls," not perhaps so sprightly as the Irish girls, more solid and matter-of-fact, yet with more unaffected zest, more generous life in them, and the kind of German good nature that my sister Katty had liked—a feeling of affluent kindness and amiability in them. Our wit was not brilliant, but when they laughed they did it with brilliant teeth and we enjoyed each other. It was a gay evening, so we felt at home when we met again and went to the theatre. This time there was Fanny, a brunette who was to go to a Catholic finishing school, a dime princess by contrast; her father a lawyer.

"Your son was very distinguished on Thursday," I wrote to my father, "in evening dress and his brother's overcoat. One of the girls proposed to me, but I refused her. Sez I, 'cash down or no bargain!' " This crude irony was to convey to my mother I had no designs on a dollar princess. And soon after we saw them off, going to the train for St. Louis, I decided to call on their friend at the convent school, somewhere on the West Side, in the Eighties.

How familiar the waxed floor was! It was like a dance floor or a skating rink. And how this young girl glided into the big room, too much as if they had begun to wax her as well as the floor. "Get thee to a nunnery." I fled from it.

George and Mabel

Angela had a cousin, distant in more ways than one, but, in fact, it was he who had brought us together. This was my Kilkenny friend, George.

George was supposed to be selling mustard on the road in Pennsylvania. He had brought with him from Ireland a simply invincible reluctance to submit to rule. He had the softest voice in the world, the most amused and wheedling manners, and an expression in his eyes that mingled lynx and faithful hound. He dressed in tweeds and a soft tweed hat, and as he mooched along, turning in his toes, his raddled face suggested the longtime, used-up vaudeville actor. But behind those wary eyes and that hovering, tentative smile there was an inexhaustible love of life, as if it had a texture that he fondled and stroked out of sheer attachment to it. He was so insinuating in his love of it that he gave me the feeling he had no bones, nothing to keep him in the awkward stiffness of men in a regular pose. He had no pose. He was totally irregular. He could see, out of the tail of his eye, that I wished him to do something about it, and under my constant pressure he did occasionally go with me to see his cousin Angela.

I met him in New York one Monday and asked, "How come?"

"I'm weekending here."

"So you're off Monday or Sunday night?"

"No, I weekend from Thursday to Tuesday."

"But, George, how do you keep your job?"

"Oh, that's easy. My pals send in the orders on the dates I give them. They're good guys. I send them my schedule."

Selling mustard by remote control gave him pleasure, and he had the top executive's ideal weekend, Thursday p.m. to Tuesday bright and early. When I deplored the risk, he pulled down his face; he deplored it himself, but when I urged him to name the day for Mooney and Medbury, wanting to pot him in domestic soil where he'd flourish like the green bay tree, he looked genuinely miserable. Still, I held him to it.

The ramrod of propriety had been inserted in Angela Medbury, as in myself, but George was something new in her cloistered life on 23rd Street, and as she looked at her cousin, a quite tender smile hovered on her lips, for those sins of his, as ruddy as his flush, could be eradicated at the proper cleaning establishment. She, like myself, wished to renovate him.

He was an object to melt the heart. Mooney said nothing. She merely noted how incredibly stiff George became in the presence of this charity. At every threat to his waywardness, his eyes went racing; then pinned themselves on the glass-hanging that dribbled in the exit. Mooney, yearning to undo the cordage that lashed her to fashion, shook her head to expel a yawn. The late Mr. Mooney may have convinced her that some males are unregenerate. Luckily Mary broke the tension; she poked in her lean head to announce tea. Tea! God! Even I, athirst for tea, could see George's dismay. And as we sat to it, Angela chose that moment to ask George had he been to early mass! His eyebrows ran up; his eyes looked bewildered. Early mass on a weekday? A weekday, yes, but one of those underhanded Holidays of Obligation that suddenly leap out from behind ambush. George, confronted by this sneak attack, began to roll his eyes. Mooney understood. Angela merely looked indulgent and beatified. The minute we stood up from tea George had to be going, and the party folded like an umbrella.

As we walked up Eighth Avenue, I tackled George boldly.

Why did he not marry and settle down? He could sell mustard, why not himself? "I can see by your cousin, the way she watches you with her head inclined to one side, that she'd think any woman lucky who got you. She never looks at me like that, George. You're an insinuating cuss. You make her pensive."

George stopped me. "You see, Frank . . ." Then, separated to let someone pass, we reunited too late for him to renew. So I didn't see. He merely said, "Turn up on Sunday like a good man."

"After early mass?" I asked.

He grinned. "She had me, hadn't she? I was up a gum tree."

George's place was in a grisly tenement, and on that summer Sunday the heat bounced up from the pavement, and the light poured mercilessly down. It was a walk-up tenement, completely down to earth. George was in his shirt sleeves when he opened the door, and there were three others in the flat. One was wearing a wrapper, a pallid baby struggling in her arms. The third was a slim girl in a tailored suit, a trim straw hat on her head. She was standing up, grave-eyed, refined-looking, delicate as a morning glory.

"This is Mabel," George indicated the mother. Mabel, one hand poising a cigarette, the other foiling her offspring, nodded her blond head to me. "Her sister," said George, and the girl in gray shook my hand. "So long, darlin'," she murmured to the baby, waved a gloved hand to us and was gone.

"Have a good time," Mabel called to the door, in a drab voice. "George, how about that beer? Rush the growler, why don't you?"

"Come with me, Frank." He took two jugs of pressed glass from a bare shelf, and we went down to the locked-in summer.

"Mabel is my girl," George told me. "Her husband deserted her."

"And the baby?"

He nodded. "It's tough. She doesn't know what's to become of her. She was a hoofer. She's a Catholic. Can't marry me."

We came back with the beer and pretzels.

"You don't take beer?" Mabel said listlessly, lifting her jug. "How can you live?"

She had a neat small body, but it was sagging, like her spirits, and the baby oozed from under restraint to grovel on all fours, his hands pasted on the bare floor. "George, pick up baby." The baby, gazing up at George with watery blue eyes that could not focus, was as limp as a bag of linseed. George picked him up and bestowed him on his mother. I was like a bump on a log, while down the airshaft hard voices reverberated, the voices of jaded Sunday, pithy remarks smiting reputations with the rapidity of machine guns.

"I told you once before—."

"You son of a bitch, you don't have to tell me. I was able to live before I ever met you. Who's to keep me from walking out, you tell me for a change!"

We pretended not to hear.

"Your sister is in musical comedy too?" I inquired politely.

"Mabel's sister," said George in his lulling, soothing tones, "she's most peculiar, Frank. She's a chorus girl, and she's still a virgin. Mabel knows it for a fact. Don't you, Mabel?"

"I sure do."

"We can't make it out. She's a nice girl. You saw her. What can be the matter?"

What indeed? We sat in the dejected gloom of the misbegotten flat, discussing the sister's virginity. Mabel was propped on a kitchen chair; I had the seat of honor, a frowzy Morris chair—one of William's saddest efforts—and George was on a stool by his beer on a table. There was oilcloth on the table, linoleum by the gas stove, but only curtains of dirt on the windows. We talked of the pale morning glory as though she were abnormal, and my feeble attempt to speak up for her, without reflecting on Mabel's happy lot, was met with frigidity and then silence.

"It beats me," said George. "Funny thing, Mabel, Frank says hot tea is best in the heat. Have a cup, now, Frank. Ah do, go on! I'll hold the boy, Mabel."

"But it's so hot!" she said. "He's hot too," and she gave George the baby to hold, going to fill the kettle.

Her drooping mouth troubled me. George grinned mechanically as I tried to be amusing, but he was watching her furtively, as she dragged herself around. The luster of the theatre, the sheen that had drawn him to her, was native to the element he had enjoyed, and out of sheer attachment to it, weary of his life on the road, he had braced himself to hold her, to fondle her child, to wheedle and beguile her, but this was not the prop she needed. She coldly felt he had no bones in him, he could not support her, and if she was sour and lacked luster, using him and abusing him, it was to punish this slave of the show business. How could that help Baby, her handicap and her care? Or restore her job?

George's meekness astonished me. As he walked over to Madison Avenue with me, he told me ruefully of his efforts to gain money for Mabel. "I'm lucky at cards, Frank. I meant to bring home a bundle last Thursday. But what do you think? We all have our little peculiarities at the club in Philadelphia, that's expected, but what did a fellow do last Wednesday? He'd fixed the mirror so he could see my hand? That's raw, isn't it? I'll clear out if they don't do something."

"But will they?"

"They must, Frank. That's no way to treat old friends."

"He's an old friend?"

A smile dawned in George's eyes and showed the gold in his teeth. "I owned a fine diamond once, and we used to work a little trick in Western Pennsylvania, this fellow and another. We were all drummers. Just before train time we'd pull it. They'd roll a few stones along the bar counter, and then I'd come in. I'd take my good one out of my vest pocket. 'Match that, why don't you?' They'd look at it, pass it around, and I'd jeer at theirs, pick it up and go to the toilet. I'd show no more interest when I came back. Then this pal would ask to see mine, I'd give him a phony and he'd buy it. That was our chance to catch a sucker, the price was so low. If they collected, leaving us just time to catch the train, we'd run for it, laughing. We always beat them to it."

"And now he chisels you?"

George nodded mournfully. "It isn't that he cuts a corner. We all do that. But to fix the mirror . . . that's unheard of."

When I reunited with Brinton I told him of the stubborn virgin. He instantly condemned her. "A chorus girl has no excuse for being a virgin."

"But she sees Mabel and her brat. She might have a baby."

"She'd have no excuse for having a baby."

"But if you saw her, Christian . . ."

"She's abnormal!"

That puzzled me. Every group has its norms, and one group's norms may be another group's abnorms. I accepted that. But was this girl shocking to be a virgin? Mightn't she be a nonconformist? To distinguish between eccentricity and real independence is a test of critical insight. There are breaches with custom, like growing a big beard, that proclaim nonconformity. But to break with conformity is not the ultimate independence, even breaking out in an odd beard, or in odd meters, or in odd poses. Lunacy isn't the ultimate freedom, though it may smash conformity to bits.

Yet if I could not fumble it out, or risk exposing myself to Christian, it did not impair what he stood for, what we had in common—all of it so unquestioned that we could reserve the other things. That was the charm of our buoyant, well-spring closeness. It was not down to bedrock, like a jarring family intimacy.

George and I were bound together by more than the link of a hometown. The very fact that I drank ginger ale, that I wore glasses, and was a child in the ways of his world stirred George to a curious fond protectiveness. I was a lowland sheep among mountainy sheep, but so obviously wet behind the ears that it touched him, and yet my talk had a maturity that really impressed him. He had a queer deference, a genuine convinced feeling about it. He never set himself up to be anything. He did not feel he amounted to a hill of beans. But the moment his eye really caught mine, his face lighted up from inside with the sudden illumination that no one can fake. That voice, as soft as Vartry water, had a caressing, slithering ease in it, and his heart, as limber as a concertina, would be mine to play on. Here we might be by happy accident together on Broadway. Immediately he would be at home with me. And you took him as he came, intuitive, vulnerable, and tragic.

Mabel's flat was of course not his home. Had he a home anywhere?

The only home he had was a small hotel in Philadelphia that was more than the Ritz to him. A few years later, not having heard from him, I went to this hotel. It was one of those bright, nippy, receptive places that smile like false teeth and sing for a nickel. I could imagine him there, proud of it, but he had checked out. The clerk was blank. The curtain had fallen on George.

John Quinn

My brother was on the road for Doubleday, Page, his territory being the South, and there were periods in which we lived in a haze of Doubleday titles, *The Clansman, The Modern Anaeus,* and *Bob, Son of Battle.* A fire-eating Southerner was then in great vogue. His name was Thomas E. Dixon. But Eddie spoke with reverence of Ellen Glasgow, though Frank Doubleday's dictum to my brother was far from sentimental. "You must understand," he was told, "that selling books is no different from selling soap." When I told this to Nelson Doubleday some years ago he said, "I didn't know the old man had so much sense." Perhaps Proctor & Gamble should begin publishing; they make best sellers so professionally and understand so well the secret of reprints—that one hand should wash the other, the right hand always knowing what the left hand means to do with the dollar edition. The Doubleday offices on Union Square were squeezed and inglorious but in spite of Walter E. Page's Southern tang, and the presence of a son of Sidney Lanier, it was the keen Yankee profile that most cut into my memory. They were a genial young outfit—the lanky, easygoing Russell Doubleday, the finedrawn Sam Everett, the pale Harry Pratt, the round and smiling Nye, and others who polished up the handle on the big front door they were putting up. They were spring-heeled, gay, and perky, and sometimes I was with them at lunch that was electric with decisiveness. They chose quickly, talked snappily, ate like lightning, and were rushing for a train before I had collected my wits. It was Saturday, and they were off to their weeding and lawnmowing. They were the first group of shock troops I had encountered in the publishing world.

Meanwhile I had myself arrived no further with books than trying to sell book cloth for the Holliston Mills. The job was, to tell the truth, my first taste of dulling security. Mr. Borthwick and I jogged along like hacks circling in Central Park, sure of our oats and our stable, and we pulled well together, but I fretted, as innumerable workers fret, because I could see no outlook. My time was employed, not my faculties, and being unable to give one without the other made me impatient and restless.

A university is well named, and I suppose that if I had gone to Columbia I might have drawn an intelligible universe out of it, with my mind better trained to use its resources. But my years at Clongowes had prejudiced me against the schools. Mediocre teachers maim the mind rather than help it, and the good ones may even maim it for a purpose, as in imperial Germany or any other nation that deliberately indoctrinates its young. It was clear to me that young Americans who came out of College could play certain mental games more adroitly than myself, just as their tennis was incomparably better than the haphazard game I had picked up at home. But this adroitness, this superiority, could only win my admiration if they went with a regard for the world, of which the university provided merely a working model. I had to take what mental food I could and prepare it for myself, without being trained for it. This made it hard since I was poor, solitary, and undisciplined. But the real world, the world of moiling human beings, was acutely present to me; I was sufficiently curious, even adventurous, to be excited to discover my sense of it, to map the chaos it offered, and to draw my own intelligible universe out of it, not to meet comparison with the academic but to use it for myself, or at any rate abide with it. I was continually struck by the enormous complacence of those who had gone to college. They missed the point so often. They missed it about Lincoln. They missed it about Mark Twain. They missed it about Walt Whitman. They missed it about democracy itself.

One afternoon I betrayed Mr. Borthwick. *Candida* was playing on Sixth Avenue with Dorothy Donnelly and Arnold Daly in the cast. Huneker who had familiarized us with so many names had also done it for Shaw. I bought a cheap ticket for a matinee. The house was so nearly empty that I could move up to a front row. How piercingly intelligent, how troublingly sharp! It was the most successful failure imaginable, a goldmine on the stage and no money in the house. New York was blind to this vividness. My Uncle Ed, for example, flipped Shaw away. He rode on a brimming tide of prosperity, hated friction, loved wine and song, was not averse to woman, and Weber & Fields, Lillian Russel, Clyde Fitch gave him solace. He viewed Shaw as the Waldorf would view a man in sandals.

The Gael, unlike Doubleday, not only published my effort, but its proprietor out of his own pocket gave me ten dollars for it. It paid for shirts and some Russian novels. And Richardson, thinking of Ireland and not himself, said, "You ought to see John Quinn some time. He has plans for an Irish literary society."

He must have prompted Quinn as well, for soon Eddie, my brother, and myself were invited downtown to lunch with this Irishman—well, this postexilian, prehensile, arch-Irishman, born in Tiffin, Ohio. He had never been in Ireland.

Quinn was affable and requested me to look him up at his office. He was a good host, gave us Corona, Coronas, and was breezy about the uncouth Irish, laughing at his own bad puns, but he was extremely serious and alert about the Gaelic Revival. He was exceptional. He might have been a duellist, fifty years earlier. He was the most combative mortal I ever knew, though not quarrelling with his bread and butter. I saw him at once as an Irish rapparee turned quickfire American. About his mouth there was a strained, famished look, and his grey eyes could be as pinched as his mouth, but he had a superb presence in spite of it. He was obviously rapacious. His grin was sharklike. But instead of being a firechief, tugging on his coat while sliding down a pole to the sound of gongs ans sirens, he was bringing this same daredevil adventure to a politico-legal future which some woman who loved him, probably his sister, had imagined for him, guiding him, nerving his arm, stirring his pride, and committing him before all to Mother Ireland.

At this time Quinn's huge desk was on the open floor of Alexander & Colby's portentous law offices. To revisit such offices made me wrinkle my nose, but in the midst of this petrified forest, "I'll be with you in a minute," Quinn was streaking through his business, on the telephone, on his feet, completely in command. His sheer power of propulsion was startling.

I watched this striding figure. Not only had he an erect carriage, but the height of his brow, the long, ascetic lines of his face, and the spare frame that his stark upright collar accentuated gave him an exterior of formidable eminence. The same might be said of a restaurant captain, but Quinn had amazing eyes, by turns cold and shrewd, then piercing and aggressive, or blazingly fierce and fanatic. They could open wide, afire with imagination. One bold flourish of his white hand, one gleam of cutthroat humor, and the bleak Quinn could be transformed. He was a master of strategy, a pirate at his prow; he would wipe out the invisible point that is supposed to divide past from future. You could not nail Quinn to the present. Within three weeks of his getting his job from old General Tracy, he was taken into this firm, seizing an opportunity as he might whirl off with a girl at a dance—by right of conquest, half-compelling, half-embracing. "L'audace" was his war cry. He was charged with energy, ambidextrous, resilient.

At times it was comic. Once we had dinner at the Plaza, a

handsome young lady and her mother being the rest of the party, and we had the privilege of listening to a long tirade by Hohn on American manners. It was almost a family party. If he thought conversation might be a bore to him, he did all the talking, which never bored him. He concentrated on the bad manners of American men in particular. He charged on the topic, gored it, flung it down, snorted, trampled, and tossed it in the air. We listened submissively. Then he produced his thin gold watch and announced that he had to go upstairs to an auction; some smart art dealer had his salesroom in the same building as the people with money. We hurried through dessert, a minor tragedy for me, and trooped to the elevator. The minute we reached the floor of the auction room, Quinn lifted his chin. He was first out of the elevator. "You fellow. Take your time!" His tall arm shot up, and off he streaked down the corridor. The young lady smiled indulgently. "American men's manners!" she said. We reached the room at the matron's pace.

He wasn't tiresome, but quickfire gentry often are, taken as human beings. I like ideas for their own sake, and the time between an idea's being moulded and being put into action nearly always amplifies pleasure in both. To amble and dawdle and idle allows life to sink in. It allows good ideas to be absorbed and to be extricated from the contenders and pretenders that try to gain attention.

Because I was fresh from the green sod and alive to Yeats, Douglas Hyde, Lady Gregory, Ethne Carbery, Moira O'Neill, Fiona McLeod, more or less, he began to operate on me to dilate my ego. We got on famously. "I'll make you secretary of this Literary Society," he said, and then he grinned, "because I *am* the Literary Society." So he said, and so would say. And if any opportunity he grabbed went to its corner, he would kiss his hand to it and laugh and pick up a new one by telephone. He could extinguish foreclosures just as deftly as Fire Lieut. John Quinn could have quenched fires. From the day he went to Washington from Tiffin, O., he had picked up speed, picked up reputation.

John Quinn

It was, I gathered, as a senator's secretary he had whipped into the capital. "I had never seen the sea before," he told me, "I had never worn a dinner jacket. I had never had a woman." He promptly bought a dinner jacket. But he left the battlefield for a battle axe, and this he tempered at the Harvard Law School. In his wake he bounced the little pleasure boats.

It was hard for me to encompass Quinn. I saw him as stranded in corporation law, that Painted Desert where custom masquerades as justice at the expense of social consequences. In his hard, raw advance he slowed down for one consideration, only one. That was his pure devotion to Ireland. Was it his own or his sister's? It was devotion to the true Ireland, which he perceived as aesthetic.

The America in which he warred was too full of gorgeous bounty to be spared. Every nickel that the meek paid for milk, or bread, or cigars, or carfare or telephone slugs, or midday coffee had been tagged by corporation lawyers for the benefit of the sharpest men in America, whose corporations, as I judged, were battleships devised, constructed, scrapped, and redesigned to combat the big fellows and despoil the little ones. War is war, said the strong, and they denounced yellow journalists, anarchists, trade unionists, cranks, fanatics, spoilsports, and soreheads, all of them misfits who got between battleships and their targets. War is hell, said the weak, and then bought a beer or a cigar. Holy Mac, what's a nickel!

Quinn was in his early thirties, a bachelor, and in the full flush of spending money. His partners valued him. He was a Democrat, not precisely of the same stripe as William Jennings Bryan and Adlai E. Stevenson, whom the Republicans had dished, but a Democrat round the corner from Wall Street. He used to laugh at "Blue-eyed Billy Sheehan." The Democrats divided the stars and stripes between them, some with stars in their eyes and the others with stripes in their trousers. Quinn went straight to the best tailors when he left the Harvard Law School, and resigned the stars to the windbags. He shot clean for his target—the moneybags. His very lack of ceremony he turned into ceremony—a crack of wit, a flash of laughter, a wave of the hand, and one bold stride to the elevator. He poked fun at the romantic old-timers, and "the year of the big wind," a phrase that he found deliciously bucolic. He was genial, yet not congenial.

But to his Irish undertakings, out of his pure devotion, he brought his ruthless managerial drive. To escape from the amused contempt that Protestant America felt for the Irish Catholics was a goad to his pride and ambition, but when he came on a book like William Bulfin's *Rambles in Eireann*, it took his hard heart in its generous flame; it filled him with a yearning that melted him. He hid this softness. He had no one near him to whom he could expose it. A corsair stripped for action fears to be maudlin.

But action relieved him. Where any other plausible Irish-American might have said, "Ah, wouldn't it be great now, if that Irish poet could be induced to come over here and give us a series of talks," Quinn could feel Ireland in the poet as a Pole could feel his sireland in Paderewski. He had this tremulous chord in him, dominated by will. One day he said to me, "Yeats is coming. Jack comes with him. I've arranged the tour. I'm sending him from here to the Coast. He'll take home $5000 or $6000 clear. He won't know himself." And he said this as he said, "two honeydew, two demitasses. Give me the check." He assumed I wanted melon as he assumed he'd pay the check.

We talked art as we talked everything. I quoted Christian Brinton, adding with admiration, "he's a big man." "Yes," Quinn sneered, "a big little man." He was not blind to Brinton's sensibility, but already he was qualifying to deal with the dealers and hunt with the treasure-hunters. What engaged him was the manipulation of sensibility. As far as the market was concerned, he disregarded it in relation to Irish painting. He obeyed his sensibility when he saw Hone or John Butler Yeats or A. E., and if he had not cultivated it through and through, he rejoiced proudly in the Irishness. But the organizer in him, the politician who picks candidates, the broker who picks securities, the policymaker who knows the plasticity of opinion, gave him a clue to the politics of taste that cajoled and bullied sensibility.

The crumbling walls of gentility, which men of native taste deplored, had protected cliques rather than adventurers, and Quinn was much too alert to let any old guard rule him. He had newspaper friends. He met painters who were in revolt. He berated "coal-hole pictures." Robert Henri, Prendergast, Glackens, Bellows, and John Sloan were men whom he hailed, and critics whose clairvoyance he had tested braced his natural vigor of assertion. He was an omnivorous reader, devouring aesthetic books, periodicals, catalogues, reading Arthur Symons and George Moore, scouring the English weeklies, and needing only a word from the right quarter to know what was "modern."

Every elite parades taste, just as every crack regiment adopts a flag and a mascot. Himself a new man, Quinn marched with the new men, keeping step to the music. But what he had really cultivated was his flair, not his taste, and to manacle the future to hotfoot pursuit of novel experiment was to substitute the chase for the goal and to prove success by auction prices, fortetting the vast synthesis of fashion which sets out not to develop but to appropriate sensibility. But Quinn was on the make and his lair was brilliant.

Yeats had no affinity with John Quinn as such. He was an Irishman in the sense that Wellington or Kitchener or Montgomery are Irish. The Protestant Irish in the Catholic part of Ireland were grafted on the tree, but they bore a distinct fruit, had a different cult, had their own schools, their own colonial stamp, and the English gentleman tradition. It was a tossup whether their careers would be English or Irish. Oscar Wilde and Bernard Shaw, for example, elected for London, and so did

Yeats's father, but Yeats himself, steeped in English poetry, was at the same time steeped in feeling for an Ireland visible and invisible—an intense, private, impassioned, enraptured perception of something haunting, rare, and beautiful, not unearthly yet not of common clay, a wind among the reeds, a breath on shadowy waters, a glimpse at twilight. This was so strong in him that it drew him back to Ireland, averting the seduction of the great society, averting its contaminations, its rewards, and its vulgarities. No poet could have spurned the world more vigorously or spread his wings more nobly.

And his Abbey Theatre abnegated pomp and circumstance. It pursued merit, not recognition. It sacrificed cash and comfort to reveal, without gloss, the vision of a heroic past and the verity of a hidden domestic present. Actors of superb talent took minuscule salaries, and the effect of this theatre was to compose by simple means a fresco in virgin colors that no chemist had vitiated or no histrion had vamped up. Yeats was an alchemist, to be sure, but he sought to transmute into gold the Ireland he had seen at dawn and in twilight, an Ireland that was from kingly days, a memory precious and vanishing.

Quinn had none of Yeats's reliance on unseen powers. He believed in slapping the baby on the back to make it breathe up. Before Yeats was to come over, he had the Irish Literary Society do three of his plays at the Carnegie Lyceum to a select audience, and these had good notices in the papers. At the head of this Society was Charles Johnston. He was a man of visible distinction with white skin and a black beard, an Ulsterman who had been in the Indian Civil Service and had written a lyric book on Ireland. His father, Johnston of Ballykillbeg, had supported Parnell, and along with nationalism his son pursued spiritual elucidations that the Indian Civil did not exist for. He was married to Madame Blavatsky's niece, a light-haired woman, charming as a fullblown yellow rose, her warm air and glow contrasting with his glassy formality.

They lived at the Brevoort, and it was exciting to meet a man who had translated Tolstoy. He looked me over, obviously taking soundings, and as we went in to lunch he made some remark, to which his wife answered, laying a kind hand on my shoulder, "He's only a boy, do you think it fair?" It had something to do with his arcane interests, perhaps with theosophy. She had a heart, that woman, while he had some sort of frigid intricacy that took its place. He looked and behaved like Gautama's secret agent.

On another visit their room was packed with Russians; their casual clothes rather Irish, but their voices, their way of looking at one another and laughing and enjoying one another and the language as happily inflected as at an Irish garden party. After tea, our hostess the natural center of it, they fell to singing songs in Russian; one of them a childish refrain to which they held as if it brimmed with sweetness for them—a folk sweetness in it, deep-rooted, but filtered through their nurseries and summer evenings. They were away from home, and in their songs was a fraternity that flowed with melancholy and tenderness, as if memory had run itself crystal clear. I envied them, yet felt at home.

But Yeats came, and I wanted to form my own impression of him. I first heard him in some private house where the hangings that divided two rooms had been drawn apart so he could speak to both rooms. He stood in the opening, his hand clasping the folds of the hanging, and he delivered himself in the measured, throaty tones of a singularly refined, self-counscious, proud nature, at once impressing me by genuine power. He was not the young dreamer whom Sargent had sentimentalized in the lithograph of which Quinn gave me a copy. He was now nearly forty, his dream possessing him but his alarm for it governed. He seemed to poise on the edge of it, as an Irish elk might scan a settled valley below him, his head lifted. I cannot remember whether Florence Farr was there with her psalter to further the work as a ritual does, but he employed ritual, less a vestige of druids than of rectories. Afterwards he was free of all convention and ready to talk.

He asked me if I knew Standish O'Grady, who had just printed a rhapsodic article of mine but signing it "Frances," knocking my "i" out. And did I come from Castle Hacket? Little did I realize it was reputed to house a colony of imps. Yeats did not take imps lightly. He was an immaterialist who, in fact, went beyond our sordid limits and explored the recondite.

It was very serious, this Yeats business. He and Lady Gregory and Hyde and Martyn had an Ireland, the Ireland of "Hell or Connacht," more Irish than our English-speaking Ireland, more authentic, more spiritual, more elfin, and more exclusive. We others were cold-shouldered, and Yeats's shoulder was very cold. At the same time he had written a play for all Ireland, *Kathleen ni Houlihan*, which was pure nationalism and pure passion. It worked on me like the sound of trumpets. The English King was to visit Ireland with John Redmond's blessing, and I sent a diatribe to the Kilkenny people; I wrote two homesick rhapsodies for Arthur Griffith's revolutionary weekly. And I slashed at a book not sufficiently national in a way that the editor of *The Gael* thought "caustic." I was paid nothing for all this. It was for "honoranglory." But such was Yeats's effect, and the effect on Yeats of his Maude Gonne. Yeats had dabbled with the Fenians, but he was far from the people. His nation was poetry.

Jack Yeats, as well as Willy, had steamed me up. He came with Byrne and myself to dinner at a German place, Scheffel Hall, and in his dark reefer jacket he was like a ship's officer—a second fiddle to his brother and a man of friendlier, sweeter tone, not giving himself airs and genuinely aware of people. We spoke of the stage Irishman, the O'Caliban, whose vulgarity made all Irishmen a laughing-stock, and Jack Yeats took an envelope, sketched on it the head of a handsome, dignified man, and shoved it over to me. "The man who looks like an ape, with a dudeen in his mouth, is a music hall caricature. There's the man you see in the West of Ireland."

I studied it. I knew O'Caliban, but this man, too, because Kilkenny had many of him. It was clear to me that Jack Yeats's Irishness was innate, and where George Moore with his smattering of French culture could be nauseated by the very idea of Irishmen, Jack Yeats could delight in them—in their every sound and sense, their donkeys, their stone walls, their fairs, their ballads, their races, their whiskey. It made me desperately homesick, yet by top-loftiness his brother would be the one to bring home to refined America the dignity of his people; he was so symbolic, so sacramental, and this because he disdained O'Caliban.

The Ship

On the letterhead it said, "The Nautical Preparatory School," and it was signed Frank Griffin, paymaster and purchasing agent, my old boss at the *Cosmopolitan*.

Mr. Borthwick was bent over his desk as I read it. We had been discussing my vacation, and I was indifferent about it, thinking I might go to Boston to see Tom Butler. But in one scoop of the eye I had dredged Griffin's letter. He had need for two assistants to begin working with him in August; the school ship would sail in September, to return next in June 1905. The pay would be $35 a month, all found. If I could write shorthand reasonably well, he would consider me for paymaster's yeoman. Did I want to apply?

The school was a private one. According to the plan he enclosed, it would take 250 boys, fourteen to nineteen, on board the S.S. *Pennsylvania*: to educate them for the Navy or for business or for college life; to cover 20,000 miles each year; to have thirty teachers on board; to voyage from one country to the other, stopping at principal ports and landing the boys to spend days ashore in principal cities, so that in four years the entire globe would be traversed, and the fee would be $1300 a year.

"Mr. Borthwick!" I stood by him. "Here's something new." He looked up inquiringly. "I have a queer offer. I told you of Frank Griffin." I handed him the letter.

He read it, slowly, as was his habit. Then he looked at me warmly, "That's what you want!"

In my wildest dreams I had never hoped to be a paymaster's yeoman, but here, at 21, the opportunity was held out. The next day I was slated to see my Irish friends, Mooney and Medbury. "I'm going to sea," I told them with a grin.

They looked horrified. They also looked unflatteringly surprised. What put that crazy notion into my head? They had never, or hardly ever, seen anyone who looked less like a seaman.

"What sort of school is it, Francis? I'm dying to know?"

"It's still pretty vague." I said this darkly, but it was a lie. The ship was a phantom, so far. *The Flying Dutchman* wasn't in it.

"Is it a school-ship for young sailors?" Angela asked. "You don't want to be a sailor. For heaven's sake!"

"It's all in the ad," I said. "It's a prep school. You know what a prep school is. It's a Groton-on-sea."

"But Groton!" Angela rolled her narrow eyes. "Groton is very high class."

"Can't this be high class, Angela? Why can't the Nautical Preparatory School be high class?"

"She means that Groton costs a lot," said Mooney with her soothing, expansive air, putting a wing over me and another wing over Angela, to keep us from glaring.

"But our school costs a lot too, Mrs. Mooney."

"What's a lot?" asked Angela, tight-lipped.

"$1300 a year each."

"Wow!" said Mooney. "That *is* a lot, Angela."

Angela pursed her lips. Suppose it was. "How do they expect to get that much?" she asked scornfully. She looked at Mooney for permission to flatten me, but her friend yawned.

"If they can get it! Who's back of it, Francis? Have you the literature?"

The only literature I had was Mr. Griffin's letter. "I don't know who's back of it," I said lamely, "but there's a Mr. Weir of the Adams Express and a Mr. Felton of the Chicago & Alton."

At last word came from Mr. Griffin. I was accepted. The school ship, the S.S. *Pennsylvania,* would soon be leaving Cramp's Shipyards, and I was to report at Providence, Rhode Island. I was going to sea. That was the idea I took hold of.

Mr. Borthwick and I parted the best of friends. Isaac, the tart elevator man, gave me a firm handshake. They wished me the best of luck as I said goodbye all around.

I left New York by the Fall River Line, and I doubt if many cadets were more upborne by their manifest destiny than I was. I did not wear a uniform or carry a dirk, but as a prospective seagoer I took a coastwise steamer without undue solemnity. I even viewed the surly roustabouts with calm. The route itself implied a sundering of land ties and a departure for new horizons. Though it turned to drizzle as we reached Fall River, and a horrible soggy drizzle it was, I had spent the whole night in that traveler's tension which is so alert for the picture that is framed by deck and gangway and dining saloon. Going from night into dawn was a constant succession of pictures. I could not afford a cabin and had a lot of baggage, but I kept moving from one prospect to another. Dignity was inseparable from this sea passage, from the soft swish of inland waters and the play of signalling lights. There were other inexperienced travellers, depressed family groups that huddled together, but I was freeing myself from that sort of cluttering interdependence, taking off on my own and imbibing liberty by the simple means of paying out space and a bit of time. We arrived in a rain that sloshed on crowding passengers at the bulwarks.

But Providence, though a manufacturing city, was not a drooling shambles like Fall River. I went straight to the Bannigan Building, which stood on a plain that was flat as a riverbed. There, on the bright tenth floor, I found the paymaster frantically busy with three secretaries. One of them told me to look for a room on Hope Street, and I was lucky enough to be housed by an ample, motherly French Canadian, who had the misfortune to be yoked in matrimony with a cross-grained John Barleycorn of Irish name and blood, an envenomed human being.

Hope Street was on a shoulder of land that heaved up from the plain, and Brown University was somewhere about, near the center of this prepossessing quarter of town, which spoke of amenity as well as money. I caught glimpses of colonial doorways, of gay, small-paned windows and warm brick walls; the houses looking as neat as visiting cards, though I was never to set foot inside any but the boardinghouse. The town was buttoned up to the neck, so far as I knew it.

Who was Brown of the University, I wondered? (He was a cash-providing Baptist.) Cash sprouted from factories on the bottomlands where the city had grown to be half the size of Dublin and ten percent Irish Catholic, some of whom spoke nothing but Gaelic.

But Providence meant nothing to me beyond the boardinghouse and the Bannigan Building. We had to work against time. We were to start around the world on September 14, and Cramp's Shipyard was putting the last touches on the ship; so Frank Griffin grabbed me as if I were a hammer or a sickle, and this was sheer joy to me. The source of my joy was twofold—loyalty to Frank Griffin and anticipation of the voyage. It was out in the blue, up in the air, full of chance and change, yet nothing greedy or empty or ephemeral—an enterprise on a superb scale. We were to have 300 boys on board and a faculty of thirty members. Boys from all over the world and from forty states in the Union were already enrolled. The project had been devised with a sailing vessel in mind. (Mr. Eiswald had, I blush to say, read *Oliver Optic* and he meant to call his vessel *Young America*) But the shipyard had only started on *Young America* when it went bust. A steamship was less romantic but more practical. Now it was our ship.

The bills from Cramp's were coming in, and my God, my

country! When Mr. Griffin handed me those astounding bills to check, printed on the best of paper, I felt my heart descend rapidly to the basement. Talk of vampires! Talk of Dracula! Talk of shipbuilders!

> *I sail the ocean blue*
> *And my saucy ship's a beauty.*

Yes, but did you ever check the bills for her? The ocean is a body of water entirely surrounded by sharks, many of them leering, but some of them solemn—reputable, portentious, grandiose sharks, lords of sea-law, commanders of subsidy, masters of combine as well as captains courageous.

Still, we had all read Kipling in 1904, and he had inseminated the *Cosmopolitan* advertising department. As a rule the advertising business takes liberty with facts, but the Nautical Preparatory School, in this instance, took liberty with the advertising business. It was as though a political columnist pouring out his prophetic soul were suddenly to find himself secretary of state, confronted by the fierce infidelity of one damn fact after another and his clay pigeons suddenly converted into real pigeons. When Mr. Griffin and Mr. Eiswald turned from writing copy to writing checks, the erratic behavior of reality compelled attention. But I enjoyed it. My target was reality. At last I could spend myself. I was committed.

There was no false geniality about Frank Griffin. He was one of those clean-cut men whose keen glance demanded prompt satisfaction. He wasted neither words nor gestures. Anything I had to spend, as a matter of fact, he was grabbing. He was up to his neck in detail and he began unloading it.

"How fast can you type?"

How fast could I type? Absurd curiosity! "Sixty words a minute," I ventured.

He allowed himself to smile.

"And you can take down shorthand?" he said gravely.

"Oh, yes," I answered. "Not terribly fast."

"Gregg or Pitman?"

The only Gregg I knew was Jim Gregg, our greengrocer in Kilkenny. "Pitman," I said precisely.

"I may not need that for the present. Now take these bids from Park and Tilford, Acker Merrill, Francis Leggett," he picked up a bunch of papers. "And those Chicago people, Reid Murdoch, size them up and report to me."

Immense lists of prices for incredible stores—with the prices curiously erratic. This was interesting. I smiled, snorted, frowned, admired. Here was food for hundreds, food for reflection. I buried myself in comparisons.

My boss really had the air of a topnotch baseball player, and he sent the ball over the plate like a keen-glancing, top-spinning pitcher, wasting no words, his tongue in his cheek, in order not to bite it. When he was in doubt how to throw the ball, he looked out of the Bannigan Building toward Narragansett Bay, rubbing his chin and pursing his lip, then he whirled around and flashed a decision. Had Hamlet known Ty Cobb, he might have taken care of his uncle more promptly since a baseball player, like a prince, has to swat them or be swatted. Frank Griffin was as lucid as Euclid. He took each leg of the journey and then said, "As A is to B," and he had the next leg. He knew precisely how many legs went to a year, how many years to a full voyage. How did he come to master this type of organization? How did he know that five coffins would be needed? He explained to me that I'd be buried in a sack—only a petty officer—but that the boys would be entitled to coffins.

We were receiving packing cases full of samples. I opened them, unpacked them, exhibited them to the paymaster, then repacked them, closed them, and expressed them. The pleasure of hammering nails into the lids of packing cases became mine. I was paid for it, and I enjoyed it. I felt proficient. Any inquiry that came by telegraph or telephone demanded an answer, and the paymaster's attention had to be hooked, even if he was sweeping from the office on a pressing errand of his own. He was incessantly active. So was I. I even took dictation on Saturdays.

But one Monday his lips twitched as he went through his mail. "Francis, come here."

I came. "New York is having convulsions. Seen these telegrams?"

I hadn't.

"Cannot furnish immediately. Will telephone." He read. "Please confirm requisition. Quantity unusual. Our stock not adequate. Can supply later." He looked at me. "What the devil have you been up to, Francis?"

"Have I ordered too much of something?"

"Is 18,000 liters of castor oil too much? Depends on what you call too much. What got into you?"

"But that's what the doctor ordered," I replied. I went for the pharmacy order.

"By Godfrey!" Frank Griffin was shaken. "I can't believe my eyes. He's no crank. Get hold of the doctor. Where could we put 18,000 liters?"

A faint smile dawned on the young doctor who had a bit of Plymouth Rock, or some other imperturbable substance, in his New England corpus. "That ought to hold them for some considerable time," he remarked.

"Dr. Brackett, 18,000 liters! New York is half crazy."

"Suppose we make it 18 liters."

Such things happen, even in peacetime. We could hear New York breathe a sigh of relief, but Frank Griffin was severe when he handed me a long typewritten document, furnished on the finest paper with lovely lines in red ink and the most imposing aspect. "Check this," he said, "it's from Cramp's."

It was the bill for the fittings of the reconditioned ship, scrupulously itemized. Little wardrobes in the boys' staterooms, little chests of drawers, costing time and overtime, the totals scraping the sky.

I could only report that the addition was impeccable. Frank Griffin gazed at those itemized pages, laid Cramp down, and walked to the window, whistling softly. He stroked his black hair, which was sleek enough for anybody, almost Indian. At last he turned abruptly. "What happened to you yesterday, by the way?" He was ready to pitch again.

"Sunday, Mr. Griffin? I went to Boston."

"Mighty nice for you!"

"I didn't think—were you working, Mr. Griffin?"

"Naturally."

"Then I'll be here Sunday."

That was my last free day. We were putting in from 8 A.M. to about 10 P.M.; why loaf on Sunday too?

One day Griffin burst in to me, paper in hand.

"Who told you to order a thousand barrels of pickles?"

"Nobody."

"Why did you order them? Acker, Merrill, and Condit—see here. 'As to your order, one thousand barrels of pickles, we are having some difficulty in filling said order. Kindly inform us if we can have some time, as the order is a little out of the ordinary.' "

Those may not have been the exact words. I was in no condition to hear the exact words. For this time I had done it, not like the time when the mistake could be traced to the doctor. What I had done, to send in an order for a thousand barrels of pickles, which would fill most of the hold and cost an immeasurable sum, left me without speech. I guess I turned white. I'm sure my mouth fell open.

"Damn it, you've upset every grocer in New York, can't you see that. There aren't that many pickles in Manhattan." He waved the letter. "What would we do with them?"

I couldn't imagine.

"Can't you telegraph them, Mr. Griffin?"

"I told you to order a thousand pickles."

So he did. A thousand pickles was right.

"What possessed you to make it barrels?"

A useless question. Only Freud could know, and Freud was not yet over the horizon in Providence. Anyway, we cancelled the order by telephone. Acker, Merrill, and Condit breathed again. So did the paymaster.

To tell the truth, I was watching his breathing. A paymaster doesn't say to his yeoman, "What ho! We're in low water." But the yeoman watches the paymaster. It was the look around his mouth, the greyness under his tanned skin, and the forgotten cigarette that burned on the edge of his desk, which hinted to me that bills are a paymaster's diet and have to be digested. He was obviously loading up with them.

"They're scared," he said suddenly one evening, picking up a group of letters.

"Who, Mr. Griffin? The mothers?"

He nodded, "The *Slocum* disaster."

Cramp's bill he had digested. Ship's carpenters don't work for nothing under pressure, else there would always be pressure. Anyway our pupils were drawn from a class with pride and substance, everything had to be tip-top for them; the prestige of the school demanded it. But just as surely as the paymaster's cigarette died from neglect on the edge of his battered desk, so would the school die if the mothers didn't keep on stoking the fires. He pulled his lower lip, scowled, and said nothing.

His concern was so real that it penetrated my youthful egoism. The school had certainly appealed to me but much as a swinging trapeze attracts a young monkey who longs to be agile. But while I meant to have this novel experience though remaining utterly on my own, still absorbed by Ireland as my Zion, the school was getting the better of me. I had to recognize it was in danger. At the same time Frank Griffin was not downed by it, and within an hour I could hear his thrush notes from the other room. I began to identify myself with the school. We'd see it through and make a go of it.

But as I was unpacking the bandsmen's uniforms the next day, Frank Griffin gave a yelp.

"Great Godfrey!" he cried, "The bandmaster will be taken for an Argentinian admiral!" He held up a frockcoat, sprayed with gorgeous frogs and looped with gold. "Look at that braid! I'll see about this. We aren't a circus."

I wasn't quite sure. There were thirty members of the faculty to be sorted out, as well as the members of the band, the ornithologist, the lieutenant commander, the pharmacist. And the ship was about to leave the yards in Philadelphia.

I didn't relax. In a few days the boys would be pouring in with their fathers, their mothers, their kith and kin. We were now dealing with the salesmen who had promised beef for the refrigerators, and they looked as beefy as brewerymen look beery. They wobbled about delivery so that I despaired. Circumstances over which they professed to have no control had to be bullied and subjugated. I used to think it funny when I watched a rawboned farmer driving his pigs to market, but circumstances were pigs with a red-eyed willfulness; I viewed them not for themselves but for their bearing on our school, whether capitalists made them, or labor, or the crew, or the nervous mothers. Our object wasn't profit. We were launching a unique school, breaking with the tradition of medieval, bookbound schoolmasters. I no more held this reflection before me than you hold an ocean breeze before you, but we were moving toward it with the zest that fills a group producing a play, and this was to be a great play, a four-year performance, and we were frantically setting the stage for it. I was steeped in it at last. By the time I started for bed I was so fatigued that my body was sodden, almost to the point of pain yet a fulfilling exhaustion, as heavy and as wooing as a drug, so that I dropped on my bed and succumbed to it.

The arrival of the S.S. *Pennsylvania* in Providence monopolized us. Even my billiard ball haircut, dismaying to the three secretaries, was no longer remarked. We were front page news. The paymaster breezed in, impressive in blue uniform. It was true that polite letters were waiting for him, on stationery that might as fittingly have betokened a big check, to give very regretful notice that little Stuart or little Billy had to be kept home until later. We could imagine those mothers fluttering in the suburbs, having second thoughts, chopping and changing. The *Pennsylvania* was no excursion steamer on the East River, but not for anything in the world would they run a frightful risk, and they just hoped they'd be forgiven. Bandages, pills, baked beans, whaleboats, castor oil, and coffins were all ready for little Stuart, but that didn't matter. What mattered to the paymaster was the exact number of withdrawing mothers.

Lieutenant Commander Harlow thrilled the secretaries by a complimentary visit to the office. He was to go along with us to shed the luster of Annapolis, no small prestige for the Nautical Preparatory school, though he'd be a supernumerary, as little in function as the braid on his hat. He was a beauty, all the same—a nervous little man, the pink of sartorial perfection, with a clear voice, redolent of authority, as fresh as eau de Cologne, and with a sparkle in his personality that seemed borrowed from blue water. He walked with a crisp click and his linen, no less crisp, had the same starch in it. Lieutenant Commander Harlow was evidently benign. I was sure we could all get along with him.

The actual sailing master, George Toon, was from the Merchant Marine. He was English, curt and stocky, shy in the unfamiliar office; he lumbered around with a roll in his gait, shambling and taciturn. There was no mistaking his character, however. His was a tough breed, and he looked game as a terrier. He was the man who brought the ship around the Horn, with a complement of four on the deck, as if it were a racing yacht. He took us in with a quick dart from his blue eyes, surprisingly keen and kindling, and when he was through with us, money in hand, he left like a shot, no longer shambling. The paymaster despatched one visitor after another. He was arranging a perfect show, and he performed like a magician. "Your uniform will be issued on board," he told me as he left for the hotel. That was where Providence was receiving our precious freight and the parents who were consigning it.

The boys, of course, gave its meaning to the school, and I would be interested to see the brats. But by this time, as with any type of organization which finally grips the soul, whether it is a new school, a new church, a new political party, a new theatre, the institution itself was the monopolist, and I was prepared to judge the boys by how well or how badly they fitted into it. The very fact that they and their parents might assume that we existed for them, not they for us, made me rather acid if not hostile. I did not want to watch them frothing and bubbling in the hotel. I had my job on the ship. We were the works. They were the stuff to be worked on.

The *Pennsylvania* was festive, bunting displayed on it from stem to stern, while the sun blazed on the blue water and the vessel's immaculate white; with the launches plying from the float, laden with self-conscious boys and their ecstatic families.

At the head of the gangway stood Lieutenant Commander Harlow, as bright as his buttons, the high spot in the proud send-off which had been dazzlingly planned. The bandmaster, with a uniform less gaudy than he had hoped for but still glorious, had agreed that the discreet music should be sweet and unceasing. The parents, probably a little disturbed themselves by the shadow the *Slocum* had cast, were now looking around them with nods and cries of approval. This was something like it! It was spotless, confident, American, reassuring. "Mighty fine!" "Wish I was going myself!" "Isn't it a darling!" "Ever see anything like it?"

These drops from the fountain were sprayed through the morning, blue and gold and silver. They were carried my way as I rushed on my errands, slipping through groups of girls, charming girls, and boys who said "Gosh!" and "look-it here!"

"That's not high. It's no higher than our flagpole." They'd come from forty-three states, by the latest count. They looked pretty grim to me. There's something about a couple of hundred schoolboys that promises no good. Held back by a family restraint, which departure was rapidly melting into tenderness, the prospect of immediate release bulged in their hot faces, and intimations of original sin were sizzling in the air. Their eyes raced around. They peered into hatchways. They glanced to the mast-top, to the crow's-nest, to the waters of the bay; then they estimated resistance in every stanchion they looked at and wondered whether the bridge could be crashed, or if not why not. Well-groomed and subdued at the moment, they didn't look fundamentally tame. They were showing the whites of their eyes. They were rearing to go, but they dismissed me with a sniff—I wasn't in uniform.

My own attitude toward authority had never been docile. I had never liked disciplinarians. But at the sight of Young America about to pass from the family cage into the Ark, I wondered how Noah had the courage. The boys ranged anywhere from eleven to twenty-one. Some had bright, pert, open faces, others looked inturned and reflecting, but the wisps of children with mother's milk on their lace collars, more or less, would have to mingle with big hulks who laughed uncouthly and beetled their brows and looked cheerfully destructive. I was not God or Rousseau, but this would be a steeplechase, not a flat race, and there'd be plenty to hurdle. Music, sunshine, buffet lunch, white paint, and pretty girls could not hide the mark of the beast in multitude assembled.

It was no joke. Frank Griffin had broken it to me that I was to be the storekeeper. I knew what that was from Clongowes where shop in an airless gloryhole filled with a rabble struggling to buy lemon plat or Fry's and Cadbury's gave meaning to the word "horde"—Livy's favorite word when describing the Tartars. Here the exigent horde would have ever so much more money and sharper demands than the half-quelled Irish. They'd plaster me with confusion and despair, roll me like a tidal wave, unless I learned to steel myself, to be sluggish in order to "deal with the public"—or first deal with my imagination.

Still, after family gibes, these little beasts had taken affectionate leave, as the launches rushed their favorite sisters ashore and the rest of the visitors. "Be a good boy." "Write home every week." Yes, the boys were human, they were being wrenched from home; they were children. Some clenched their fists, never lifting their eyes from the launch as it cut through the water.

I had taken a long look at the headmaster, Mr. Kent. He towered above the deferential parents who had clustered about him—a dignified man and a trifle stooped who parcelled his heat among them but more like a stove than an open fireplace. Curious, the academic dignity and reserve. John Bates Clark had it. You asked them for bread, and they gave you a dehydrated biscuit, as much at variance with this brilliant day on the open deck with the open prospect before us as a sober alpaca would be at variance with the bunting, the uniforms, and the music.

In spite of all his burdens, there was nothing dehydrated about Frank Griffin. His dictation was worrying me, since now I was his secretary; I might not be fast enough; I was no John Quinn, but he interrupted himself to say, "You're assigned to the petty officers' mess, Francis. I think you'd be more at home with the junior teachers. I'll see if I can fix it for you." But after dinner he shook his head when I met him. "Can't be done. Everything here is cut and dried. You're to mess with Chips, and the pharmacist, and the commissary yeoman, one or two others. That's your rating." The men who got $40 a month or thereabouts. Well, you don't go to sea to be with schoolteachers. I felt that this was part of the icebreaking that I was looking for.

But something about me, my manner, my positivity, rumpled

several messmates. Cramp's had crowded the messroom into a meager space and given it an oak finish that reminded me of the Kilkenny Workhouse. We went right at the business of eating, emphatically sincere about it, but Frank Biederstadt, the commissary yeoman, seemed averse to me. To his earthly envelope the pig had contributed not only the hams but small, suspicious eyes, and he sat next to the electrician, who proposed to strip the long voyage of any ceremonious nonsense and to get down to the naked bulb from the beginning. He was rawfaced and rawvoiced, though grinning for approval, while Chips and the others, many years at sea, reserved judgment and held aloof.

The weather, I thought, could be ventured on, and I spoke of the Atlantic in October. The electrician took it amiss.

"Ever been to sea before?" he said with pained forbearance.

"Only when I crossed from Ireland."

"That all?"

"Unless you count going to Albany on the night boat."

"So you don't know what you're jawing about?"

"Opinion is free," I said.

"What's free got to do with it. You're talking a lot of bullshit."

Fresh air was welcome after that. We were coming toward Bristol, Rhode Island, and we were to have a marvelous sunset. The day had been so full of emotion that most of us were exhausted, but as I stood alone on deck, soothed by our stately progress down the widening bay, my anger yielded to the indefinable solace of a September sunset in New England. Serenity had settled on the year. It was auspicious to have such affluence of changing color and a lingering caress from summer as we glided along. The most homesick could not deny that it promised well for the years ahead of us.

But we were slowing down, then coming to a stop. We must be parting with the pilot at Bristol.

"How far are we from Providence?" I asked a hurrying deckhand.

He answered over his shoulder, "Thirteen miles."

By this time we were paying out the anchor chain; ship's noises became audible again, and a nauseating smell spread from the galley. The gulls screamed as refuse was jerked into the sunset water.

Pretty soon I went down to the big cabin that I was to share with another petty officer. I climbed into the top berth, and the ship's immobility stuffed in with me.

It was too stuffy for long. I was up early to find a thin mist veiling the gray water. At that moment Lieutenant Commander Harlow rapidly crossed the deck and was going over the side; I watched him step deftly into the launch and wheel around to cast up a look as his suitcase was slung down. He was wearing English tweeds, his hat cocked at a saucy angle.

"Where is he off to?" I asked one of the ship's officers, a lanky New Englander, with a quizzical face and a long, clever nose, Mr. Crowninshield.

"To Chicago, I guess," he said laconically.

"What for?" I burst out.

"To raise more dough," he muttered. "Give way," he shouted over the side. So that was it, Commander Harlow was going to milk Mrs. O'Leary's cow, with the help of his brother-in-law, President Felton.

To scare up money ought to be a simple matter for the Nautical Preparatory School. It was such a fresh idea, and we were so far along; there'd be no difficulty. Perhaps Commander Harlow wasn't the most forceful envoy in the world, but he was no doubt going straight to the influential, eminent railroad president. The fog was already lifting; all would be arranged for.

We were busy that clammy morning. The paymaster had to get through a lot of work, and he looked the way my father often looked when a case was serious. Before he left he told me that we had 200 boys on board out of the original 300 acceptances. "About a hundred have cancelled." That was $130,000 we would have to subtract out of income.

We were so busy in the first few days that the commander's return did not preoccupy us. While we lay at anchor I had to organize the shop and list the boys' deposits, which averaged about $100. That made a tidy sum to take care of. Classes commenced, and Mr. Griffin was back to his accumulated accounts. That gentle, incessant music with which we'd started the cruise, the flags dancing above us, had changed to sharp bugle calls and stark structural lines. I began to identify people, even the smooth-faced, elderly engineer, who'd once been in a boiler explosion and kept squeezing his eyes together as if to expel the steam. His name was Gallagher.

But the Chicago mission was being prolonged. It got under our skin. The boys grew restive. When would we lift anchor?

At last, after twelve days' absence, Commander Harlow reappeared. The ship's mood became hushed. Everyone was tight-lipped. But the next morning, staid as a wooden Indian, Mr. Griffin said, "We're to weigh anchor." "We're on our way?" I exclaimed. "Yes," he said, "back to Providence." I couldn't speak, and he left me to glance out of the window. "Yes," he added, "here are the tugs for us." The ship was to be unloaded in Providence, and I elected to stay with it, and in the richest human company. Except for Harry Kendall, I had never rubbed against New Englanders before, but here were Chadwick and Crowninshield, a different kind of man. They were to stay with the ship, and we got on well. They were just like me in one essential particular: people were people to them, not things to hang a sale on. They wanted what they could get, but not to be mackerel, not to be eternal scavengers. They lived in another universe, a very different breed from the Providence receiver, Mr. Post.

To know Yankees is admittedly a deep human experience. It is like hunting for ticks after a walk on Martha's Vineyard. You never can be sure when you've reached the end of the inquest.

Some New Englanders are sour and hard, as if crabtrees had borne them, and then you can think of such pleasant, rich, and companionable natures that you might liken them to the apples of the Hesperides. In the course of half a century, I was to meet enough of them, from Justice Holmes to Oscar Flanders of Chilmark, to learn how dangerous any generalization would be. The Maine Yankee, the Connecticut Yankee, the Boston Yankee, and the Yankee from Cape Cod—Henry Adams, Calvin Coolidge, P. T. Barnum—make it impossible to sort out any human trait that is common to all of them. Yet something in the shape of the Yankee soul is different from the Irish shape. The Irish find it foreign. No, let me be more direct. I find it foreign.

Now I look back on a number of those I met later—Phil Littell and Robert Morss Lovett, with whom I worked, Howard Hart of New Britain who built a house simply to please Signe and myself, Louis Dow of Dartmouth, Henry Beetle Hough, Ellery Sedgwick, Robert Frost, The Eddys, especially Norman Eddy and his mother, and not a few others—the term Yankee touches no common trait, only they couldn't have been Irish.

Very often in dealing with an Irishman, or a Jew, or a Negro, I am aware of a fluency of spirit, an interchange of our notions and positions, which gives me a certain relief from the necessity of maintaining my own notion and position. And in trading an Irishman may say, "I won't be hard on you," which really means that he can yield a point for your comfort and advantage. He puts himself in your place for a moment and enjoys the commodiousness of it. So Julian Mack's father traded in diamonds. He did not find out what the traffic would bear and then exact that. He sold in relation to what he had given when he purchased his diamonds. It made him happier.

Most New Englanders, as I have found them, have a different isothermic line, a moral climate in which they keep from melting longer than the Jew or the Irishman, and take longer to come to the boiling point. It is not that they are cold, or even "tied up." But they are circumspect about another ego to a startling degree. They cannot intrude or obtrude. They hold aloof.

⁂

The school-ship had promised a new world, which at least would ease drudgery, and now I saw drudgery claiming me again. The best, the only thing, was to join the Navy. So I got leave to go to Boston, taking letters to show I was a paymaster's yeoman.

I made myself as spruce as possible when I presented myself on board the *Constitution*, "Old Ironsides," which was the recruiting station. That vessel, lashed to the quay in South Boston, I approached with reverence. It had been commanded by Admiral Stewart, in the War of 1812, the grandfather of Charles Stewart Parnell, my hero. Parnell's American mother had been a striking figure. Her influence on her son was charged with fiery feelings that the struggle for American independence had engendered a struggle that was in dead earnest, no matter how blandly the English Whigs talked of it. The Whigs, with all their wise blather, had no more ended exile for Irishmen than they had secured peaceful separation for the colonies. It was time for a new allegiance, and I boarded this venerable vessel with a stab of recognition. It stood for a self-possessed will, a great act of clarification, as against pious professions of liberal spirit at grips with thick-skinned stupidity.

The ship's timbers were weathered. Daylight filtered to a mellow haze through the small-paned windows of a cabin. The official to whom I gave my papers was low-spoken and attentive. Berths for petty officers were available in the Navy at the time, but he indicated two obstacles in my path. The first, that I was not a citizen, might be surmounted, but he shook his head when I explained I had poor vision.

"There's no way around that, I'm afraid," he said. "Good eyesight comes first. It's too bad. I'm sorry to have to tell you."

The tight passageway seemed to have shrunk as I hurried

along it, denied any enlistment in the navy, but I admired in passing the somber massiveness of the old tight *Constitution* itself, and the candor of the officer I had dealth with.

The coziness of that old ship, its rugged timbers and yet its trim details, left an impression I cherished. A ship has pride and elegance after a masculine pattern, and that lingered in memory. There are morose ships, sick ships, ships without self-respect, but the ones I saw with love were staunch, comely and harmonious. How beautiful they are, and how fitted to their mission! They too educate the imagination.

But we couldn't see eye to eye, myself being myopic.

The big word for what had happened was frustration. But what did the word really contain? We had caught sight of a rainbow, and now it had dissolved. The jobs we were losing were not the only ones. The boys could go to other schools, and the seamen find other ships. It was more than jobs and a school and a ship we were losing. We were losing the world, a large experience of its continents and its waterways, a myriad faces, and a thousand cities and their skies. We were to be confined, brought back to the treadmill, to the streets men spat upon, to the unclean air and the mob. That was the pain we thought we had escaped from. We were to wear a galling harness again, and our dream was dissipated. It seemed as though we could never find another such chance.

The death of this enterprise was no less painful because it had been a gamble. Such a venture must always be a gamble. The longer I was to live, the more I was to see of rainbow-chasers, and the great art of life is certainly to keep a clear vision of some such ultimate aim. This aim forever recedes, but the pursuit of it, granted a sporting chance, is the only consummation to be hoped for.

For the younger teachers, too late for positions in their own field, Mr. Felton had openings on the Chicago and Alton railway. I wondered if Mr. Felton could give me a job punching tickets.

On one thing I was determined: I'd never go back to New York, that was certain.

It looked as if the rainbow had receded to Chicago.

Chicago

To have a job in sight, that is the great when you arrive in a city, and I had been promised a job with the Chicago and Alton Railroad. It was December 1904, too late for the St. Louis Fair. All the professors and instructors from the school-ship had been offered the chance to be conductors on the railroad, but I had missed my chance. Still I was sanguine, because Mr. Samuel Felton had told me to come to the Railway Exchange Building and ask for his office. I had the feeling of relying on myself and yet wearing this safety belt. I was escaping from New York, from the leading strings of a family, and the tentacles of the church.

My reception when I got off the train was enough to blanch the ruddiest cheek. The sleet was in deep dirty furrows through which the traffic wallowed and floundered. The wind was like a whipsaw. On the black faces of the buildings were big welts of misconceived ornament, and inside these buildings the air had been cooked to a withering heat. I don't think I had formed any picture of Chicago except that it was a prairie city on a lake, but I was overpowered by its strangeness. It rushed at me like a clanging brigade vomited from a firehouse. I was overpowered by the dark huddle of the streets, the infamous congestion and dirt, the incredible noise, and worst of all by a rapidity of movement, a roaring vitality, that zero weather could not daunt. Nothing daunted Chicago. It went ripping along, like the Goths and the Huns.

Usually a city's fervor is mitigated and soothed by the body of water on which it lies. But Lake Michigan had not been wooed by Chicago with any success, and at that time it seemed to be permanently estranged. Of course the heroes of free enterprise had grabbed the waterfront. All the way from the water tower to Michigan Central Station, a couple of miles or more, so much territory had been impounded by the first comers that no water could be seen. You just observed wasteland, a cinder in the city's eye. And when you did come on the water, on Lake Shore Drive, it had not forgotten its extrusion. In winter, without being actively malevolent, it had an impenetrable melancholy, an expanse of inhospitable chill, that Chicago had never subdued. It seemed to hold secrets baleful for mankind—memories so remote that man was insignificant in his puny effort to harness it. Lake Michigan has a wilderness of eons in its cold bosom and waits to be alone. You speak to it and it says nothing. It has no wish to speak, or so I felt when I came on it that winter.

Because I had so little cash, I was resolved to play safe. I set out to find a "furnished room for light housekeeping," picked from the *Tribune*. As it cost too much, I walked against the lake wind, till I saw a scribbled sign, "single room, one dollar a week." This was on East Superior Street.

It was an execrable room; the bed was shaky and poorly covered, and the windows were gray with dirt. The house itself was grimy, cold, and dark. "This," I said to myself, "has a sort of perfection; it does not fulfill a single aesthetic demand." I paid a month in advance. I had a home in Chicago. I was apparently the only roomer. The proprietress, a sack about her waist, and her dark hair wild, took the cash eagerly. She was American.

Chicago's wickedness was a legend the world over. This legend I had to combat, so right off I wrote to my mother, "Chicago is a very handsome town to look at in the business section." Damn cold, too. But I pushed on manfully. "I am prepared to like Chicago. And here in this freezing, strenuous, virile town I expect the stimulus which in the social half-warmth of New York I never would have had."

As I got into bed that night, my teeth chattering, the floor sinister with velvety dust, the radiator without heat, and the water cold, I put on the pea jacket I had so fortunately stolen and a wooly watch cap. Home was never like this! Chicago was at grips with winter, and I was at grips with Chicago.

My hostess knocked in the morning. "I put a bucket of hot water in the bathroom." This angel with smudged wings was a farmer's wife, born and bred in Illinois. Maltreated and goaded by her man, she had gathered up their small boy and fled to the city where her Church housed her as a caretaker. She stood five feet from me, as wary as a she-wolf with her dirty, shapely hand clutching her black dress at the throat. I went to the dark bathroom, and I stood in the tub, trying to remove deposited Chicago, sponging from the bucket. We made a deal about breakfast, and I resumed the pea jacket, nestling in the trough of the bed.

Then I put on my new suit, for which I had sent $15 to Ireland, and strode out to the Railway Exchange Building for my interview with Mr. Felton.

The railroad business, I am sorry to say, did not come up to my expectations, but it was my own fault. Or, rather, it was one of those comedies that lie in a young man's inexperience and his failure to judge character correctly. I saw Mr. Samuel Felton, the president of the railroad. He was not, as I supposed, the owner of the road, a man of great wealth and therefore formidable in the sense that a great Irish magnate, a landlord, would be. He was a paid executive, earning a big salary, but not at all a financial superman. He was, in fact, so little a superman that he had not been able to find the hundred and fifty thousand dollars that would have saved the Nautical Preparatory School. But, unfortunately, Mr. Felton looked like a magnate. He was a big man, almost monumental in size, and he had a manner so reserved and so parsimonious in human fellowship that he appeared uncommonly severe. I don't suppose he had built himself up to be severe. He was just a New Englander walled up on the top of a hill. His coloring was warm and brown, but his manner froze me. And after a few words in which he noted that I had come too late to be a conductor, and that he had a place for me for the present in the clerical department, I was turned over to the porter who led me down a corridor.

At that moment I did not realize that Mr. Felton was not cold at all. He had my dossier, and he had flatteringly concluded from it that I was a graduate of Trinity College, Dublin. He was putting me on the treadmill, but it was his way of "taking care" of me, and he had something up his sleeve. I was given a job in the waybill department, at $40 a month.

"Un caillou, c'est une pierre, une pierre, c'est un caillou, un caillou c'est une pierre, une pierre c'est un caillou." That's the waybill department. Rows of files held little slatted bundles of yellowing waybills, turned in by the freight agents along the line, and when a shipper had some claim to make, sending in his copy of the waybill, it was my job to dig out the original for comparison. It was straw foot, hay foot, straw foot, hay foot, all day long, and whether you walked on the ties or between the ties, the rails ran straight ahead into the horizon, into eternity. Centralia to Sedalia, Sedalia to Centralia; waybills, waybills all the way.

Forty divided into weeks made $9 a week. You can't marry on it. You can keep a goldfish, the most virtuous of liaisons.

The other slaves in the waybill department seemed apathetic to me. And they were hostile sartorially. They did admire the pea jacket, but they laughed raucously at my woolen watch cap. I wore it defiantly, but inside I was not very loyal to it, and in time, I fear, they would have ground me down. It was very like those nightcaps that Daumier made look funny. After a while I weakened and sullenly reverted to a Derby hat. It was hard to understand how so unbecoming a shape could look so sportive and convincing on certain shapely heads and so potty on me. These things are infinitely puzzling to the young, but at last I made my way to the center of a vacant lot off Goethe Street, assured myself that no one was in sight, and left my Derby hat there, admitting defeat.

❦

Lake Michigan might be alien to everything human, but I had human friends. Mary Prindiville was much amused at my turning up again, when we had so recently parted for four years, and she welcomed me in a domestic frame that recalled my own home in Ireland. Her mother was recognizably Irish—fined to a point by the cares that God provides so unfailingly for anxious shepherdesses. Captain Prindiville, on the other hand, a free patriotic Irishman, was a pioneer Chicagoan, wearing a jutting Uncle Sam beard that declared him fearless and independent. The Great Lakes had no terrors for him; he had been a skipper on them.

Meeting this family made me realize Chicago was a melting pot. Kilkenny, at the time my father was born, was three times the size of Chicago. These two great cities ran neck and neck for at least ten minutes after Chicago hit its stride; then Chicago drew out in front, to put it delicately, while disconsolate Kilkenny went into reverse, even contributing to its rival so that by 1905 Chicago had two million and Kilkenny 10,000. To trace the effect of this growth on the Prindivilles I had only to look at Mary's older sisters. Hard times were perpetuated in their strained and arid visages. They had been early schoolma'ams, dark evergreens against the sand, whereas Mary and Tom and their willowy sister Cora had put out eager leaves to the sun, disloyal to misery.

Native America, culturally linked with England though democratically at variance, found in Chicago rather more than it could cope with. That its sons and daughters should reunite with the East through Harvard and Yale and Princeton and Bryn Mawr, was a natural outcome of prosperity. Its matriarchs, fortified by millions, inevitably moved to and from the Europe with which New York kept step. But where New York was a national auction hall, its hard hierarchy flashing its bids for keen talent to adapt and incorporate, Chicago had no such multiplicity of interests. I had only to walk from Michigan Boulevard to Division Street to drink in a different air, to feel that stratification was disrupted, that feudalism was nominally discounted, and that, a thousand linear miles from New York's well-trained croupiers, the prodigious beauty of the West was being spilled into a beer garden, permitting a promptness of return, a fresh-water innocence of spirit, a cordiality, a hospitality that overflowed in confidence and exuberance. "I won't," said New York. "I will," said Chicago.

Through Mary Prindiville word was shingled along that a young man newly arrived came from modern Ireland. Yeats had spread the light, and this unfamiliar aspect of the Irish still excited curiosity in a city where the famine Irish had risen to unmanageable political power. Cocktails were not in vogue, but I was asked to tea at the Little Room, a stockade of native American literature. It should have been called the Fort Dearborn.

On Christmas Day, after a feast with the Prindivilles, I returned to my home. My landlady heard me come in. She had made an effort to dress for the occasion, and she said, "I am cooking dinner for myself and my boy. I'll let you know when it is ready. Won't you take it with us?"

We ate in the basement, the three of us. She had lit an oil lamp with a reflector, and we sat up to the table in stoic festivity. I had not thought to give them a present, but she heaped on my plate the fare she had labored to make palatable —great mounds of cabbage, mounds of mashed potatoes, and scrags of meat which she and the boy devoured—while I strove to diminish my portion. I could not bear to eat it. The wolf was at her door, and she was feeding me.

The Little Room was a polite islet in brawling Chicago. Out of the city's two million, half a million spoke German. At least forty other languages and dialects were spoken, and there were ten "foreign language" papers. A third of the people were born in Europe, half of the voters were foreign born or born of foreign parents. The Germans were 30 percent of all Chicagoans, and the Irish about 13 percent, of whom 12,000 spoke Irish, while there were 50,000 who spoke Yiddish. There were 170,000 Scandinavians.

The English ritual of tea was attuned to the pleasant, homelike clubrooms, and Miss Clara Laughlin was the smiling priestess who officiated. Those were native Americans in the Little Room. They were sincerely trying to disclose themselves. They were entirely different from the business men, not wanting to utilize me without instinct or tact. They held out a hand because I was a young, would-be writer.

Clara Laughlin was the only liaison officer between this clearing and the actual business of living by the pen. She had visibly brooded over me as a foundling. Throned before her samovar at the Little Room, she exercised a deft practicality, without at all disturbing her flush of surprised innocence as, at her very feet, she beheld a Moses in the bulrushes—poor little kid. By rights she was a Rubens, on billowing pink with maternal curves, but her tenderness was Scottish. As she explored her heart one day in her house, privately divulging James Whitcomb Riley while her mother took a nap, the volume of her trancelike utterance cloyed me with the good, the true, and the beautiful to the point of glassy-eyed stupor, and yet she could suddenly shift to mischievous mirth, whisking away the communion cup to give me a snifter.

But it was Clara Laughlin, literature shimmering for her afar, bright across black water, who was impelled to probe and to help. Matronly in looks but young, romantic, and credulous, she cast herself to be a literary godmother, and her presence was warming.

The atmosphere of the Little Room was a solace to me. Miss Laughlin murmured introductions as though they were a minor betrothal, and it was all so tolerant, so affable, that the members seemed as carpeted as the floor. I knew nobody and was made to feel I was known to everybody.

A tame, leonine veteran, Franklin Head, received court from his juniors. Lorado Taft, the sculptor, inclined attentively, his profile mournful and sublime. Henry Fuller fluttered about, a white moth, even his wispy beard evasive, but from under his deprecating dots and dashes, his deploring submission to the juggernaut, he shot incriminating darts of intelligence, gently absolute in his perceptiveness, half-dissenting, half-purring. Hamlin Garland was pacific and benign. An equable presence, he had known the rolling prairie and had enough of it, another kind of juggernaut, but his acquiline dignity and keen glance from under bushy brows had not been impaired. Emerson Hough glinted his ax, swinging it around as briskly as "Fifty-four Forty or Fight," letting the chips hit you in the eye. At no time in New York, outside Mrs. Pomeroy's, had I felt myself so much in indigenous America, and so sympathetic with it.

There was, of course, a feeling that even if God had been extracted, like a superfluous wisdom tooth, there was still a cavity that the tongue kept seeking. Whitman's dithyrambics about Man, John Muir's efforts to give to the sequoia what Whitman meant for Mankind, and Edwin Markham's desire to attach it to the hoe, rather than the sequoia, all had the evangelist, the revivalist, tucked into it somewhere, and now Charles Edward Russell, his face flushed with tea, was quoting Swinburne as the Evangel. But they abstained from asperity; they withheld from collision. The Scots from Indiana were equally absorbed and absorbent. George Barr McCutcheon said little; he was content to simmer. John, the other side of the McCutcheon, had a liquid, impressible eye, a disarming mellowness that invited advances which did not corrupt his reserve. Quite different was Robert Burns Peattie, who was pointed and black, married to Elia Peattie, gushing, beaming, admiring all the new literary babies except the odd, unwholesome ones whom she had to expose on Starved Rock. She was a literary power on the local *Tribune*, her perambulator padded for best sellers. Mr. Peattie was on the news end. Roswell Field, whose brother Eugene was the poet, was finely chiselled, thin, acidulous, both sharper and flatter than his brother, yet kindly to the young man. And George Barr McCutcheon asked me to lunch with himself and Herbert Stone, who published Shaw, Maeterlinck, in most personable editions.

Three or four times I was asked to the Little Room where I soon met Harriet Monroe and Edith Wyatt. Robert Herrick, too, I met; he was a novelist teaching English at the University. Dry and shy, reminding me of my brother Bat, he made remarks tipped with New England irony, and his laugh was a bit rueful, shaken out like castor sugar. But the good taste that saved him from gush left him thwarted, ridding him of the Evangel, yet nipping out his flame.

I went to the library for a novel of Herrick's. I stayed in bed to read it, Marie Bashkirtseff, Yeats, *Dead Souls, The Tragic Muse,* the *Imitation*, Marcus Aurelius, Gummere's *The Beginnings of Poetry*, and Brandes's *Shakespeare*. Even if I said to myself that the Little Room was a bit lacking in distinction and genius, it was an attempt at a literary lighthouse; it was a godsend, and literature was everything, but "forever to be referred to the humanity which it strives to represent or to direct." And by "humanity" I meant even the birds who bashed themselves against the lighthouse.

Florida

My ultimate conviction seemed to be that life was for happiness. I could never be happy checking waybills, and no one indicated to the private in the ranks how he could ever be promoted. I had not come to Chicago, hope personified, to be a mole in the Railway Exchange Building.

But one day Mr. Felton's porter—I am ashamed I have forgotten his name—penetrated into the corner where I was working and said his boss wished to see me. I did not know what to think. About two weeks had gone by. Maybe I was to be reprieved.

"I understand," said Mr. Felton, "that you are a graduate of the University of Dublin."

"No, Mr. Felton, I'm afraid. I matriculated for the Royal University."

He looked at me sternly. He evidently preferred to have it the other way. Who was I to contradict him.

"My boy, Sam, hasn't been well, and the doctor says he's to go South. I'll send him either to Pass Christian, Mississippi, or to Ormond, Florida, and you should be able to tutor him. His sisters will be going along. Could you take this on? It would be fifty dollars a month or so."

"I'd like to try, Mr. Felton."

"You were with the school-ship. I think you can do it. We'll try it during the month I'm in Cuba. Now go up and see the boy's mother. It's for her to decide."

The Feltons lived in a house on the North Side, not far from the Lake. Mrs. Felton was the sister of Lieutenant Commander Harlow, who had brough the prestige of the U.S. Navy to the Nautical Preparatory School, and where her husband was the locomotive, she was the tender. She was the very reverse of that driving executive. Though she had three daughters and a son, and was evidently the one who had interested her husband in the school-ship, she was like a bird that dared not reveal the secret of the nest. She had appealing eyes and a gentle, fluttering, indecisive manner, an air of seeking to propitiate the male. Her anxiety to keep Sam from overwork and to have a tutor just to protect and companion him was something I accepted almost too eagerly. The prospect of being a tutor was already curdling my blood. But we looked into each other's eyes, and she concluded I wouldn't wilfully hurt her boy. He was called in, and we clicked like—well, like two billiard balls.

Sam was pale, with a nervous twitch, and a degree of inaccessibility that appeared to shed my presence almost as we shook hands. Only twelve, but a weedy five-foot-five, he was tense as a steel wire. His bony frame was in a white tissue that no sun had tanned, and he knitted his brows as he jerked, his palpable intelligence caught in some snag I had no clue to. And who was to tell me, with a father so executive, a mother so mute? The boy's confidence had to be gained, obviously, and he sized me up with the finality of an addict who rejects the wrong bottle. He had none of the leniency that, in a juvenile European of a certain meek tradition, at least puts you on probation. Sam could smell. I didn't smell right.

I didn't smell, that is to say, of gasoline. The zest that devoured Sam, that brought him to trembling keenness, was for anything that propelled itself mechanically. And at the first hint that a Pope-Toledo left me unmoved unless I was riding in it, he had little genuine use for me. Sam's rapacity was merciless. If you didn't see motorcars as persons—or more personal than persons—you were mud.

All I could hope to do was to be his watchdog, his attendant. Still, on that basis I was accepted. After a few more days— aerial—on the treadmill, the porter told me that Pass Christian had been ruled out. We were to go to Florida.

Bad weather never strives so hard as when you are setting out for the South. The station was gusty and the platform cold, but a number of young men had come to see the Felton girls off. They were extremely pretty girls. Their eyes sparkled, they dimpled, they opened their arms to bouquets, and their gloved hands held boxes of candy. They were in that period of decorative receptivity which has a charm for any young man, so they seemed to me, but by this time I was in a stew. I boiled with confused emotions in which my Kilkenny dinner jacket, my inability to dance, my fear of seeming uppish, and my being uppish, and my funk at the prospect of tutoring Samuel, joined with the proximity of three pretty girls, creating a self-consciousness like prickly heat. We pulled out of the station, and I averted my eyes from the farewells. I began scowling into a big book, Brandes's *Shakespeare*.

That was a hell of a journey. The girls were perfectly uncomplicated. Sometimes they chirped to one another. As we rumbled into the South and the long train moaned its way through the resinous forests, the girls sat dangling their legs from the platform at the end and singing in light voices that had a shy gaiety in them. I sat behind, in one of Pullman's more unfortunate efforts at an armchair, burrowing my nose into Brandes. I was taut with my decision not to get into the family group, not to presume. They honestly didn't know what was the matter with me. It was a disease called youth, an attack that had been fermenting since my first crash in relation to a girl.

Winter was left behind, spring was overtaken, and the sun brought fragrance from the earth that was prisoner up North. As a paid tutor I had a duty, but how to go about it was baffling to me. At what time I was to teach and on what subjects was not yet decided. Mrs. Felton made no move. We were all so excited to be in the hotel and at the sea that the evil day was never mentioned.

Florida was having its own difficulties. It had on its conscience to give us sunshine, but every morning the sea was shrouded and could not bring itself to peel away its vapor. Restless guests hovered at the windows muttering, "It's impossible!"

But for me, after Chicago, there was a lightness I had hardly dreamt of. While it was not mine by right, as I firmly reminded myself, and as youths in tennis whites or with fishing tackle or with canoe paddles reminded me by their brisk gait, the Ormond Beach Hotel itself was so far from the asperities that I could not help being inundated by it. Outside the air gave a caress, a horse and buggy ambled on a road of dried earth, and I saw orange trees, more slipshod than imagined but bearing fruit, with dust and dead leaves around them. But it was inside the hotel, three stories high and built of wood with big verandas, that the Loop and the Stockyards relaxed their menace. The care that shone in its woodwork, on every waxed floor and glass and stair rod and crisp apron, the rhythm of New England will and conscience in this serene example of the Florida resort, and the fascination of these Northerners at play had a deft and fastidious practice that lifted my spirits inside my awareness of not being entirely legitimate.

It could be as precise as it liked, this punctilious hotel, with its regular hours in the immense dining room and the scarcely less immense bills of fare that spread out incredible variety and delivered it. It was all so bright and starched, so neatly creased and accomplished, that I could feel behind the veils of morning mist the promised resplendent sea, the Gulf-stream blue, and overhead the incomparable brilliance. It was assuaging after boardinghouses. Such bounty had hardly been on the cards in the slush and brutality of Chicago.

However, my time was Sam's, so I dutifully took him out fishing—he caught many more than I did—or walking, yet I could see that in the eyes of the three girls I was more and more a dud. It troubled me that I was costing five dollars a day and living with the family, but after grim soulsearching, and as the girls began to meet friends and form a circle, I decided to pull back social feelers I was tempted to send out. It was against my nature. Sam and I never bickered, but we were like two goats chained together who could never nibble at the same time. The situation was utterly false, because it called for intimacy and a personal feeling, or else for a professional training and technique. I was incompetent as a tutor, and the other thing, the personal response, was hopelessly restrained by the innate prejudices against a family that I involuntarily identified with those who had induced hostility in Ireland. They, poor dears, could not understand it, because at the same time I ached to have them overcome these prejudices, which the exhausting, the punishing contradiction in their tutor's attitude induced. He refused to play, and he urgently wanted to play. I knew it, but at least I did not begin twitching or biting my fingers or avoiding the cracks in the garden pavement. I simply burrowed harder into Brandes's *Shakespeare*, and wondered how long it would last.

It lasted no longer than the day the father arrived, and the family got at him. He was bland, as became a large imposing personality, but as we sat together for ten minutes alone after lunch, my awe quite visible; he preserved an absolute silence which I knew to be awkward. In a way it was a relief when he finally said that the experiment had been a failure.

"You come back with me to Chicago," he said without rancor. "I'll take care of you."

Take care of me! In the waybill department! This was a cheery prospect. Vandalia, Centralia, Centralia, Vandalia, a crate of iron gratings, what happened to them?

They saw us off. Our private car wiggled and twitched at the end of a lot of public cars and at times showed a slight inclination to hop the track. My soul boiled. Mr. Felton read typewritten reports, and the scratchy Florida landscape receded; parts of my self-esteem holding fast to the job that I was irretrievably torn from.

But what parts? Only the ego. While I had not gone out to win the Felton girls, and had, indeed, girded myself against their charm and their fresh vitality, their definite verdict that I was no good to Sam was a hard lump to digest. And their father was going to "take care" of me. Not much! Yes, I boiled, I stewed, and at the same time I sizzled.

I knew the Feltons had flunked me. But why? I suspected it was because I didn't really know about America and Americans. But couldn't I come to know it? If America was going to flunk me I had to know it, especially if I meant to write for it. And I was down to my month's earnings—fifty dollars.

But I was free. Free to make my own world. But how to balance it with the world as it is? If it had been possible for me to retreat to an ivory tower, I might have done it. Certainly there was in me a fastidious prig who sneers at everything, and by the method to which the Jesuits tied a tag—*omnia suspendens naso*—looking down my nose at a world to which I wished to be superior. I was a critic. But I could not live without somehow repulsing forces that were pushing me around, and a smirk was not enough. I wanted to have a true idea, a real measure, of the American system as it worked for the underprivileged to whom I belonged. I wanted to learn at firsthand what, as a class, we small people, the white-collar workers, were honestly up against. I had seen a bit of it in the waybill department, and it opened my eyes to a massive stupidity of management. I wanted a concrete idea, and then I could express myself not as a prig who drew away from the struggle but as a witness. The common lot, what really was it? Why could I not find out for myself in my own person? I would not try being a tramp or a farmhand, a day laborer, or a mechanic. For me that would have been playacting; I could not be a Tolstoy disciple. It would be natural to take city jobs and make up my mind about the society clerks had to live in. Then I'd have something based on experience. I couldn't use experience I'd gained from people who trusted me as a person. It must be impersonal. I must make myself a guinea pig.

I looked at the receding rails that ran together as they sought the horizon. They lied, if one were to go by appearances. I had to get behind American appearances, to escape from the spider web that native Americans weave for immigrants. How to do it? Nothing could make me go back to waybills.

Then I thought of the Little Room in Chicago. These native Americans were themselves caught in the spider web. I remembered that Clara Laughlin had spoken rapturously of the Bobbs-Merrill Co., Indianapolis, particularly of their editor, Hewitt Hanson Howland, who had started a monthly called *The Reader* magazine. A job was vacant there, and she had urged me to link with him.

That decided me. I wrote a little note, thanking Mr. Felton for his kindness, and at Indianapolis I shook hands with my fellow conscript, the porter, and got off the train. Goodbye slavery. I declared myself free. But that was just it! That was what I'd write about, white-collar slavery, the American rainbow twisted into a dog collar. I was ready to see Mr. Hewitt Hanson Howland.

Bobbs-Merrill

Now Bobbs-Merrill, as George Ade (who was the child of English parents) so smilingly put it, frankly catered to the family trade. That was the toboggan to perdition, if I knew anything, and I wibble-wobbled at the prospect of this interview. The manumission of a slave never brings a pension with it. I was now no further along than a chicken that has just pecked itself out of the egg. Carefully removing the last scrap of eggshell, I entered the Bobbs-Merrill office.

It was a charming place, carpeted and suffused with tranquillity, cozy as a club; and the quiet smile of Mr. Howland went with it. He put me at my ease, being innately gentle, and while he was protecting himself by the reserve that every intelligent writer has to expect in an editor, he was as cordial as he was clement. This, I said to myself, is not New York. This is America. No wonder America has never elected a president from New York City. That city lies outside democracy. Here at any rate its wolfish zest could be forgotten and the diamond glitter in its eye.

It was hard to convey the nebulous idea revolving in me, and I was so shy about it that I feared Mr. Howland might bark and frown like a busy New York editor.

" 'At the Foot of the Ladder?' That sounds interesting. How would you go about it, Mr. Hackett?"

"I'd go out and look for employment. I'd take jobs—jobs

anywhere, but not to work with my hands, jobs in offices and stores and that sort of thing. How do you get a job? I'd try to get it in Chicago, in San Francisco, anywhere. Just to report what a beginner is up against. You know."

Whether he knew or not, he gave me my head. He'd have to talk it over, but he encouraged me. He might print five or six articles. "We'll write you."

My courage ebbed in the next few weeks. These editorial decisions take time, and I had only $30, which meant very light housekeeping in my execrable room in Chicago. I was low in my body as well as my mind, and I resorted to eating a gross meal in a nearby saloon, which cost 25 cents. Then Clara Laughlin invited me to dinner at her home. She was a wondrous cook. Miss Laughlin revealed she was in the literary kitchen as well. She was D. Appleton's literary deputy, and she could commission me to cook up a book for them. This was amazing. I never drank, I had not smoked since the beginning of the year, and I abstained from carnal delight, but such news on top of Clara's dinner made me tipsy.

Yes, if I could deliver a manuscript of 70,000 words on Beauty and Hygiene, Appleton's would buy it from me for $250. Think of that! "You don't have to do it out of your head," smiled my angel. "You'll find all the books in the Newberry Library, and it's a lovely place to work. Let's see, 2,000 words a day, 10,000 a week. Could you deliver it in seven weeks?"

Seven weeks! Oceans of time! I jumped at the offer. At the end of May only the chapter on home nursing had to be written. Miss Laughlin had been charming all through, and I asked my mother to select for her a handsome streel of Irish lace that some poor soul could smuggle in for me. It was to be paid for out of the check, the wonderful check.

It was August before Appleton's made their decision. When I

went to Miss Laughlin to hear it, her eyes were enormous and full of kittenish apprehension.

"I'll read you what he says. Here is the gist of it. 'Mr. Hackett tells girls not to eat pie if they want to be beautiful. We want a book that tells girls they can eat pie and still be beautiful.' " She watched to see how I liked the guillotine, and when I said nothing, she laid down the letter. "Of course the manuscript is yours."

"But the idea was yours," I grumbled.

"That makes no difference, none at all. You sell it anywhere you like. I'll see if I can't persuade them to give us $100. Or I'll pay you myself."

I smiled, though decapitated. Meanwhile I turned to an aesthetic topic. I wrote a long article on Douglas Hyde, since John Quinn told me he was soon to visit America. Mr. Howland rejected it for *The Reader* magazine, but said it was "too long but beautifully written." Good discipline, I said to myself.

Brute economic anxiety was wearing me down when, toward the end of June, Mr. Howland asked me to come to Indianapolis.

<hr>

Indianapolis was a harmonious city, early American, and the Bobbs-Merrill office was in a "residential district," more or less. The trees lining the street were in leaf; the air was warm. The surreys dribbled along the quiet avenue or stood lazily parked, gold flecked under the play of the leaves. It was something that Irvington-on-Hudson had intimated to me, and even if the horses were to chuck up rebel heads and break loose, tugging their lead weights after them, I'd remember the jerk of their tolerant heads, the nonchalant flick of their tails, and the spill of sunlight that gilded them before they went daft.

Mr. Howland received me genially. He had arranged for me to stay the night at the Editor's Club. He said he wanted my articles. I was to keep what I earned, and he would pay me

$100 for each article, a sum I thought handsome. As we dined on that delightful evening, he held out a quiet prospect that I might become a writer-in-ordinary to his magazine, and while he suggested Buffalo as a good place to begin the study of clerks, he conceded that Chicago would offer me more scope. Our talk was easy and sane. He was sorry he had not seen his way to take my long Douglas Hyde article. Perhaps the fact that Chicago had ten times as many Irish, proportionately, as the capital of Indiana made the Gaelic movement look more remote there. He gave me $50 to go on with, since clothes in America cost money, and as I was wearing my winter suit, this touched me. I went away treasuring H. H. Howland and his lenient, reflective temperament. He was willing to see me buck the Colossus.

It was no good starting before the Fourth of July; Chicago has to bang itself deaf with fireworks first. They were busy that morning of July 5 in the Stockyards. Beside myself there had arrived 27,000 cattle, 33,000 hogs, and 18,000 sheep. As I walked along the pens, the sun still radiant and benign, the cattle were lamenting, the sheep were mourning, and the hogs were in woe, for they were the principals in this drama—poor children of nature. They had been unshipped with brute practicality, the broken ones thrown aside to die as they saw fit, prone under the sun. I watched the stockmen. Theirs was a natural dignity as they went riding or stirring about, their gait easy and their togs carefree, not men who would be cruel. Their bronzed faces and keen eyes contrasted favorably with the nippy aspect of office men who hurried by. This was the vortex of the Yards, sucking in the living yield of the prairies for purchase, its livestock a massive offering to Colossus.

The butchery was productivity at its crudest. I ought to peel off my collar, I said, and ask for a worker's job—the sort that Maxim Gorki had grappled with. Then I recoiled. Even if I possessed a grain of Gorki's talent and could screw myself up to such tension, it would make my nerves scream so loud and fill me with such loathing that I'd infallibly misrepresent it. A butcher splattered from head to foot with blood would think no more of it than pump water, whereas I'd blanch and vomit.

Then I went into Swift's and filled out a card, asking to be slipped into the hopper. For half an hour I sat waiting my turn, dulled by the familiar clatter and ping of typewriters, the pellets of sound hypnotic. But there was no vacancy. My application was put on file. It wanted a full account of the ten preceding years, taking me back to the age of 12. It asked certain questions about home life, liabilities, debts, sources of income and salary expected. At Armour's even an application blank was not issued.

The next morning I betook myself to the First National Bank. I'd like to be a clerk in an American institution of the highest class. They only wanted experienced men. Along with even more searching questions on the application blank one had to promise to "devote my entire time, energy, and ability to the exclusive service of the bank."

Marshall Field's

At last I got a job at Marshall Field's. His wholesale house at Adams and Fifth Avenue was doing the biggest business of its kind in the world, though my part was only to act as one of the incoming turnstiles for packing cases, entering them in big books. We were only 25 out of 2,000 in the clerical end, but a quart of water can disclose a lot to a bacteriologist.

Ours was a filthy hole; part of it was under the sidewalk, said to be freezing in winter and certainly stifling in summer. We worked by green-shaded lamps. The wooden fan, supposed to stir up the musty air, was out of order. We sweltered in our shirt sleeves nominally till 5:30, but for $2.50 a week extra we kept going till ten, five nights a week. Counting the half day Saturday, we put in some 75 hours a week.

The work was nothing itself. "What are dowels?" I asked the clerk who broke me in. "I don't know what the hell they are. You don't have to know. Enter 'em up." He'd been on the books for ten years.

On night work, when the manager was absent, it was an established male custom to speak of each other's wives, of women in the wholesale house, and of the girls their buddies meant to marry with complete and dashing indecency. They thought a rude crack the height of wit and a homosexual crack the cleverest. They refused definitely to be prissy. "No, sir, I ain't one of them guys that smokes a cigarette and carries a cane. I speak right out, I do."

Yet the pivotal question in every clerk's mind was the question of marrying. Their filthy talk was bilge from stifled sex, and sex had to be stifled by these underpaid clerks, who, once they married on $11 or $12 a week, were doomed to drudgery forever. Before marriage the clerk tried to have "a good time." He went to amusement parks, to the Olympic, or the Criterion, or the Bijou on Sundays, to fish in the lake, or to take a girl to Milwaukee or on an excursion boat to South Haven or to Cedar Lake and came home "full."

But marriage is a hazard on low wages. A thin, palefaced man with delicate blue veins showing under his eyes spoke vehemently to me of the conditions inevitable in all these great wholesale houses and of marriage after four years on less than $14 a week. The clerks might talk filthily, but all their natural craving for comfort and happiness, all their shy aspirations about marriage, were hopelessly thwarted by the iron ceiling that pressed into their economic debasement.

There was one ungainly, obsequious, short-strutting clerk who had an ineffectual high voice and an anxiety to "stand in with the boss." Everybody baited him. He was nicknamed "the deacon" because he had a very large head with a bald spot on top. He had been married for two years on eleven dollars a week. The office had long twitted him on his wife's pregnancy, saying he'd have twins. This never got a rise out of him. But one morning he arrived late, carrying a box of cigars, wreathed in smiles and distributing to all of us. It was a girl. The air was thick with comment, and even the lamest joke about race suicide, diapers, and midnight squalls made the Deacon beam with pleasure.

One broad-shouldered, square-chinned, high-colored man, Johnston by name, was watching this narrowly. He turned to me in disgust.

"The Deacon," he said, "that fool! He's able to beget children the way his father did. He'll probably have half a dozen, and he'll bring them up nohow, without education or anything, on his miserable pay. A man is a damn fool to get married until he's thirty, anyway. And still you hear boobs, like Sandy too, say that a man can live, raise a family, buy his clothes and save a hundred a year out of thirteen a week. What do you think of that. He's crazy."

Dan Sullivan had the chest development, the red neck, and the choleric temper to make him a typical extra policeman in the teamsters' strike. He'd been ten years on the books and Field's had kept his job open for him; but if his mother hadn't begged him to return to quiet, decent Field's, and if his "friend" hadn't said she would marry no policeman, he'd have remained in uniform.

"Keep your mout' shut here," he warned me. "Tell nothin' to nobody. These guys here are all damn sauerkrauts. They're all right to your face, but they're tricky and clannish as hell. You're Irish and that's why I'm taking the trouble to talk to you."

Eventually I asked Sullivan should I remain in Fields.

"There's nothin' in it. It's a man who's ten years in it is tellin' you. Get out as quick as ever you can. If you have a drag, it's all right unless your man is canned himself. They call us the pigpen down here. I call them the $3 a week dudes. And I'll say this to you. I feel as good as sunshine when I come down here of a mornin', and I'm not here but one minute and I'm feeling like hell." Johnston concurred in this. A man of strong character, he stood out from the Germans in this pigpen. At 22 he had been partner in a small drugstore, but overwork had injured his health; he had been three years in Field's. After three months he had sought a raise.

"You have nerve, haven't you?" said the assistant manager.

"Wasn't it nerve made you boss?" And he got two dollars more.

Every time I left the romanesque building that H. H. Richardson had built for Field's wholesale house, I thought of those who admired it as architecture. We who were smelted in it were less admiring. If we wanted air we had only the back to open to, where to the grinding of trucks, the grating of crates, the rattle of handtrucks, the yowling, bawling and clamoring of shipping clerks and "teamsters," we could drink in whatever ozone and exhaust we desired. We were negligible.

Hearst

My first two articles covered searching for a job and getting one at Marshall Field's. To my enormous surprise and delight, Mr. Howland liked them and accepted them. Now I wanted to discover on what terms William Randolph Hearst had gate-crashed into circulation. That he failed to become mayor or President proved he was no vote-getter. That he gained immense popular circulation proved nothing till the nature of his appeal was studied. Hearsay, prejudice, mob hysteria, flag-waving gain great circulation. I was intensely interested in him as Ibsen was interested in the waterworks in "The Enemy of the People." Did he foul the water supply?

Quite near to Field's, under the dingy elevated railway at Madison and Fifth, I asked a newsboy, "Where's the *American*?"

"Middle of the block. Y'can't miss it." I came on a grimy building of soiled white. Sprawling gilt letters named Hearst's *Chicago American.*

A Corkman at City Hall who knew Hearst's managing editor had given me a note of introduction. The instant I presented it he scribbled a line, "Look over this young friend of Lahiff's as a candidate for the kindergarten. He looks likely to me," and shunted me off to the city editor. An office boy sat me down while an attempted murder was being dealt with. Word had just come in by the tubes from the City Press, a blob of delicious honey around which they clustered before dashing into action, one to his typewriter, another to the telephone, one grabbing his hat and coat, another strapping on a heavy camera outfit. This was a "front page."

I sat on, the whole works exposed to my greedy gaze—hunched illustrators under window light, reporters and editors in the center under nervous incandescent lamps that flapped and flopped against naked whitewashed wall, linotype operators in the rear, and the vast floor strewn with trampled paper. From the ceiling idly dangled Mr. Hearst's obiter dicta. "The policy of the *American* is to please as many as possible," "Thieves' slang and slang of all kinds must not appear in the *American*," "The *American* is to speak as a gentleman should," just like Mr. Santayana, and then a sign that hid a smile, "No exaggeration."

Then the city editor saw me. He was a fat, white-faced man with sleeves rolled up, neck bare, an imposing brow, and an unimposing chin; Mr. Koenigsburg was it? He motioned me to sit. Running his fingers through his thick mane, he leaned back in his chair and puffed a grudging look at me.

"Can you use a typewriter?" When I said yes, his face was as blank as the sole of a boot. "Why do you want to go into the newspaper business? You know it is the worst business on earth—there's no money in it."

This was the old song and dance. No money in it for Hearst, who was to boast of himself as the richest man in America. Marshall Field twaddle, respectable twaddle for Lilliput. But this editor had to utter it. "Well," he added, as if to himself, "I'm running over my salary appropriation already, but I'll take you on trial at fiteen dollars a week. You've had no experience, you say. Written a little, had a story accepted or something? Of course, that won't do you any *harm*, but grace and deportment in English—they're not exactly what we're looking for. You'll have rough work in the beginning, but if you make good I may be able to take you on at a better salary." He called over Charlie Fitzmorris, who shook hands with me. I liked him right off; he could have magnetized steel girders. "Sit down by the door till you hear your name called."

I sat down. I could hardly breathe. I had a job on a newspaper!

The work itself indescribably quickened my feelings. I was inexhaustibly keen as a reporter. It demanded direct contact with people in the throes of action—a woman whose husband had tried to kill her with a butcher knife, a woman whose son had shot himself, a woman stripped of her valuable belongings, the parents of an Italian boy killed by a street car, a woman whose ex-husband refused alimony, and a woman who was cruelly slashed as she fought with her lover to keep him from cutting his throat.

What moved me was to find people so simple and pellucid in trouble. Their whole lives bared to a reporter before their bewildered, stunned, or frantic recoil after a hard clash with fate threw them on police attention and on public notice. The newspapers sucked their drama from police news. They were surfeited with disaster and catastrophe.

But to make it palatable, it had to be cooked up, and a gang of rewrite men, working for the prince of lies like fallen angels, did the cooking. Hearst's *American* adulterated and fabricated the product to dish up melodrama and stereotyped burlesque.

The mad mastiff was typical. This brute weighed one hundred and fifty pounds, the Sunday papers said, and a patrol wagon pursued it a mile on Saturday, shooting fifty times and not killing it before it had torn the clothes from two men and bitten a woman. I hurried to their addresses, comparing all the stories. Nothing seemed to fit it. I went to the police station.

A foaming mastiff? Had anyone heard of a foaming mastiff? "Go round to the school and see Gallagher. He might know about it."

Gallagher was a lame policeman assigned to watch the children at play.

"Mastiff?" he regarded me pityingly. " 'Twas no mastiff. A miserable little cur dog about as big as a minit."

"How big, you say?"

"About as big as a young cat. It wasn't mad at all. 'Twas poisoned the creature was. I walked after it half a block not to frighten it, and when I'd found a soft place—less the bullet'd glance off it, do you know—I put two shots into it. I did indeed. Sure it's down under the Elevated yet. You can go and look at it."

I started off.

"Say, there."

"What?"

"Look close or mebbe you wouldn't see it at all."

I found the little dog, curled up as it died. Gallagher was right. The story was what he called a "pipe." The rewrite men had dreamed it.

I went to Desplaines to get the picture of a young woman on her honeymoon. She had come to a Chicago court, we were told, to ask that her husband, selected on a jury, be released. Actually she had been married three years and had a two-year-old baby. "I do not particularly care for the *American*," she said, and would not give me her photograph. But we stuck to the story. " 'Free husband from Jury' is Bride's Plea to Judge," and the rewrite men gave the dialogue. "It will be too bad to wreck your honeymoon."

The next victim parted with her photograph. She told me how an express company had lost her suitcase, containing clothes, a silver-mounted toilet set, and Sir Philip Sidney's poems. This detailed report went into the enormous wastebasket. "Do no more work than you're ordered to. It makes work for others." We printed wrong initial and wrong address, the suitcase became "a chest of silverware and heirlooms, valued at six hundred dollars" (picture of a man struggling with heavy wooden chest), gave the wrong express company, and carefully stated that the chest bore the (incorrect) address. Why the rewrite men did not supply a wrong photograph was a lapse of inattention; the *American* had thousands of them.

Our pulp writers stuck in revolvers where they could. I

interviewed a young woman at her bedside about her husband's trying to steal her baby. She spoke indolently from her tumbled couch. Yes, her husband was hanging around, but she hadn't laid eyes on him, and her mother, pulling on her stockings in the next room, relieved her mind about her son-in-law. She did not want her daughter's picture printed but, out of spite, gave me the husband's, and added the baby's when I pleaded that all babies look alike.

This was hatched by the rewrite men into a striking melodrama. "Mrs. Janzen is today staying indoors in deadly fear of her husband, whom she expects to come at any moment to steal her babe." He "made an attempt to steal the child Sunday, and after being outwitted by the mother, fired several shots at her. One of the bullets just grazed the woman's head.

" 'Who's there?' came the response to a knock at the door of the little Janzen home today.

"Mrs. Griffin, mother of Mrs. Janzen, finally opened the door. Mrs. Janzen, trembling and frightened, stood by with her baby held tight to her breast." The pulp magazines pullulate with babes and bullets.

"Yellow journalism," said Arthur Brisbane, Hearst's Pooh-Bah, "is simply real journalism." The mad mastiff, the Desplaines bride, Mrs. Janzen frightened and trembling, the chest of silverware and heirlooms—Mr. Brisbane's "real journalism."

Two-thirds of my work was fruitless, and I wanted above all to make good with Fitzmorris who, while handling me without gloves, seemed ready to give me every chance. When I telephoned to him, for example, that a house on Chicago Avenue gave no answer he said, "Can't you break in?" I answered, "It's opposite the police station." He was silent, and then he said in a patient voice: "Is there no back to the house?" I went around. It was nailed up. When I came back empty-handed he despatched me to see a lady in distress. Her ex-husband refused to pay alimony as long as she retained her star boarder.

Her niece, a soft, unsuspicious country girl, described her

aunt's struggle to support herself and the children and "Uncle Fred's meanness" to her. The day before a reporter had come saying her aunt had sent him for the one picture she had. "Auntie was mad. She gave me 'sand' when she came home," said the niece. I telephoned Mr. Fitzmorris how the *Inter-Ocean* had got the picture. He said, "You go to the aunt and get an order for it. Take it to the *Inter-Ocean*. Say you're a friend of the family and get the picture."

"I'll try and get the order, but I won't lie to get the picture."

Fitzmorris could hardly believe his ears. "It won't kill you to tell a lie."

I said, "Probably not."

We had a talk about it. "Do you adopt no subterfuge to get a picture?"

That stumped me. I used smiles and wiles, but just plain, honest-to-God lying stuck in my crop.

"What do you mean by a subterfuge?" I asked.

"Well, if that woman gave you an order, that would be a friendly act. Why would it be a lie to say to the *Inter-Ocean* you were a friend?"

"Yes, but a friend of the family? That's absolute sophistry."

"It may be sophistry," he returned with an Irish grin, "but it's a damned good argument."

"I don't want to be pompous," I said to him. "I'll be as smart as I can, but I draw the line at direct lying. It vitiates the whole thing. But I can expect to be fired, I know."

"But if you have such fine ideas about editing," he answered, "why don't you do what you're told till you get where you can use them? The idea of firing you never entered my head, but you're the first man who told me he wouldn't lie, and I wanted to see your point of view. I never ask a man to do anything I wouldn't do myself. I never ask him to do anything mean or low that would hurt anyone."

So he put me to investigating appeals for charity, but he interspersed a comedy and a tragedy. In the comedy a "bandit" grabbed a girl's handbag and slapped her face. This "bandit" was a boy who snatched and ran without slapping anybody. The rewrite man had dressed it up.

The tragedy was a 7 a.m. suicide. I was at the police station at 8 a.m. and I said to the hard Irish lieutenant on the desk that I'd like to speak with the woman, pacing back and forth. Her lover had cut his throat. His blood was on her skirt, her hands in white bandages.

That knife-edged Irishman stabbed me with a look. He leaned forward. "You'd have the heart to ask that woman for her picture?"

I shrugged. I was dogged. "Go ahead," he sneered.

She was sobbing, trying to clench the bandaged hands with which she had tried to prevent her lover's suicide. The splotches of his blood glistened freshly. "Send me to somebody," I begged. "Oh, go away!" she said wildly, "Go away." I went to the desk and telephoned.

"Too bad about her," said Fitzmorris. "Wait half an hour and ask her again. Hold on. Is she good-looking?"

She was so exalted she was flown with beauty. This time I lied wholeheartedly. "No," I said, as dully as I could. I could hear Fitzmorris talk to the city editor. "He says she isn't good-looking." Koenigsberg muttered something. With profound conviction Fitzmorris replied, "No, he wouldn't be able to get it." He spoke up. "All right. Come in." So I went in to the chopping block.

"It's a thing I never like to have to do," he said. Chop. The guillotine came down. I was still alive. Then he added, as if speaking of the Next World, "perhaps you'll find it more congenial elsewhere." Yes, I said, sitting on a cloud and playing a harp. I drew $37.50 for fifteen days' hard labor.

The game was vivid, tough, and exhilarating. I had wanted to "make good." During that month the sworn sales were 8,207,251 for the daily, and 3,060,797 for the Sunday. A few months before Arthur Brisbane had declared, "I have no doubt that Hearst in his influence on public thought and action is the most powerful man in the United States today. That is because he owns the present meeting place of the people—the yellow journal—*and he presides at all the meetings.*" This was rubbish. He was not powerful enough to be elected mayor of New York; Brisbane anticipated that. "Yellow journalism is war—war on hypocrisy, war against class privileges, and war against the foolishness of the crowd that will not think and will not use the weapon that it holds, the invincible ballot." These audacious words were often echoed in Chicago. A streetcar conductor showed me in his home a free gift from the *American*, a new dictionary. "The *American* is good to the poor." Fifteen teachers said to me in their school, "The *American* is fair where we are concerned." I heard praise of it from a bricklayer's wife, a steamfitter's wife, a janitor's wife, from Colinski, Pantek, Simadis, Olsen. A great big section of adult Chicago workers absorbed Hearst's ink and the propaganda with which it was loaded, and this did give him importance. Had there been guns behind him he might have disrupted America, but while Brisbane spoke of voters who don't "think for themselves," they thought enough to defeat Hearst as a candidate. But as newspaper owner his quackery gave a lead to yellow journalism the world over. By magnifying fear and hate, stirring mob hysteria, bemusing the uncritical, he promoted war—class war. Wrapped in the spangled banner, he spouted patriotism at will. He smeared himself with the Sermon on the Mount. His crew dabbed in fillers from Turgeniev and Thoreau, counterfeiting culture as well as democracy.

When Mr. Howland accepted that article on Hearst, he did more than he knew. I walked up Astor Street and over to the Lake to take in the news. I grappled it as one grapples a firm staple after a long swim, and I let myself admit the truth, "I want to be a writer."

For three years I had kept afloat as a clerk, too ignorant of America to write for it. No intelligent alien can disguise from himself the difference that makes a native American one thing and an alien another. The British subjects who founded the Republic had set a bench mark on it when they decreed that no alien could be President. As a nationalist I saw its deep wisdom. Every nation is rooted and its intimacies become so instinctive that the new arrival has to imbibe them as he would a foreign language, and he seldom reaches down so far that he can write good fiction. Fiction lets intimacies well up, group intimacies, and in their absence even an imported caricaturist like Tom Browne was quite lost in Chicago; what welled up in him was England. I was too new to write fiction.

But in tackling Hearst, "incestuous Herod discoursing on chastity," I had broached a topic peculiarly American, and a native magazine had consented to it. It was a small magazine, a small triumph, but it opened into the New World. I felt as an American in writing it, and if I thought Hearst a bad American, I proposed to say so, and had a right to.

I could not think it out. The Catholic answers were no good to a writing Irishman. In Ireland imagination was manacled by Catholic editors and publishers. But more daunting still was England's proximity. It made Ireland a dependency. Either its writer abandoned nationalism and let Ireland fend for itself, as did Shaw and Oscar Wilde, or he turned to Abbey playwriting, short stories, or journalism. But, in America there was also a dependence on two sorts of masters. The polite tradition depended on England, and the base popular tradition depended on mercantile inventiveness of the Hearst stripe.

I struggled to shape ideas in relation to America as a literary field. It was all very well to talk of a "common stock," but I believed that what was natural for Oxford and Cambridge was exotic for the University of Wisconsin. Walt Whitman spoke for unborn America when he scorned the literature of feudalism, however beautiful and true it was in its own time and place. It could not meet the proclivities of a child trotting to school down Dearborn Avenue or hopping the Union Pacific sleepers to a Nebraska schoolhouse.

America had a new set of associations for its imagining, a special social content, at variance with the furniture of professors and professorial critics who absorbed English culture. No wonder they were popularly termed "highbrows." They sought to impose a foreign culture on a country that could share in universal genius but must have its own Milton, its own Shelley, its own Daughters of Albion, and its own Alastor.

I was not talking as a visitor. I was not priding myself on Europe. Kilkenny was my Europe, and I was hardly equipped to pat America on the head or to take Chicago solely on the basis of its aesthetic performance, which would be captious and premature in view of the flux required by the democratic experiment, its dispute with privilege, and the absence of caste. America had to hold itself in solution to keep new privilege and new caste from condensing. But the promise of a rainbow could not be redeemed if human life as organized by inventiveness were to cramp imagination of necessity. Let the nation be and do what it will, juvenile and unformed by polite European reckoning. it could still fulfill its promise. But this could never happen as long as it confused successful organization for the mass in the measure that gainful inventiveness proposed with those individual experiences that imagination proposed and perfected. The seductions of mass facility were America's greatest seductions, whereby it disregarded the single American as the final experiencer.

Works of imagination were witheringly exposed in America, and whenever they were produced the critic should be found to sustain them, as against the preying commercial jungle and the parching academic desert.

Probably at the suggestion of John Quinn, I became secretary and press agent for a meeting at which Dr. Douglas Hyde was to speak on the revival of Gaelic. It was not a writer's work, but I took it on. It took a month to organize. It was a cause!

John Quinn was as hardheaded as anyone, and he knew no Gaelic—a language that you should creep into on your hands and knees in early childhood, an intricate language as resistant as Basque. It was as remote from most Chicagoans as the wearing of kilts, but the Chicago Irish did not fail Douglas Hyde on the appointed night. They filled the auditorium.

Dr. Hyde came through as a messenger, not that he was born to sweep an audience from its moorings, but he did what was in him as a scholar and a teacher; he defined the Gaelic movement and won accord and support.

When the moment came for collecting the support, we first stood up to cheer the speaker, and I was so carried away by the desire to whoop it up that I could hear lugubrious primitive wails emitted from me as from an animal in pain. I had never known I was so Celtic. My coat was plucked, "Stop, man, you'll disgrace us." But on waves of cheers the subscriptions were launched.

Douglas Hyde told me I had been a help, "invaluable," he couldn't have done without me. But the results, contrasted with $20,000 subscribed in San Francisco, were far from glorious. Yet this tour of his netted nearly $60,000 for the League. At a time when the dreamers behind it did not have that many pence, it gave them the means for maintaining a central office, the League's journal, and help for their organizers. The flame would possibly have expired unless protected methodically. It was a handful of intellectuals in the Gaelic League who spread this fire from which the torch of rebellion was lighted in 1916, though socialists like James Connolly gave their lives from motives equally lofty and very different.

Hyde kept his mission unpolitical, but when I mentioned in private that my brother Bat was now doctor at Mountjoy Prison in Dublin where political prisoners were sometimes confined, he looked at me with depth in his black eyes. "He may be of good use there, some day." It was in January 1906.

The departure of the Hydes left me in a "state"; to call it

confusion would be too mild. Everything Irish in me was stirred, and I whizzed with plans for returning to the land of my birth. These frothy ideas I had to combat. A "renegade" Catholic might go back to France or Belgium, to live in free association with men and women who felt as he did, to have access to free thought, to exercise free speech without arousing legal antagonisms, but, however Ireland needed free play of the mind, a born-Catholic who did not toe the line would be daubed yellow. He would be shunned by his own people and forced to spend his vitality in fighting the chill. No such penury had to be endured in Chicago.

Chicago Evening Post

At the beginning of 1906, finding myself in this critical tension and having no money for a try at creative writing, even if I'd had the courage and the capacity, I decided to have a go at book reviewing. I went to the office of the *Chicago Evening Post* to see the literary editor, Tiffany Blake. He had heard of me from his cousin Henry [Blake] Fuller, and took me to be a young Irish poet. He handed me a batch of poetry to review, published at the authors' expense by Badger and not worth tuppence at McClurg's, where reviewers sold review copies as their sole recompense. Toward the end of February, however, delivering some reviews to the *Evening Post*, I was startled to hear that I might be colliding with a job. Tiffany Blake said to me solemnly, "We have a small staff. We cannot afford to keep anyone unless he gives immediate satisfaction. But see the managing editor, Leigh Reilly. He may take you on trial as a reporter." I was not cut out to be a reporter. On the local American scene I was befuddled about unfamiliar issues that made news, nor had I the audacity to extract details on the surface. At best I might manage to hang on. But Mr. Reilly said, "I can start you at $15. We may possibly be needing a literary editor, and if so I'll see if I can't work you in and pay you better."

The pay was small. Willie Kenealy on the *Daily Mail* in London was earning about $30 a week. But I went to work at the beginning of March with a tenacity fiercer than I had so far generated. I was 23 years old, admitting myself to be dolefully ignorant and abominably undereducated, but with a grasp on the opportunity that was positively prehensile.

Reviewing books for the *Post* was done on the outside, and however hard I took it and however much I put into it and whatever weight I gave to Tiffany Blake's liking or disliking the reviews, it was a private affair. It was quite another thing to join the staff as a reporter. The *Post* was not an awe-inspiring paper to Chicagoans. It was a small paper. But if you are in a battle, even a small battle at $15 a week, it's your skin that you are risking, and it's your imagination that is excited by it. A generation later I sat in the Supreme Court, watching a young jurist, William O. Douglas, the day he was seated as a justice, and the play of imagination on his face, at once troubled and exalted, pale and flushed, swept by sun and shadow, was intensely evident. The stark altitude of his new office gave him an overwhelming sense of human inadequacy. But that was exactly what my job on the *Post* gave me. I was scared.

When I went up to the city room and told a boy that I was "the new reporter," he took it in his stride. That is to say, on the hop and without its making the slightest difference. So I sat there, in the backwash of the busy office, trying to report that I was the new reporter and proving by my failure to break through the routine what a feeble reporter I would be. I expected someone to pay attention, instead of securing it by hook or crook. A reporter who stands on ceremony is a gone gander.

And then a thing happened I never forgot, protocol in a newspaper office. A reporter in his shirt sleeves came up to me, his hand extended. "You are the new reporter, aren't you? And you're looking for your typewriter." This was Julian Mason, still redolent of Yale, born with a passkey and then promoted to snatch as snatch can. He had a nervous trick of fidgeting with his cigarette, smoking it as if imbibing it and then knocking off the ash. A blue haze on his chin would have made another man untidy, but Julian was out of a bandbox, his hair meticulous, his tie miraculous. I blessed him for that kind greeting, and in a minute he appeared with a venerable typewriter that had arthritis and the staggers. All I now needed was an "assignment," a job of reporting.

The *Evening Post* wore mittens. Among the murderers and thugs who distributed Hearst's sheet and the *Tribune*, the *Post* was a journalistic freak, a refined spinster, and it edged along with its eyes cast down. Luckily for us, the big afternoon paper with which we directly competed, the *Daily News*, was the least sensational in town; it was a vast acreage of small type that left the impression on a passing stranger of a thickly populated cemetery filled with neat little items and with gravel on the paths.

Our city editor was Joe Sheehan, a fretful nervous kind of man, who looked like a thin Catholic curate, and when the pressroom demanded copy from him he would tighten his lips and come behind me as I pecked out a story on the typewriter. Then he'd wrinkle his pale skin and utter a bitter cry, snatching at a page of copy. I was too slow. I was fit only to write editorials. And this was so indisputable that I lost no sleep, though it pained me not to have a "nose for news."

A berth on the *Post* was what I desired and needed, and the fact that it was not a moneymaker was in its favor. It meant that, so long as we took very small salaries and tried hard to achieve some sort of excellence, we could at least give our proprietor the prestige that paid him instead of cash. If cash were his underlying object, however well disguised, we were dished from the beginning.

Our managing editor, Leigh Reilly, was an ideal skipper. On the business side he had to deliver prestige to John C. Shaeffer, the Indianapolis newspaper publisher who footed the bills, and also keep Dave Towne, our business manager, out of hot water. On the editorial side he had to save us from the more thickheaded and brutally conservative Chicago bigwigs who might frighten Mr. Shaeffer, and this meant understanding the pathology of the Illinois Manufacturers' Association. His argument to Dave Towne could usually be that, at the salaries we were paid, we had to have some leeway. Leigh Reilly wasn't one of those grumpy, cynical, "tough and icy" managing editors who chew their words and their cigars, at once truculent and serviceable. He was a fine-grained, keen, and imaginative boss with a baton he employed sparingly, a manner that did not permit intrusion, but had warmth and humor. He was neither bulldozer nor piledriver. He crunched down nobody. And the size of the enterprise suited him. In consequence he was as welcome in the composing room as in the city room.

One of the economies of the *Post* was to make the literary editor an assistant to the editorial writer. This was my good luck. Tiffany Blake was then the heir apparent to the chief editorial writer who was just resigning. Tiffany took his job, having meantime put me in the offing as a reporter.

These things seldom happen. The venerable gentlemen who inter their ideas in editorials are very long lived. Their assistants see them down in the little plots where they bury their thoughts and often have the impulse to tap them on the head, but this is hard to reconcile with editorial decency. The old gravediggers go on, saying the last word, but never for the last time unless some fatal editorial slides in on them.

To be writing editorials on the *Chicago Evening Post*, under Tiffany Blake, was an invaluable schooling. Tiffany did not teach by admonition. He taught as do all craftsmen with keen eye and good hands who give the benefit of their own experience to a willing apprentice. He, McEachern, and myself had to fill the daily three columns lickety-split. The book section was Tiffany's job but I assisted him at it, and I had feature articles to write, such as "Little Talks about Big People." I sometimes felt there wasn't another fresh editorial topic in the world, my brain wrung out until not a bubble was left. But I had the greatest of all boons in an editorial job, a perfect reliance on the man I was working under.

Tiffany Blake was by long odds the best chief I ever had. A single glance at him as he hurried with quick step and fixed gaze to the pressroom revealed the concentration he put into his job, and as he stopped for a word with the managing editor, Leigh Reilly, sweeping away the lock of thick black hair that drooped down when he was vigorously in action, the whole accent of the man's personality was of unaffected sincerity. He was distinguished in his dark clothes and white linen, but the fineness of his distinction was in his mournful, dark, deepset eyes and the poet's sensuous mouth. He was physically frail with deep hollows in his cheeks, but that did not impair his responsibility as a maker of editorial policy. He gave it powerful direction, using rich resources in national history, full acquaintance with state and local affairs, a reasonable approach in general, and also on certain issues with hard-hitting fire behind him, but he scorned the "vim, vigot, victory" school of copywriters that was beginning to vulgarize America. The Illinois of Lincoln was a massive, steadying presence in the midst of the dead-end kids who were waiting to run screaming into journalism. The men in the city room did not go in for eulogy, but they had an unqualified respect for him.

Mine was an arduous job, but what made it hard was refusing to be a hack. More and more I ran the book reviews as well as the three short or two long editorials a day and the two feature articles a week.

Added to this were the two evening classes a week I taught at Hull House, for I had moved there in the middle of 1906.

Hull House

A Hull House resident was a voluntary worker who paid for room and board in cash—$7 or $8 a week, which even my sparse wages could stretch to. My duties took three evenings a week. I taught English classes twice a week, and on the third evening I attended the door.

The old Hull mansion on Halsted Street was symbolic of the "social settlement." Built by a prominent Chicagoan in his affluence at some distance from the city, it now stood islanded in the inundating slum, immigration having deposited successive waves of Europeans at its portal. Without secluding itself from Greek or Italian or German or Russian or Irish, it offered contact on its own ground, investing it with dignity and decorum, being not an intruder on the immigrant so much as an intermediary and next friend. The impulse behind it was that of all bridge builders and ferry services—to carry the displaced to their proper destination rather than see them fall prostrate or go astray. They were often dumped into America, these immigrants, shipped wholesale under consignment, but even those who could depend on natal colonies or friends were frequently stunned by the upheaval in their lives. The strong immigrants victimized the weak and native America, talking of free enterprise, started these newcomers from scratch, just as the early settlers had been obliged to start themselves. Chicago was a harsh free-for-all where many an immigrant ousted the native-born. Amazing goodwill permeated this rough and tumble, but victory was to the strong.

For myself, after private skirmishing as an underpaid worker, this chance to encounter the real rough and tumble, to study a class of Russian Jews, for example, could greatly help to show what America was in for and what it proposed to do. The essence of it, whatever sociologists or political economists might say, would be the inner convictions it must breed about the United States, and especially the United States toward which I had a leaning—the one that promised harmony and delectation. For where could harmony be, and in what form could delight be embraced, if the great country itself betrayed its people? I sought rank experience, however it went against preference to react with these innate Americans to the goad of conscience.

Did the United States nullify its political superiority by its economic perfidy? Could the thing work out? Could politics referee it? Or would rapacity overthrow the referee?

Nobody at Hull House, so far as I could see, gave adequate heed to the arts. Of course the arts whiled away exciting hours in the theatre, and Hull House had its own beauty, its scrupulous regard for culture. But I mean that the usury exacted by fine art, whether in painting or writing poetry or creating in any known medium, was not merely refused but repudiated as out of keeping with the convictions that possessed this women's argosy. That Jane Addams and her fellow workers were engaged in an adventure, in the quest of a golden fleece, was precisely what drew creatures like myself in their wake, holding on by any grappling-hook that could be slung into their bulk or frame and never confused about the magnitude of an enterprise on which I was the merest transient or stowaway. Hull House was itself creative. It was born from women who had detached themselves from a traditional role and pose. These women, in the course of time, would become museum pieces to snippets whose bobbed hair and stained fingernails and eternal cigarettes, or whose ferocious Communism or Lesbianism or Mercantilism, owed not a little debt to the creators on Halsted Street, as much disallowed as the debt of any gilded grandson to a daguerreotype.

Hull House broke ground for these heirs to an emancipation and did its grim work at a sacrifice. At the same time, given the immense demand that any more personal creative art must levy on its servant, Hull House elected to shut its eyes or else gazed uncomprehendingly, and even Jane Addams, then writing her significant books, assumed that the left hand could serve her authorship when she needed the right so badly for steering Hull House or for the myriad activities that grew from it.

Of course she wrote from her heart, sensitive in everything she undertook. She was incapable of spiritual infidelity and tragically aware of the drama in which she was sometimes to look like Duse, a sociological Duse, diverted from the career associated so often with Helen of Troy or Cleopatra or the great Catherine—females who would compromise a Hull House that was much nearer to a Teresa, an immolation of private self being preliminary to an assertion of the Good.

Miss Addams had a strong feeling for literature as it unrolled itself day by day. I remember her wistful expression as she praised *The Mirror of the Sea*, a new book by Joseph Conrad. She could have pursued a quest in that direction. But under the burden that Chicago heaped, and that she shouldered with such valor, she could only let her eyes follow it, her hands employed. With a meekness quite misleading in view of her iron purpose, she would sometimes consult a writer of reputation to see how her own books might spread their sail. Henry Fuller, whose eyes and hands and voice and beard could all quail and flutter at once, so plaintive in a wind-swept cosmos that everything threatened to blow away except his point of view, would grip with the tenacity of a storm-tossed butterfly to the vision he never forsook.

"Those titles!" he said to me deploringly. "She can call a small book *Democracy and Social Ethics*. What a title!" The elephantine footprints of that fine, high-arched, quick-moving spirit completely overwhelmed him. He had pleaded with her in vain. Those worn words—democracy, social, ethics—were ardent and burning words as she conceived them. She could not change democracy or social or ethics.

Once, in the impatience of a youth that could not forgive Matthew Arnold for his reference to the "ineffectual angel" I spoke of him as "only a glorified book reviewer." To my distress Miss Addams chilled and darkened at these slighting words. To me there was nothing ineffectual about Shelley, though he was clearly deficient in the instinct of self-preservation, and Matthew Arnold swam in a life belt, or so I judged by his shivering refusal to plunge into Tolstoy. Yet where Miss Addams valued the Victorians—Arnold, John Stuart Mill, Lecky and so on—was on that broad prairie where the passions could become cyclonic unless governed by—democracy and social ethics. Miss Addams belonged to the world, but the prairie had bred her, the so-called good earth that is liberally diversified with badlands and dust bowls, and it was the men of level temper and of wide outlook and constant purpose who gave her confidence in her own dealing with the gusty, greedy, irrational males who dominated the scene. She had Rousseau less in mind than Rousseau's bastards, donated to the Great Society to be put in chains though his heart bled for humanity in chains. The woman in her took cool stock of romantic revolutionaries.

But art is in itself a revolution, whether romantic or the contrary. It cannot be harnessed to the immediate goodness that occupied these admirable thinkers. It must conscript the whole man, ask him for his heart's blood, and judge him by the consummate performance and achievement.

George Twose, the English architect, was the one artist who pervaded Hull House. My long acquaintance with the Jesuits had prepared me in some degree for this mixture of the monastic and the urbane. There was an incipient anchorite in Twose, who had retreated from an all-devouring clan at home to the desert of Chicago where he should have worn sandals and a tonsure. But the urbane Englishman is ineradicable, even in the petrified forest, and Hull House inveigled Twose as the right alternative to petrifaction; the urbanity that Chicago had stiffened in his veins beginning to thaw and liquefy in its atmosphere. He was a tall, rangy Englishman—his dome eminent and bald, his coloring an attractive brown, his teeth large, and his eyes snapping and sparkling with vitality. He was a nervous critter, just the same, skittish and verging on the irascible, not rebellious against the snaffle but tossing his plume and giving a wild lunge when things chafed him. But if things really went all wrong, he was all right. He laughed at the idiots and brushed them off like crumbs, He had not espoused Hull House forever. He was footloose.

He rather piqued me by this airy unprofessionalism and negligence, but to do a thing in nonchalant style, to be at home in his own element without effort and stress, and to have the negligence of mastery, was the very essence of his nature which was tameless and volatile. He hovered near Miss Addams in a sort of chivalrous hope that his light hand could relieve her of inordinate claims piled daily on her unprotected conscience. His own conscience he wore loose, like an open collar or waving tie, and he said "rats!" if the precise stopped to tidy him. Twose never really fluttered in the void; he saw Hull House as a most concrete court of conscience, but one that he would not permit to harass him. He desired a plaisance, first of all, to be enjoyed and to be enhanced by enjoyment, and if Hull House lent him such an opportunity, he generously improved on it.

As my own room branched off the same landing as his, I saw a little of him. Our rooms revealed a lot. In mine the oatmeal paper and the dark mission furniture were regarded as given; I deferred to the heavy hand of government. Twose reacted to his room as to Hull House itself. No less penniless than I was, he secured silvery foil out of boxes, probably from Guiseppe in the restaurant, and his walls gloomed and glittered for his amusement. He could see that I was "bitterly young," and he laughed at it. "It will all be the same in a thousand years," not that he believed it. Nothing was the same two days running. But he took no responsibility for the universe as such. Everyone else might be agitated about First and Last Things. Twose disregarded the keys on the ethical machine; he used a touch system. And this clarity in him, not secured overnight, permitted him to go privileged through the ever-shifting intensities of this group. He did it ex-portfolio.

This had nothing to do with ambition. Twose lacked all desire to make his mark, if it meant carving it in the tissues of his competitors. But he had an inexhaustible desire to have Hull House gaily realize itself as a going community, an absolutely innate social gift that gave him an art of intercourse quite aside from mere geniality or sociability. He had that invaluable English sense of people which makes snobbishness in the majority of cases but a Borrow-like humanism in others. Twose had imagination for the lame and the halt; it was only the intimate young things he shied away from, set parties, and set sentiments. His gift especially showed itself on certain public occasions when Hull House was the host to big groups or that sort of thing. But it was for the sake of Hull House itself, of Miss Addams and her original partner, Miss Waite, that he drew on abilities any theatrical producer might have envied—whirling shy or awkward people into a circle that swept them out of themselves and with such prompt humor and amused grimace and offhand skill that no one was left his debtor. Twose could not be explained by the purposeful. He was not visibly motivated or determined any more than a prize canary. He gave. He gave, not as a social worker or as an ideologist, but as a Twose, particularly to the non-self-starters. People like Twose have no formula. They flourish in England. They transform a group, or at least aid it in transforming itself, with a felicity that has no unction in it, no damn sweetness and light, but a fineness of touch that would make the fortune of anyone who could devise it for mass production. A Frenchman does it in his own way, so does an Italian, but Twose had a tonic quality, a verve, and a fund of social sense, which made him at once sound and festive. Where Twose was, there was birdsong.

On his way home to England, seeing his native shores once again, and visualizing his Set, he bundled up his evening clothes and pushed them through the porthole into the sea.

He was excellent for Hull House. When they acted Shaw or Yeats, when they got up a dance, or when people who came were interested in the Labor Museum, Twose rose to the occasion. But there were things he wouldn't do. The afternoon James Bryce came, Twose was making his own tea, and I couldn't get him to budge. The ambassador downstairs was important to "tote," but not as much as that. And when I asked him to tackle Belloc in a book review, I was surprised he could not organize it. He gave me the feeling that he perceived everything; he was so lucid in conversation, so prompt and audacious with people, but on the humble workday task of a book review, which required him to isolate that factor in the Hillaire Belloc equation not yet detected and established, though of course as simple as any puzzle, once it was made familiar, he gallivanted with it for weeks and then threw it aside. Contact with a mind could not engage him like contact with an organism like Hull House, nor could it absorb his interest or demand his energy.

And yet, a book review, what's that? You read the book, you write it up. Nothing to it!

George Twose was to die of typhus in Russia where he had gone to help in a famine.

Jane Addams was then in her middle forties, dressed as a rule in severe gray, but with a touch of femininity here or there and with the ample short figure singularly ennobled by the poise of the head. She had eyes of indomitable sincerity, though frequently somber and sometimes absent in apparently hopeless quests for a way out of a dilemma, however brisk and plausible the course that might be recommended to her. Her voice had no great resonance, and at times it had a high, almost querulous insistence on the difficulties her companions had overlooked. But there was nothing torrid, nothing heavy or stifling, about her convictions. They were formed on reflection, and she could expose them to any inspector; the breeze of inquiry only refreshing and invigorating them.

She had disengaged herself from orthodoxies by the aid of men who had found their way through the lightless night, and Mill, Arnold, Lecky, Morley were the critics of society to whom she subscribed. Hers was the heritage of rationality that alone had directed women to educate themselves, break away from church-children-kitchen, become citizens, take responsibility, vote. But the objective was a new society as a whole, a society attained by other means than blood and death.

That she should be set right, even patronized, by a lot of local bigwigs, their wives, and offspring, was of course to be expected. Chicago was bosomed on prosperity, and it had a buoyancy that carried it over the cobbles. But it was one thing to take an interest in a social settlement, playing the dairymaid in a Petit Trianon, and another to hear the words "anarchist," "communist," "overthrow of society," "class war," "ideals of peace." "She's going too far," they said, "she's in bad hands." Plenty of men and women were ready to support her on condition that she should not wave the banner of the ideal until they decided as they saw fit. They were ready to smother her with kindness, so long as they could smother her, but at no time did Jane Addams confuse the intransigence she pursued with any hostility to her fellow citizens. She was even to sit on the platform with Theodore Roosevelt, that timebomb. Her antiseptic was by no means supplied out of a tolerance that came from a lack of moral discrimination. She thought of T.R. as a militarist.

But the categories that leave no room for participation were excluded from imagination as long as possible, and when she adopted them, she was never a protagonist who had to harden her heart. She took up causes with no reference to whether they were popular or not, but she took them as part of social participation. She was a co-worker, a member of a group. And in this habit of democratic association her leadership could not become narcissistic. She could be wounded, but never self-poisoned. Her America, even, was never an extension of herself. It had to be an embracing inclusion, a responsibility. This power to suffuse every issue with a consciousness of the other fellow is technically known as love, and it was her great attribute. But of course she bumped up against a war that no more responds to this approach than the obsessed lion. She knew that. She made her home in a jungle.

One night a burglar burst into Miss Addams's room. She had her little nephew staying with her at the time, and he was so far from well that she had taken him into her own bed, so that she could watch over him. They were both asleep when a cat-burglar climbed up from the courtyard and let himself in by the window. She sat up. She could feel there was a strange person in the room, but as he rushed for the window she called out, "Don't jump! You may kill yourself!" He stopped. In a low voice she added, "My nephew is asleep, here. The little boy is ill and I wish you'd do nothing to frighten him. You'll be all right if you go down by the stairs."

"All right, Miss Addams," said the burglar, being a polite neighborhood boy. He knew his way out and left obediently.

Some time later she was placating someone else when her nephew said, "Aunt Jane, that's just the voice you spoke to the burglar in!"

I told this to a religious editor once, and he loved it. He thought it might be improved by having it come as a climax to a talk earlier in the evening in which Miss Addams had been explaining to her nephew the power of religion and the nature of God. But I never heard any curlicues on it.

~~~

If Bernard Shaw had invented Jane Addams, he could not have created a better incident to illustrate her character. The solicitude which most of us have for our private property she had for the property of others in their health and sanity. She really had a strong neighborhood feeling for that young gentleman visitor, and she didn't want him to get hurt.

The essential fact of Hull House was the presence of Miss Addams. This is strange, because while one was living there she was away a good deal of the time, and when she was there one did not have a great deal to do with her; yet Hull House, as one clearly felt at the time, was not an institution over which Miss Addams presided; it was Miss Addams around whom an institution insisted on clustering. We often said, "Without her, it's—nothing."

It was contact with the residents, not with the neighborhood, which seemed to me more real at the beginning. We were a diverse group, mainly young, and meeting each other no more intimately than shipmates and messmates, outside the important residents. Yet my recollection is of vivid personalities that managed in some way to harmonize.

There were two sets in Hull House: we named them the Noble Set and the Frivolous Set, but I cannot imagine a diverse community in which there was less division and friction. We did not behave like business partners, trying to round the corners of each other's silences, or like huddled intellectuals, or like a rasping literary group, or even like those theological seminaries and college faculties whose members develop vested interests and are full of gossip and spite. Our probation, I suppose, did result in a real selection. Certain thorny people were not admitted. We who were there at any rate were in harmony.

But it did not root out difference. I can see the residents now: Miss Benedict in her effacing dress, like a Holbein print, her hands busy, her tongue silent; Fraulein, bigboned and almost Mongolian looking, with an occasional positive utterance; Mrs. Britton, ample and active, her eyes quickly responsive and soft, yet very articulate; Mr. Britton, with a Raphaelic smile, big and brown like a St. Bernard; Mr. George Hooker, steel-rimmed glasses, hair a little untidy, myopic, and crammed with statistics on municipal ownership, unoiled, dry, and good; Frank Hazenpflug, almost unbearably aesthetic, dancing pliantly, hard at work in the Hull House theatre, painting, nailing, and doing make-up, with a nervous giggle to hide his inarticulateness; Miss Nancrede, devotee of Henry James, skilled in vanishing from the successes she contrived, and disciplined as only the French can be disciplined; Von Borosini, the Austrian, naive as the dawn, kindly and rambling, vague as the mist; Carl Linden, the Swede, who talked in a slow growl and brought with him the outdoor feeling, the stubborn fight, the unsentimentalism, the strong color that he put into his paintings; Charlie Yeomans, with eyes squeezed up when he laughed, solid worth, twinkling with humor yet subsiding into gloom; Miss Gernon, solid worth, too, puzzled at life; Ned Yeomans, with a crackling laugh, full of the same Saxon manliness as Charlie, also an inchoate soul; Miss Alice Hamilton, clear as an etching, liberally intelligent, with a voice of such fine music that could only be matched by the candor of her eyes and the fine hands; Miss Norah Hamilton, shy, sidelong, original, and a Brontë, looking at one like a deer through the brake; Miss Clara Lonsberg, of Bryn Mawr vintage, valiant, tense, *souffrante*, at once impatient and remorseful, indefatigable, and worn-out; and Miss Mary Smith, wise, tolerant, and unspoken.

And of course there was Twose, of whom I have spoken. His full banner of a name was something like George Mortimer Randall Plantagenet Twose. His teaching job sat very lightly on him. He gave one the impression of laughing at life and yet skipping away from it. He wanted above everything to be free, and at the same time to satisfy a conscience which had the disadvantages of being fastidious and social. But of course he concealed his conscience as he clothed his nakedness.

To me, the literary bird of passage, they were not "copy," and yet after twenty years I can remember casual things they said. Ned Yeomans, quoting, "walking alone like the rhinoceros," and of course wishing he had a similar hide, which was in vain. Miss Lonsberg, commenting on George Eliot with scorn unfathomable, "Of course she could say to Cross, 'I need you to tell me you love me every hour.' It was just like that woman."

This was far from social work, and I wonder now what Miss Addams thought about her residents. We were well-behaved; we did our classes and so on, but we were not yoked oxen. Yet in Miss Addams there was no reproof, though I always had the feeling I did not do enough. I can well remember how often, with residents passing through the room where people sat around the common table on occasion, Miss Addams would say, "Mr. Hooker, you can help us. What do you think ... ?" Her attitude was, "You can help," and because she elicited goodwill in a common cause, that cause preoccupied the residents. In other groups where social idealism brings its practitioners very liberal funds, high prestige, and flattering publicity, the will-to-rule is likely to be stimulated, which in a hysterical period like the present leads to intrigue and politics and ends in the will-to-war. But this irony never confronted Hull House where there was little prestige or publicity and no pay. The House not only recruited strong characters, it was excited about them.

In 1906 or 1907, I was told "Miss Lathrop is coming! Miss Lathrop is coming!" as if it were an occasion for public rejoicing. I had never heard of Miss Lathrop; the name was a fashionable one in Chicago, and I thought this was much too fawning. I did not know Miss Julia Lathrop of Rockford, Illinois, who brought with her such force, such warmth, such an almost roguish sense of the tragi-comedy of American politics. You felt she enjoyed the game and through the game could bring into being the Children's Bureau or anything else without losing sight for a moment of the big end she had in view. Her brown eyes, so sincere, but with a sparkle lurking in them, her slow redolent voice, and her flavor of Illinois, gave her a richness which was valued by colleagues who had less vitality. Yet that almost Italian salience was only one kind of strength. There was a variety of strong characters. The group that included Mrs. Kelley, Miss Lathrop, Dr. Hamilton, Miss Grace Abbott, and Miss Addams has made itself objectively important in the life of the American people.

A fine group of people, of course. A neighborhood that seethed with things to consider and do. But we returned to the personality of Jane Addams for the overwhelming reason that our own personalities gained in value through contact with hers. She had the power to value human beings, to appreciate them, and to feel in terms of them. I do not mean to manipulate them in the fashion of a Disraeli, who, simulating that interest and that respect, twisted human beings around his jewelled finger. This is a trick to which human vanity lends itself and which innumerable public men employ, the Lloyd Georges and the Roosevelts, the makers of a "personal following." It is a trick which accounts for the inferiority of a "personal following," but with Miss Addams it was not a trick; it was depersonal and disinterested. It really was her way of life.

The world being her neighborhood, she had the same solicitude afterward about the war. For to her, after all, as to Frenchmen like Anatole France, as to Englishmen like Bertrand Russell, as to Germans and Austrians and Italians who could be named, the war was truly civil war. She knew the combatants. She could not have made Hull House without knowing them.

Hull House was American because it was international and because it perceived that the nationalism of each immigrant was a treasure, a talent, which gave him a special value for the United States.

We were flooded by nationalisms. How many nights did I stay awake while the interminable whine of Greek folk music came across Halsted Street to my exasperated ears. Miss Addams had gathered Greeks by the hundred to come to the Theatre during their unemployment so that English words could be taught to them in chorus and en masse. The Greeks were to her a Presence, a possibility, no doubt, of human suffering, but also a group that was suffused with reality for her, a group with a cluster of warm and ripened associations. She felt the aura of Greece when she dealt with them. She had a heart for them or rather an imagination for them, a grasp of their difficulties and their fractured loyalty.

And if the Greeks were neighbors, with their sharp profiles and sharper wits, the Italians were not less neighbors. An Italian family lived in the House—the handsome matron who ran the coffee house, her signorial husband who was an editor, and the two boys, one chiselled Latin and the other a ball of Nordic-Italian energy. But there was also a stream of Italian life from the neighborhood—the black eyes blazing out of immobile faces, the withered mothers, the gnarled fathers who seemed to carry with them the parched heat of a beating sun; and out of these indurated workers, these people made over by their toil into something like terra cotta itself, an occasional revelation of an inner life hued by time so fantastic and so tragically passionate that only a Miss Addams could find a clue to it. She has herself told the story of the Devil Baby that was torturing her neighbors within sound of factory whistles.

In the crisis of many lives, Hull House was an asylum. I recall one late night I went down to answer the door. Elsie Smith, Miss Addam's secretary, had arrived first, and she had let in an Italian woman. I shall not forget the crouching woman in the swathing shadows below; she had run away from a house of prostitution. I see Miss Smith in a long gray robe on the broad low stairs that led up to Miss Addams's room; her face with that look of stilly starlike calmness, of self-collection never lost. In the quietness the woman knew she was safe, and Miss Smith made plans with Miss Addams in a low tone.

The Irish did not come with quite the same magnificent gesture as the Latins, who make a large free donation of their helplessness and who keep marvelous capacity for dramatic entry and surprise. A few Irish remained, to enliven the neighborhood. One afternoon I came back to Hull House to see crowds in the street, or rather a few torn wisps of a crowd that was scattering. In the House itself there was a sense that the worst had happened. Mrs. B., her brown eyes full of suppressed fire and her jaw set, looked forward to court. One of her Irish friends apparently had loosed the passion that was in him under the very walls of the House, had started a bloody and wondrous fight that was only halted by the arrival of the patrol wagon. Still sweeping the air with blows and curses, the little bantam had been taken away to cool himself, leaving Hull House shaken and unhappy.

What shook it was not the normal householder's dismay over unruliness. It was the difficulty of doing the right thing that Miss Addams later expressed in *The Spirit of Youth and the City Streets*. Here was Youth, flashing, wrongheaded, and turbulent; Hull House was on its side, and yet the young devil asked for the patrol wagon. Still what could you do with him? His mother would be around in a mood of despair that only Peter Dunne could describe. What could she do with her firebrand?

One thing at least was done on the highly traditional occasion of St. Patrick's Day. Though many of the Irish who were once thick in the neighborhood had become better off and moved away, they came back on St. Patrick's Night to a dance that showed Hull House at its most exciting.

For people like myself who could dance in every way but with their feet, it still was a festivity. The preparations for it occupied weeks; the North Side helped, Crans Baldwin, B. Poole, and others, and grave residents like Miss Benedict working like beavers without a word. The music was daring for that low stairs that led up to Miss Addams's room; her face had that look of starlike calmness of self-collection which it never lost. In the quietness the woman knew she was safe, and Miss Smith time, and the on-and-off lighting a great feature. But the main thing was the dance itself which, in spite of its congestion and tropic warmth, had a way of seeming fresh and free, a way of seeming choral, and of releasing everyone into a hilarious mob. I suppose this can be done by any kind of group play, mass, revival meeting, or fighting. But Hull House did it for the Irish and the North Side guests with music and lighting, festoons, favors, streamers, and dancing.

One evening at Hull House it came to the sort of showdown you do not forget. Miss Addams had two guests who had escaped from Russia after the revolution of 1905. One of them, as I recall, was a rather thin-faced, mild-mannered youngish man who went by the name of Tchaikovsky, and I think that the other was Gershuni. These men defended assassination, and it was very real to me because of Ireland where the Tories still pretended to believe in parliamentary method but actually took by the yard and yielded by the inch. Miss Addams has herself told of Gershuni—how the worst outrage of Russian Czarist tyranny had been to drive a man like that into terrorism. She was moved by the simple revelation of his own attitude—that of a man who had never punished a child, a naturally gentle human being, a vegetarian, but who accepted murder as his weapon. Yet when he and his comrade had said their say, she spoke as Lord Acton might have spoken, not refusing to see their disinterestedness and nobility, but affirming that they were assuming a grave responsibility: they were using force in a way that would be imitated by men of less scruple and restraint.

Within three months Gershuni was killed. I believe Tchaikovsky became a Menshevik and opposed the Leninists at Archangel. She was more farsighted than they about little people, powerless people, the deprived, and the enslaved, the discarded, and the pawns and the puppets. Her whole career was an admonition to Samson that in blind virility he would multiply disaster, though in blindness she would wait for him to speak and heal his wounds. The enormity of man's blindness was no abstraction with her. She lived with it.

She realized that Danton, Robespierre, Marat, Saint-Just, are perennial to the casting lists. In the wings of history, there are always the dethroned who await "the call." The center of the stage is to be theirs, even if they are to avenge one inferno at the cost of making another. Give them the cue, they will inflame their audience, sweep their epoch by the volcanic power of perpetual revolution that lies dormant in pastoral interludes. Under sufficient repression or other incitement, their will to power can burst into magnificent eruption, open the Bastille, arrive at the Finland station, or the promise of the millennium, the Day. It is not current ideology that gives insight into a volcano. It flames with the will of God, Mahomet, Marx, or the Empire. Murder spurts from unslaked hearts, and if statesmen have made the world tinder, then conflagration rules. Out of the black may spring fresh green for them, but those who measure suffering as Jane Addams did, and try to mend broken lives, do not invite holocaust. They fear it, because they can imagine it. Bright trumpeters shout, "Ten days that shake the world!" Easy for them to say later, "I beg you to excuse me. I was mistaken."

Not mistaken, irresponsible.

Russian Jews came in great numbers to the classes at Hull House and had special leanings towards literature. Whenever Miss Addams got a handmade tragedy by an aspiring girl, I had the privilege of reading the manuscript. I was even allowed to read Miss Addams's current book in proof and to make suggestions. The skill with which she extricated herself from suggestion always amazed me. After a whole night combing one of her paragraphs into an order that to my weary brain seemed superlative, I'd find that bit by bit, with perfect uncombativeness and humility, Miss Addams would have restored all the snarls. She liked them; they said what she had to say, and she was right.

It was Sheldon of Dartmouth who defined the type of philosophy that "gains by yielding; its spirit is not aggressive, but meek; it rules by love rather than fear. Its code is that of nonresistance." But he made the mistake of seeing the outcome as conservative and compromising. No, in Miss Addams, as in Fridthjof Nansen, there was no mush of compromise. Their humanity was warm, clear, and free, but it was anything but soft.

To be hard on herself was, indeed, just as much an instinct with Miss Addams as with Nansen. There were times at Hull House when the disgracefulness of Miss Addams's hat led to protest and when her united friends forced her to reform. Her asceticism, however, was part of that self-scrutiny which was alive to what is due—to others. Like Nansen, again, one felt in her presence that to be an "other" was in itself a title to her recognition. Like him she included Turks, Greeks, Soviets, Reactionaries.

I do not say that she did not have twinges of conservatism. We had a baptism once at Hull House, a kind of vegetarian baptism. I think Jenkins Lloyd Jones officiated, looking like a benign old Druid, and the baby was the progeny of the James Weber Linns. I do not know whether they handed that well-behaved baby a white flower, but I have a vague recollection of the kindly patriarch's tickling the soles of the baby's feet and adjuring her—it was a her?—to walk in the paths of seemliness and righteousness. The name of God was avoided with a prudishness that delighted me. A baptism without God was so chic that I closed my eyes to the anomaly of there being a baptism at all. But I remember Miss Addams looking a little lost, a little mournful and thoughtful after the ceremony. She confessed it was rather "queer," to her sense.

You could picture Miss Addams as a person solely of good works. I have been talking to her when, in answer to a ring at the door, she would let in a "bum" who wanted a cup of coffee. And she herself would lead him into the Coffee House, and, with her curious air of pleading politeness, would say, "Mary, would you give this man a cup of coffee?" To the hobo and to Miss Addams nothing seemed more natural, but these incidents of humanity never meant that Hull House interposed mere charity between itself and the rough-and-tumble world.

Hull House lived in a bracing, not a mawkish, atmosphere. It met the world vigorously. I don't think the child-labor gentry would say that the opposition which Hull House generated was mawkish. Miss Addams on the School Board was not precisely mawkish when my good friend P. Shelly O'Ryan wanted to put something over. And there was nothing mawkish when she went to the Big Bazoo of local journalism at the time, Jim Keeley, to ask him to print the truth about Gorki. "Marriage, you know, Miss Addams, is a Sacred Cow!"

Miss Addams came away from that interview with the air of slight puzzlement which she often wore after encountering the formulas by which men like Keeley kept their public and their jobs.

Hull House had a grip on me that I found absorbing. Miss Addams remained impersonal, but the whole climate of the place was temperate for that very reason, and we revolved around her. No power of will decreed the influence she wielded. It came on the wind, never blustering or overbearing, yet penetrating the house in a breath of faith and wisdom. When you live on the French Riviera and travel within a certain distance of Grasse, the fragrance on the air is unexpected and astonishing, and it was at the core of Hull House that the nature Jane Addams had cultivated should diffuse its own vagrant, extraordinary essence. In the course of life, I was to meet a few other people who had come into possession of themselves, or of a comprehension beyond the ordinary that was as real as the brilliance of a star or the grace of a fawn. To say they were good and therefore like that is pure nonsense. I have known shoals of good people who were as little like Jane Addams as the products of high-minded arts and crafts are like Bach.

Virtue in Jane Addams was not anything the *Ladies' Home Journal* can teach well-meaning young women to creep up on. It was a state she achieved by obedience to laws of harmony that only she could arrive at. It was a kind of genius. And I dare say I recognized it, as all the residents did. But this particular transcendence in an individual is more like the habituation to a tableland of comprehension than it is a faculty for producing great effects such as characterize grand opera. She was a citizen of Illinois, like Lincoln, but a native of another clime, of which Illinois could be the beneficiary. It wasn't a matter of brains, particularly. It had something to do with social techniques. But it came from deeper sources. One has only to read her marvelous account of her father in *Twenty Years of Hull House* to have the material for discerning the burning glass that led her to focus the distant rays to a point that lit a flame in her. Her idiom was of her time. She was a gentlewoman who went to college, a correct spinster; but Bach did not have a grand piano. She carried democracy beyond Lincoln. She carried it beyond racial bounds, yet held it on this side of war and murder. And still what Chicago feared, and what America in general feared, was her breach with current thinking. Why, being so obviously a lady, did she have to break with Received Opinion? The Manufacturers' Association asked it. The Bill Haywards asked it. Or, it they didn't ask it, they washed her up by calling her an "idealist."

But, while Hull House and Jane Addams were my real introduction to the meaning of America, and while Hull House was the first real home I had, it was impossible to go on with it and earn a living apart from it in journalism. The residents varied greatly in occupation—one a doctor, another a pump manufacturer, several architects, and a number of them teachers—but in the end, unless a man could gain his livelihood from "social work," he would be drawn more and more deeply into an activity that could not support him. People who have not a penny of capital cannot devote their lives to any occupation that doesn't feed them. The occupation may be uneconomic, but someone has funded it, whether it is a begging brotherhood, a research foundation, a museum, a college, or a music school, and all these institutions demand is your time in return for your keep. But Hull House was not endowed. We had to pay for our keep and contribute our time. That was an impossibility for me.

I was then writing three editorials a day and doing book reviews as well, along with feature articles and some news stories. Only by sitting up all night could I do good book reviews, and I once had the strange experience of going to bed after working round the clock and sleeping from 10 P.M. to 4 P.M. the next afternoon.

At times in this period, I was so exhausted I could hardly endure it. I don't believe I ever crossed the Chicago River without being tempted to jump in. At a station once I dared a friend to jump on the third rail, to see if it were charged with electricity. He wouldn't. I did. Nothing happened.

Apart from the difficulty of two jobs, however, and the pain of separating from Hull House, I did not want to absorb myself in the techniques that social work demanded. There was no end to the problems that trade unions and the I.W.W. brought up.

You could not touch on any aspect of welfare—hospitals, mental hospitals, old age homes, nurseries—without running into a labyrinth of sociology. The regulation of vice was a vice in itself. It would not let you go. And neither would municipal ownership or state ownership. Sooner or later professionals must take over many of the cases to which amateurs were applying first aid. Already I heard official certitude, professional jargon. Social work would be organized and standardized. Like medicine, like religion, it would have practitioners—it would have dogma.

When I left Hull House, however, though it was after little more than a year's residence, I was by no means the same man. Since leaving the Catholic Church, where I had been as crippled as any foot-bound Chinese, I had necessarily struggled to think for myself with whatever apparatus came casually to hand. I could not live without a faith. Nobody who had been intensely Catholic in the simple emotional God-fearing Irish way, going frequently and scrupulously to confession, taking communion with absorption in its solemn reality, making retreats, and genuinely believing in the Church's discipline and sharing its abhorrence of sin, could very easily abandon the habit of self-scrutiny on rejecting the particular objects that had excited it. Our emotions don't work by thermostat. The self out of its old habit, no longer gratified or mortified as divinely ordained and certified by the Church, was still as urgent as ever. I was inured to a self-conscious life, and I wanted by fits and starts, to live a meritorious one. In order to roll up merit, a necessity that had been rubbed in by the Church as a practical requirement since I was seven, I had to devote myself genuinely to something true, beautiful, or good—all three if possible. And if I could not do this, I'd be baying the moon and would be miserable.

My neighbor Twose would sometimes gaze at me. He had an

even longer face than Lord Halifax, reminding one of a benign horse with big teeth. His eyes could dance when he was amused, and as he had the Englishman's unwillingness to be caught off guard, to be detected in a process, except shaving, he sometimes could scarcely control his smile at the round-eyed, startled, and confused young man whom he surprised in the deshabille of self-scrutiny. He would laugh and say, "Cheer up! Wot's the odds so long as you're happy." And he'd bolt downstairs. But this buoyant April Englishman had embraced a simpler faith than I found possible, more abundant though more capricious. I desired the whole world to be coherent, whereas Twose asked only to be coherent in himself and to take untroubled any hand that was dealt to him. England had prearranged bouyancy for him, while Ireland had queered confidence for me. Only now and then could I jig with him.

This lack of confidence—and confidence is faith—never related to Hull House or Jane Addams. I came away with the first strong belief in democracy that I had formed since I crossed the ocean.

It was belief in a process, not in a state of being, and this process, as I inferred from Miss Addams, was vulnerable. She knew the galaxy of economic princes that had emerged above the government and beyond its power to limit and regulate by fiat. She never lost sight of the requirements of humanity with which these princes and their industries and businesses were so often in stubborn conflict. America, however, was the embodiment of a faith for her. She was too close to the Lincolnian America not to conceive that a "good"—the ultimate great good of the people—could probably be secured, though so far it had not been secured. Ever since the industrial revolution it had been compromised, and "economic royalty" put their prowess above the ultimate good of the greatest number, as Hull House would testify from the neighborhood. But it would also testify that a revised process could be vitiated by those whom the conflict had vitiated, and in her criticism of a prowess pushing toward monopoly, Miss Addams laid enormous stress on the means by which its victims should arrest their vitiation and keep from substituting a new callousness, a new viciousness, and a new profanation for the old.

Her democratic faith was a "reading of life." It did not espouse the proletariat as the repository of political wisdom and thereupon decide that its interests required the bourgeois to be placed under a dictatorship. Miss Addams was bourgeois, and for her it was given that she might be bourgeois and still true citizen with the proletariat. She did not assume that she or anyone could have an indefinite option on stability. On the side of the economic princes labored a vast number of sophists skilled in mass-seduction, but on the opposite side, as Miss Addams scrupulously observed, labored apostles of remorseless change, no less skilled in mass-seduction. It was her view that democracy was the only political contrivance by which this primitive remorselessness could be curbed. In fact, her enemy was the enemy in man that vitiated democracy in the first place and then generated a revolt that hotly denied common humanity to its offenders. Her concept of common humanity transcended class, as it transcended race and creed. It embraced the enemy, combatting the enmity. It did this with thousands of "cases" before her, idealists who meant to murder, fathers who had committed incest, boys who had sold their sisters, immigrants who had ground down their kind in sweatshops, young men who thieved from their mothers, petty criminals out of hand, the demented, the hysterical, the skilled procuress, and the loan shark. She saw into a tragic darkness that the proudest torch could not illuminate, and it was the powerless in this black night whom she both loved and feared. Power had given them bad models.

This is what I took away with me. I had no clear idea of how amelioration could be brought about. I felt our magnates had lost sight of humanity, and that I wished to avoid the high cost of making money, if it meant working for magnates—Hearst, for example, or even old Marshall Field. Did not Theodore Roosevelt wobble over the chalk line in the etiquette book when he said that "guilt is personal"?

At the same time, polite Chicago opened its arms, and I returned to the complex in which magnetic intellectuals work secretaries to death, and radical authors pay sweatshop stipends, and nuns exploit laundry workers, and bishops own whorehouses. High-minded Gradgrinds, low-minded philanthropists. Get rid of the profit-motive, and you bring in army discipline. Get rid of army discipline, and you invite profit and anarchy. It was in fact utterly confounding. And in Chicago it was more than hearsay. We lived with it.

North Side

In describing my move away from Hull House, I find myself tempted to titivate the perception I had and to arrange the past so as to flatter my insight. With ingenuity I could keep up this edifying vein, especially since to edify is never objectionable and often profitable. But my frame of mind at this period, in spite of some clear convictions, was more open than I rush to admit. I was tired of Halsted Street. I wanted to have fun, and I liked immensely to be with people who were pleasant, attractive, and affluent. I did not prove very discriminating at times. I chose paste instead of diamond.

Tiffany Blake had just married Margaret Day of Lake Forest and was in touch with the North Shore. He promptly did me a great kindness; he introduced me to his friends.

When I came away from Hull House and its severe discipline, it was a new chapter in my life to meet people in easy circumstances. It was the first time in America that I was thrown with a group that in respect of money could more or less conform their lives to their desires. Out of the early struggles in Chicago, they were among the inheritors, not on a grandiose scale, but emancipated, at least to all appearances, from anxiety about money and pleasantly, liberally equipped to have a good life. Some had Chicago homes, but Chicagoans radiated into an immense variety of suburbs. The ones I knew best were Winnetka and Hubbard Woods.

These were still near open country. They had their own

civility and yet the enticement of nature on the border of the Skokie swamp, away from the Lake. I had known the Dublin suburbs a little, but they had been patterned directly on the city, most of the houses being, in fact, city mansions incarcerated in a walled park. They were built of stone, with greenhouses jutting out, screened by sullen bushes and neighbored by lugubrious trees. Even when near the sea they were often grimly secluded, though a quite luxurious and ceremonious life was developed in these inner suburbs with good vintners behind it, hushed servants, rich man's gout.

Entirely different and with much more of social invention were Winnetka and its satellites. No walls shut in the houses which stood on open lawns in a gay freshness, and the grounds had privacy without walls. The trees were less portly than the Irish trees, thin, aerial, aspiring to the sun. An evening haze could pervade in autumn such as had so often enamored Weir and Innes,, and in this desuetude the hush of nature was all that one heard. Chicago was nothing. Halsted Street ceased to exist. But in summer it was the swimming pool at the Hibbards which made Saturdays and Sundays an actual lifegiver. Summer in the city could be ferocious, thumping in its heat and bestial in its smells. One morning I fled to Lincoln Park after a contorted, restless night, and the heat was already so punishing that I looked desperately for relief. Then the lagoon caught my eye. It had a fence around it, but no one was in sight so I crawled through. Putting my watch in my hat, I slipped into the water, fully clad, and for the first time in days I felt cool as I swam across. My clothes dried on me. Mr. Jerrems, however, had glued the cuffs of my light trousers when he turned them up, and as I ran home they flapped to my heels.

It is one of the fabulous illusions of youth that established places and people seem to be at rest while one is oneself in motion. I went to Hubbard Woods in a state of becoming, all agog and all recipient, like a dog with a quivering nose. I ran around the teacups and cake plates with my eyes on stalks and my tail ticking. It was at once agreed I was "Young Hackett." But if I took it for granted that I was revolving around their sun, why did I suppose that their sun wasn't revolving? These people were none of them static. It wasn't a solo on my part though so many of them had the attitude of being set and stationary. It was relativity, a dance. Because I was without visible property while they were anchored in real estate and cemented in income, perhaps they could not help solidifying an aspect of being staked down and impregnable just as much as though they had high stone walls around them and iron gates in front. Property often is an unconscious bully.

But it was Yankee reticence, not economic condescension that would project its fenders against my collision. Any immigrant might say, "these are privileged," but "Young Hackett" came out of the blue, and they instantly extended the privilege. They made friends with me.

By reason of innocence, Chicago was much less hostile to a newcomer than New York. Had I married on my own economic level on the small *Post* salary and had a wilting wife and dejected children, I rather think we'd have found Chicago less inviting. But I was single, eager, and receptive. It was delightful to feel welcoming warmth and uncomplicated kindness. Because of Tiffany Blake I had begun with his friends, but the circle was widening. I moved buoyed in a light and unresisting hospitality. I was "asked out," and accepted with the simplicity of a fish that joins a school and arrives at the feeding grounds.

That this involved any domestic effort or machinery I never took into account. I assumed that cooks, maids, linen and silver, motors and boats, and gardens and flowers were happy incidents of delectation which kindness simply provided. I particularly liked the soap. It never occurred to me that my foible of never drinking alcohol was depriving me of free enterprise on a grand scale, but the unencumbered bachelor is a gullet, and mine was open both to devour and to express. The opportunity to dance with one's feet was not important, but to dance with one's mind or dance in attendance was continuously diverting. "They say? What do they say? Let them say." Janet Fairbank had inscribed Shaw's legend over her fireplace in Geneva, and her energy heightened the excitement with which everyone said everything and all at the same time.

Beyond any particular group—at Lake Geneva, in Winnetka, at Wheaton, in Chicago—the entire activity that Chicago's affluence released had some sort of meaning implicit in it, and I suppose that Lake Forest was even more active on these lines. Chicago in the first decade of the century was about the same size as Cleveland is today, with much the same focussing on its orchestra, and art institute, and art school, and university. All these cities contrive to lift their dinners and week-ends to the level where the home group is diversified by visitors or transient stars. The young may prefer chit-chat, and some of the stars long to display their peacock tails, but in the chastening of bores and pedants, in reducing the thumps and whacks of political wisdom—"You know what I'd do with Bill Hayward?" "Theodore Roosevelt is a traitor to his class"—the hostesses of this innocent age were cheeringly serpentine. They were not reigning in a principality, nor was Chicago the great-grandchild of a court, but even in a midwest city they could confer prestige, enjoy gallantry, reward prowess at the tournament, murmur to a troubador, smile from the balcony.

The expatriate in me was attracted to Winnetka. It had not the slightest resemblance to Ireland, but it had the semblance of a leisure class, and if you notice the Irish in America, they cannot easily desist from their fondness for a desultory, intensely personal and persistently defeated quest for a ramified employment of the organ they take to be the heart. Joe Patterson wished to combine this with the horse, and at Libertyville he built a house that was worthy of a farmer in Tipperary, except that he kept a volume of Nietzsche near the lulu. The house gashed the landscape when it was planted and in Tipperary might easily have done the same, though it was full of another Irish quality—a citric Ulster trait of obstinacy and defiance.

Very far from this was the incorrigible Irishness of Finley Peter Dunne, whose sting was so quick and deep, and yet its victim wreathed in balm while it still tingled. Mr. Dooley was a shanachie, a courtier with no duty but free speech; he cared nothing for a limitless audience, everything for a circle.

But there were other Irish who zigged in the American sunlight, men of lost horizon like Scott Fitzgerald and in some measure John O'Hara. The emphatic Donn Byrne actually succumbed to his longing for that vanished home, pursuing it to the fatal end. But for Scott Fitzgerald it was perennially elusive, a reunion with midnight swans such as were never seen on Long Island—the arched phantoms of his private sense of perfection. Scott Fitzgerald was the grenadier who wards an empty patch where the Queen had once posted a soldier to protect a flower. The Queen was gone, the flower forgotten, but the order was never suspended. The Fitzgeralds, the O'Haras, the Philip Barrys, the Sylvesters, are not without these unintelligible promptings.

And my own, little as I knew it, was to conform Winnetka to the life I had never enjoyed and yet taken into my hidden wish before I left Ireland.

Louise and Ned Burling were intimates of Tiffany Blake, and they welcomed me on his account.

No one could have been more Yankee than Ned Burling. Just as the hot sun draws an elm out of the earth, so he was pulled up, high and thin, with an extraordinary length of limb and the wiry frame that is classic in Abe Lincoln. By profession a lawyer, Ned looked to me like a pillar of society, and my deference to him was not unaffected by my previous servitude in a law office. But, oh, the difference between this thing of flesh and the ones I had known before! Ned Burling had a temperament.

From Tiffany Blake he elicited poetry that had successively made Tiffany a music, a dramatic, and a literary critic. Tiffany, married to a superwoman, was to be headed toward another goal, his ineffectual wings to be pinned and his feet to be kept to the ground, if her common sense could guide him. While that was in process, Ned Burling, born in 1870, the same year as Tiffany, turned to my young self with an eagerness that distinguished him among all the adjusted, smiling, exteriorized Winnetkans. I was in luck. In ten years, when he was to be chief counsel to the U.S. Shipping Board, his enormous law office would become a grinding possibility for him, just as in ten years Tiffany would be chief of the *Chicago Tribune* editorial page. But this was April, all fools' day for me and plowing time for them. They liked, even loved, my supposed naivete.

In the jargon of America's psychological pop-eyes, Ned was "maladjusted." Into this duffel bag you can put anything you like, but it simply would mean that for a restless, ambitious man with a whirling mind, he allowed himself the relief of free speech. Where I was revolting against the genteel and had a saucy attitude all around, Ned was more generally mordant. Very early in life his father, a parson in Iowa, had sunk the family in gruelling poverty. Maybe the panic not long after the Civil War had downed his father, or maybe he was a feeble soul, but those joyless years in a small town hurt the boy's pride and made him bleed for his mother. He delivered groceries and earned what he could by chores. But that premature struggle with hard times and his intense wish to support his mother caused a strain that now showed in Spartan silence about himself, but in pointed observation and in vivid paradox about the world at large. He had not been irreparably neglected. He was sent to Grinnell College by an older friend who saw his gifts, and he had gone on to Harvard where his keen intelligence was plied to the law, and he had a walking tour in Europe. But harsh wind had cut into that tender growth. His confidence had been hurt. Now he was quick to mock at overconfidence in others, skeptical and ironic about himself, and within him, as within so many Americans of that parched epoch and region, he had an actual bleakness that he craved to overcome, giving him a driving eagerness for a dancing partner.

But he was a lawyer, and a lawyer's dance is in dialectics. He pirouetted with a balanced ball on his nose, and when you are young this game can outlast the day. And underneath, when it has companionship in it, the human being comes to light. I found Ned human. He had no particular interest in the kind of convictions I had brought from Hull House or in the tragic effort to arrive at values. Poetry gave him sensuous pleasure, and for the rest he rejoiced and chuckled with glee at the wit and dexterity of impish criticism. As for society, there should be rules as in a football match—perfectly agreed on, perfectly merciless. Step over the line and—biff! He asked no mercy. His mind was schematic in this manner, and he rather excluded any topic that lent itself to moralizing. He practiced the fine and shading art of negotiation and compromise. But with his unsparing comprehension of the monkey in man, he was avid for any kind of true story, touchingly alive both to comedy and pathos within the limits of the subject's probable insignificance.
Only rarely, gazing into the gulf, could the diminished monkey pluck his heart. At times, I do not doubt, he more than raged and sorrowed, but this was solitaire.

Not long before I met him, he had been arrested. He was happiest when he could take off his shirt and feel the wind on his bare skin, and as he perambulated along Lake Michigan singing heartily, "Tira-lira, by the river sang Sir Lancelot," a local constable rose up out of the bushes and came lumping toward him.

"What's this?"

Ned could not explain. But at that time, when gentlemen went bathing in two-piece suits and ladies were obliged by law to don black stockings before sopping in Lake Michigan, the disclosure of a man naked to the waist, singing in a lusty voice, and wearing vine leaves in his hair to discourage the midges was virtual proof that he was insane. It delighted Ned Burling's soul, but he got out of it for the sake of his law partner.

We took long walks together. We'd start late on Saturday afternoons, heading toward California, and would arrive at some place like McHenry after dark. We'd eat beefsteaks with fried eggs on them at some hotel where the coffee came in a blue enamel pot and the cook doubled as waitress. We devoured pie and hot biscuits and jelly. And then we'd take whatever bedroom was offered, getting up at 5 a.m., usually in a drizzle. Our breakfast we'd take in whatever farmhouse would receive us. The Irish farmhouses I had known had homemade bread, fresh eggs from the loft, buttermilk or Indian tea, and butter from the churn. Here it was often a run-down farm in North Illinois with thin milk for the disconsolate coffee, bread with pernicious anemia from the store, and from the frying pan some section of the pig that he could never have desired to sit on. What meals!

And out of troubled eyes, barbed with suspicion, the poor farmer would mull and growl as he clawed his broken cup; his woman tousled at the stove, his dog bored with hunger and yawning.

We did it for pleasure.

It was only later in the day that the great sun would bang down on us, and then we unlimbered. The country roads we deserted if they ran gruesomely straight, and we went cross-lots, sometimes discovering a swamp where the tamarisks were in water to the lowest branch, and we could plod and squelch without a single thought, enchanted with this incident. Or, on a gorgeous day, exhausted after fifteen miles, we might find a country stream. Once, to our amazement, a run of water we discovered was about five feet wide and rippling over pebbles. Could Illinois give this? We tore off our sweaty shirts and heavy boots. Never did weariness give more joy than as we lay in this swift coolness with brilliant sun above. Our thirst we saved for another mile, and then we guzzled chocolate sodas.

Ned knew the country. We covered about thirty-five miles in these walks, and when at last we got home, when we smelled the honeysuckle at his house and lay at rest after a bath, the prospect of Louise's dinner was before us. The candles shed little light, but we dressed more or less formally, and six or eight might come. Then Ned, stimulated by his day in the sun, would begin to toss opinions in the air, wildly and fantastically retrieved, until the whole room would join and sometimes a felicity of phrase would give us that Dionysian pang which comes in the dance of ideas.

But Winnetka, so excellent of its kind, with such admirable hospitality, such fine feeling, and such good soap, had a banality that was in its (vegetable) marrow. It all came to light about seven on Monday morning. Up to that moment school was out, and everyone poured forth his mind if he had one, cracked wisely if he could, and intensified the jollity or the intimacy of being together. The women had swum and played tennis and walked miles in the afternoon. They came to dinner resplendent or seductive or radiant in their fashion, and when you flicked the glass it chimed. If you enjoyed harmony, here it was, and we did enjoy it. It was an amusing, a polite, kind, and generous society.

But Chicago, probably like Manchester or Hamburg, or others of the big cities in the provinces, was intent on the main chance, and this was business—the tremendous business of meat, bread, nuts, bolts, printing, clothing, boilers, ropes, coffee, dry goods. On Monday mornings the toys were put away and the lessons began. The suburbs gave up their men in three great train loads, "the clerks, the works and the shirks." Out came the little electric car, once the exodus was completed, and the smiling hostess "tribbled" off to see a laundress. Lunch was prim and waspish. The males, the capitains, had departed.

This banality was basic. The women had not yet followed the men into business, and they were shut out of politics. They were in purdah. College was beginning to be a possibility after Farmington or the other schools that finished the women off, but it was tentative. The specific femality that could rejoice any man who loved women, where the brain stays fallow but the response to the male is direct or abundant, was reserved for the West Side or the South Side. On the North Side the men cleared out to business and the women devised a life of amazing insipidity that was eventually to be heightened by lipstick and hair-do.

Julian Mason told me a fable of Lake Forest at this particular moment. A spifflicated Yale man reaching home late, fumbled upstairs to bed. When he came to in the morning he woke up the little darling beside him. She shrieked. "My God!" he said lamely. "The housekey was the same. The silver-framed photographs were the same. The fourpost bed was the same. You're sure you're different?"

Conformities did not always go as far as this, but their existence could not de disputed. On the South Side, for example there was a highly sophisticated Jewish society, but it took another ten or fifteen years before Jews came into this clannish society, and when Frenchmen were mentioned, it was as termites who got into a woman's moral fiber and left it in powder. Chicagoans studied art in Munich, not in wicked Paris. They thought of Edgar Allen Poe as if he were a spark in black litmus paper. They spoke of absinthe as if it were nitroglycerine. When I uttered the inflammatory words "free love" in the house of a tight-lipped host his wife came to me afterwards and said, "John won't have you in the house any more. Isn't he silly?" The truth was, the men were crusaders, the Loop was the Holy Land, and they hoped to find their chatelaines the way they left them.

Chicago had to have an orchestra, an art institute, an observatory, a library, and a university, but the notion of having a Rive Gauche, or a Bloomsbury, or a Greenwich Village, not to speak of publications and the various types of exhibitions and concerts by which local artists are enabled to survive, was wholly outside the imaginative grasp of this community. No art is possible unless it can begin at the breast and be weaned and taught to walk. But the Chicago bigwigs began at the other end. They did not go to creators in the early stages. They went to dealers, since that is the way to do business. Those with a great deal of money went to astute dealers and sometimes to good purpose. But the supreme need of Chicago, a society in which women could engage men in the creative art of life, as against its mere amenity and self-glorification, was beyond their experience. Only out of an honest erotic life, generally speaking, can the woods resound to song. The nightingale is seldom a member of the Board of Trade, nor is the lark a sociologist. And Chicago-on-the-Drainage-Canal, willing to have its erotic life in a separate fireproof compartment in case that had to be, seldom deserted its main chance for that brooding idleness which earlier Americans turned to expressive end, around which scholars pour the best preservatives.

Vachel Lindsay killed himself in penury. Sherwood Anderson earned $400 on his first four novels. Henry Fuller, I. F. Friedman, Edith Wyatt could not flourish in a dust bowl. Stone gave up publishing. Ogden McClurg refused to go on. "I make ten times as much selling stationery." And this happened at a time when Chicago rolled in wealth and was fat to the ears with it. But this was wealth incapable of discerning the miserable germ from which an art can be developed. The recognition of its own possibilities as a rewarding center for manufacture amounted to genius in Chicago. But in the art of life, it was an exporter of goods in transit or a wary consumer. And the women could not take the aesthetic lead if the men held back. Spirited and discerning men who could build an institution were soon to be found, but not the progenitors of the arts—the men and women who dare to adopt the illegitimate baby.

One of the Chicagoans whom S.S. McClure particularly wanted in his magazine was Edith Wyatt, or Edith Franklin Wyatt as she came to sign herself. She had written *Every Man His Own Way*, but the swagger of that title was entirely literary. Edith Wyatt was no apologist for Billy the Kid.

By this time I had come to know the Wyatts intimately and to visit them on free Sundays. As I walked up to Sheridan Road in the dry sunny autumn, with sumac so vivid in the vacant lots and basking crickets so joyously chirping, it seemed at last I was in America. The city had not yet devoured this strip of coast. Above Lincoln Park it was still almost wild, and one could breathe in freedom from people, though at the end of the walk there was the Wyatt home, an ample frame house on a lawn and the American supper that Sunday allowed, never voluptuous in any Continental sense but served freely, full of light little dishes and grandly diversified like the conversation that preceded it.

This conversation, I must admit, was often at cross purposes. When at times the Wyatts threw off a reference to "the cranberry bog," it was to a family property that they went to visit, a place they cherished, and if I could not see a cranberry bog in my mind's eye, or with any glow of joy at any rate, it was only one of many enthusiasms, many presumptions of knowledge, that are not shared unless the stranger rises to it. The Wyatts were saturated in their own sense, and it was this fullness of saturation that attracted me to them, but in spite of their spiritual hospitality and the spice of its novelty, I had really entered into a foreignness. The core of it, I think, was that amazing and excluding specialization in right behavior, which springs from the Puritan conscience, and yet they welcomed me in an obvious absence of it, perhaps believing it was latent in me just as hunters feel sure you'd shoot a raccoon if you really were put to it.

Edith had taught at Miss Rice's school, and I think her subject was Greek. In this we had no ground in common. My education could scarcely have been as conspicuously irregular as my teeth, but the gaps were equally evident when I opened my mouth, and at times Edith would gasp, "Well!" and then laugh too generously. I had exposed ignorance. This drove me into wilful positiveness when I felt sure of my ground, and then she saw she had to be kind. With eyes as gentle as a doe's and a sudden gush of compunction, she would make up for the strain she had put on goodwill. It must have been this soft, wary, infinitely persuasive manner which led the virile to regard her as a frail young lady who could be shooed aside. But there was nothing frail in her spirit. Like steel she could recoil, but the stuff in her was unbreakable.

Her father she adored. He never said much. He was one of those massive, slow-spoken, honorable men who remind one of sea captains. He was possibly in heavy weather financially when I knew them, but he would never had swerved from his line of conduct to gain a crown, and yet the sunless days that had descended on the house did not extinguish his kindness. He had a ripple of humor in him. His wife was an anxious little lady. Apparently submissive, her somewhat plaintive tone had a certain fretful and exigent will behind it, even if it wore a wintry shawl and gave a wintry smile and a sigh of resignation. It was a family so high-minded that I ran the risk of frost bite; the altitude was sustained by an underpinning of lofty literature and by the vigilance of the New England conscience. Yet behind its lyrical intensity and its moral intrepidity, there was the simple fact that the youngest daughter, Phyllis, was threatened with death. She had tuberculosis. The whole house on Sheridan

Road lived in passionate devotion to this dovelike girl, the darling of the family, and they circled about her to ward off the enemy.

The big silent father had been in the Civil War. He had been a spy for the North, or in the intelligence if that sounds better. And like so many who had been born in Illinois in the seventies, Edith was a child of the national divide, perhaps more so than the shy middle sister, Faith, and the fight for Phyllis was a continuation of Armageddon, another spell of warfare. The Greek word ethos, if I may bootleg it, would cover Emerson, Thoreau, Harriet Beecher Stowe, the "underground," down to Henry and William James, Walt Whitman, Melville. And America was all alive under this roof, not as reminiscence but as an almost fulsome presence laden with significance, the drum taps still beating. I think Edith's imagination was forever fired by the national convulsion in which her father had participated, though the mellowness of William Dean Howells, whom she knew through his daughter, was a sunlit patch beyond. And her spirit rose like the lark when she thought of Stephen Crane, not simply from kinship with the Civil War or from humane tradition or American fraternity in general, but from the excitement that his purity of taste, his clean line, and his exquisite vibration stirred in her attuned and susceptible nature. A story like "The Monster" could not have more pleased her if she had written it herself. Her own writing was, in fact, of the same timbre.

So when S.S. McClure asked her to go to Cherry, Illinois, where there had been a mine explosion, I proposed myself as her comrade, to carry her bag for her. It was the period in which American spinsters always promptly produced their nickel on a trolley. But she did allow me to be her porter. It was a journalistic assignment to which she could bring a keen eye for the facts as well as a social perspective. Her father had had an experience with Edison in regard to an invention that enabled her to enter into Ida Tarbell's criticism of a high-handed or underhanded monopoly, and in the coal industry the owners had a bad record. But when it came to any blanket indictment of capitalists, Edith compressed her lips and shook her head rather like a child who was offered strange candy. Had she been forced to frame this indictment it would have changed her whole life. She held to her convictions as others do to real estate. But her father was an employer; she knew employers, good and bad, and the American situation invited her scrutiny as a tableau of many colors rather than black and white. She was not using it as an excuse for indulging suppressed feelings, a sponge for a psychosis. Hence, she respected its complexity.

The hamlet of Cherry was 50 or 60 miles from Chicago, but it was a complete surprise to me in the March of 1906. Miners walked the village street, lamps in their caps and coal dust around their weary eyes. Their lives were meshed in a lifetime occupation that was as alien to my notion of the prairie as a regiment of hussars. Their town was in jeans like themselves, slapped together by hucksters and stuck in the mud. It squatted low, a cheapjack, ramshackle outcropping, and its hotel was as drab as a funeral parlor. Cherry stared at us with a look still stunned by disaster, estranged by the recognition that it was all over, and we were as powerless as themselves. Small and remote it might be, but Pennsylvania, West Virginia, Kentucky, Ohio, and Illinois could reveal similar grim settlements spewed around the mouths of the coal pits, and it was only disaster that for a moment loosened them from the clasp of the mine and exhibited them to America. No matter what danger or subjection the job entailed, it was disembowelling coal for subsistence, and this horrible absentee town, mained at its birth, a municipal bastard, was a foul witness to the conscription of coal digging. Martin Luther had been a child in a mining town. And only recently a wealthy coal owner, full of amelorativeness, had been visiting Hull House. Clearly the misbegotten town was something that neither Christianity nor Capitalism had gotten around to remedying. Cherry was the American rainbow at midnight.

One evening I went to Sheridan Road to see the Wyatts, and a stranger was with them. She was then a little over thirty, with a pair of luminous and comprehending eyes, a kind of gallant breeze that forever gave life to her manner and at times a ribald gale to her laugh. The Wyatts had in themselves a natural sedateness, their light diffused gently from a cool gray wall. This friend of theirs, Virginia Tracy, was incapable of one moment's inexpressiveness. As I said to her later, "Virginia, you stuck out like a corner saloon!" I never met anyone to match her for her fund of response, and that evening began a friendship which lasted forty years.

Her emotions were unpremeditated. They possessed her to absorption and often to worldly detriment, taking for their form and content the vivacity of the theatre, and divorcing her more utterly from hard calculation for that reason but making her one of the tribe whose allegiance secures the survival, perhaps the triumph of good theater. She still pursued in Henry James, in Stephen Crane, in Turgeniev, and in every modern novel she could read the answer to that sensibility which I call "romantic" for short.

Perhaps life gave it to her, too, but a romantic woman may not be a flirt, and if she does not dangle a ladder but waits for the male to arrive with one, she may actually miss that kind of enlistment. Virginia was not like the first young actress whom I visited in a dressing room. "Now," she said, "be a good boy and turn away." She added, "Now don't look. I haven't a stitch on." Anyone who lets down the gangplank with this bump is not likely to be boarded, but in Virginia's eyes the ignition could only come, I imagine, when she was overwhelmed by pity.

Even Virginia's hair was romantic. It would have been sandy but for some miracle that had let it attain a light apricot in color. Had it not been one of nature's sprightly efforts, no bottle could have kept it uniform. When woman improves on nature, nature often becomes sinister. Virginia in this respect was authentically romantic. It was not in her nature to titivate, try as she might.

She was a dauntless partisan. On the periphery of her embracing loyalty was America. America was something she had, as it were, sweated for and earned all the way to the Coast, down in Washington, on one-night stands, in trains, cabs, buses, and on those rather high heels which made her progress staccato, not that she was kittenish for a second. Her American periphery was, in a sense, a trouper's, but hers was a glorious, a famous troupe. Her father was John McCullough. When you play this name as an ace and start to take up the trick with it, I wonder how many would concede it. It would be a bluff on my own part, but he was one of the Shakespearean actors that gave luster to his theatre and dominated San Francisco in his heyday. Virginia saw her America with her father, then her mother, both of them in high repute; Helen Tracy being lead woman for Augustin Daly at the very start of her career.

Next in Virginia's loyalty, after America, was the unaware city of New York. That began at Union Square, where the theater district was centered and moved by stages to 42nd Street. For inside New York, and nearing the core of her heart, was the theatre, a vivid rim of movie houses fringing its actual core. And, at the heart of it all, Jack and Lionel and Ethel, succeeding their father Maurice Barrymore.

Virginia was by times an actress. "Virginia," her mother said to her, "you are the kind of actress who looks around to see if the chair is there before you'll risk sitting on it. An actress *sits*." In Helen Tracy's case, the actress sat, not on a chair, but on her daughter. They lived together on Eighth Avenue and 50th Street, where only Benjy, to whom the name cat can no more apply than the name dog to a four-footed bayard, was the one rival to a Barrymore that ever entered Virginia's affections. How pale that word for the gladness, the merriment, the utmost reciprocity, and hospitality of spirit that came effortless from her radiant self. That she could bang down a sentiment that disappointed her, or scorn an affront to her loyalties, or meet with wit and indignant fire the torpidity of a criticism, was just as much part of her as her appreciation. She knew, and to the last poignancy, the faults and follies of her objects of perpetual adoration. Behind that level gaze were vaults of comprehension, sealed by her pity and her charity. Virginia ended by compassion for her mother before she put that afflicting mortal in a more appropriate vault.

Her way of escape from that parental octopus was, of course, by earning money. But there are situations in life like those in which a person who has lost his glasses can't find them until he has the glasses he lost. At any moment that Virginia became sufficiently absorbed to write a story, since the parental glare withered her talent for the stage, she was no sooner well started than a tentacle gathered her to her mother's bosom, a tentacle of illness, of chores, of haste, of worry.

Norman Hapgood was to print most of *Merely Players* when he was editor of *Collier's*. Into these stories went Virginia's skill in catching the beams from the footlights, their evanescence and their magic. But, like her mother, she started with a promise that she could never keep. And it was not her mother who contrived to enlace her in obligation; it was some vagrant to whom she became guardian angel. She was first and foremost a giver. She gave to her father, to her mother, to these clients who made her a one-man Alcoholics Anonymous, and to her friends in the fullness of her incredible attention.

But when it comes to reclamation, she was the one who ought to have been taken hold of, not the soaks and swamps and the sloughs of despond in which she waded. Her talent was of a rare quality, if I am any judge, and while it would have required time for the discipline of its abundance, it had the richest, most personal validity, the most lucid color. Her adored New York, however, could only note that her brocade was an awkward width and length, and even after her mother's death her most feverish submission to the rules of writing books as sleeping pills—detective stories—could not bring her a livelihood. She went on relief. She did it in furs, since Chicago never forgot her, and I had noticed that this rather acrid comedy could rattle her. She had accidents, a frightful one that set her lovely hair on fire, and with age she accumulated, instead of years, a variety of campaigns for health that had doctors at one end of town, dentists at the other, and problems in logistics that only Hanson Baldwin could explain. But she never deranged those loyalties that made the war worth her valor.

Meanwhile, with Margaret Wycherly her friend, and Actors' Equity to lean on, she was suddenly surprised to find the curtain going down, her inextinguishable self vanishing in black extinction like a firework star. Virginia's show was over. I could not believe it had to stop. Relief could write her off. Her little room had overlooked Bryant Park and flagrant Sixth Avenue, with vacant lots below, caged in by blank walls, staring with chalky faces toward the East River. These gave her clamor by day that was music to her ears, and she loved New York diamonded by night. On her wall by the bookcase was a Barrymore. But for me the comedy of Virginia Tracy has horror in it, a life squandered by drunkards she befriended and spendthrifts who left her in pawn. It is a wealthy civilization that can throw such jewels away.

At the same time that Virginia came over the horizon, another sparkling romantic appeared at the Wyatts, named Harvey O'Higgins. He was on his way to Denver, I believe, to write articles about Colorado.

Harvey was a lean Canadian, twinkling, alert, audacious, honest. He had broken into the magazine field with spirited stories about New York's fire-fighters, and he was now going out to muckrake with verve and tenacity. He was in the second flight of those who were showing capitalism in collision with labor, especially in the mine fields. Edith Wyatt was about to write an article for McClure's, and the actuality of this conflict, so heightened by Lincoln Steffens and such fantasts as Thomas Lawson, made Harvey O'Higgins a man we could not help wanting to know. He was not a sprawling and puzzled amateur but a highly paid professional. He soon was making as much with one article as I earned in a year. And at the same time he was unspoiled, with a quick chuckle, a bright insight, and in every way as open as a post office. He was brisk and yet easy, astute and yet invitingly frank. That he was unsophisticated, outside his floodlight, I rather think Edith Wyatt suspected.

But Harvey was infectuous and extremely lovable. He was so much a knight errant that one really longed when one knew him to put up a sign in front of him, "load not to exceed ten tons." He was soon battling for the young Authors' League, and for Theodore Dreiser, though he had found Dreiser rather a twister as an editor. He showed pure glee, however, in talking of another editor, Ellery Sedgwick. "I gave Sedgwick a story," said Harvey, "in which the climax was the breaking of an engagement. That was the point of it. And Sedgwick said, 'This is a story I want to print, very much. But it hits me personally on one point. I happen to be engaged. Would you mind very much changing the end?' "

To pink Ellery Sedgwick amused Harvey legitimately, but if an editor who wants to hobble a big audience departs from standard formula, it must be under considerable pressure, and this Boston Yankee that the young man from Canada ran into was uncommonly shrewd. He could sell Leslie's by having the pretty girl borne down only if she were to pop up again like a weighted doll, and his aim was to sell. He wanted to buy the *Atlantic*. He had his lariat ready, and his swinging it to catch the populus was only a preliminary. He was out to rope the carriage trade.

Harvey's aim was quite different. He had already written his novel of love in an attic. He was securing his grip on the big public. He was sanguine; he could write to please the big audience and himself. I must say I sympathized more with my blithe friend than with Sedgwick, for though the new *Atlantic* would be laid out adventurously, with the polite fairway widened and the bunkers made harder for gentility, the solid obstacle to all magazines had been created by editors who sweetly falsify for millions. Harvey respected not only himself, but also the big magazine audience, and he aspired to do something reputable in it. He would be the first to acclaim from this viewpoint the comparable triumph that Charles Chaplin achieved in *The Kid*. On this reckoning, though the adventure was to break him, he was less canny, and more truly romantic than the architect for gentility, since gentility also has its beauticians and morticians and no apprentice to *Leslie's* quite loses the touch.

These two, Virginia Tracy and Harvey O'Higgins, brought New York excitement into the air. They talked of Norman Hapgood and *Collier's*, of the *Century* and Douglas Doty, of what was happening to S. S. McClure, born in County Antrim in 1857, and John Phillips, born in 1861, like McClure a graduate of Knox College, but parting from his old friend and the ructions that only McClure's Ulster nerves could thrive on. How could Edith Wyatt begin writing for these brilliant editors? Idle to think of it, but Bill Hard was leaving tame Chicago for it, and it made book criticism seem the pale etching of a rainbow. These magazine writers were, in fact, bringing to an end the genteel era because of their impregnation with Marx. "Dialectic Materialism" was a jawbreaker, but it was coming to America through Jack London, Lincoln Steffens, Scott Nearing, Theodore Dreiser, and the rest in dialect form at any rate, and it posed new questions to everyone who could think. Thorstein Veblen's sly *Theory of the Leisure Class* was rejoicing Robert Hamill in Wheaton. The economic origins of the U.S.A. were not going to rest without having some Chicago historian interrogate Jefferson and Washington. "Say 'Aaah.' "

The Erskines

The easiest mode of living for a newspaperman is a good boardinghouse. Except for Mrs. Hatch's in New York, I had generally—without premeditation—selected a house run by an Irish woman or an Irish-American, and I had good luck. Mrs. Meagher's, Mrs. Murphy's in Providence, (she being French, but no matter), Mrs. Coffee's in Flushing (which was to be a great bond with Charles Dana Gibson, because he loved Flushing and made me an honorary Flushingite), and in Chicago Miss Leary's and the Fannings. At the thought of any boardinghouse the fairest cheek might blench, and in London we were to know how it can rasp. Those dusty fans in the empty grates! Those drilling eyes and rheumatic claws. Those gas jets! Those towels! That muted cat with the sunken flanks! Those sour plums and that custard!

But literature of adversity, like George Gissing's, could not apply to Miss Leary's beefsteaks, or to the gentle solicitude of Mrs. Coffee, or even to the sometimes breathless and distracted Fannings. The Irish may not observe all the laws of the successful restaurateur and may fail in differential calculus, but my experience of these houses where bachelors board and brood leaves a relatively gay memory. They were remorselessly bourgeois by my preference. On the next level down they would be active with insects and sickening with kerosene. Below that a greater ill-fame could be deserved since dearth compels anarchy. Fridthjof Nansen I once interviewed, and he told me of the blockade famine in Russia, where parts of human flesh were hanging from hooks in peasant huts. But even down below much depends on the surprise of human quality. I have talked to a man from death's havoc on a raft, and he saved his men from anarchy. Torture by boardinghouse can be excruciating, and it can also be exaggerated.

At the Fannings' an English family with five children arrived from California. They had a huge round table next to mine by a large window, and I gleaned my impression of them as surreptitiously as possible, but it was soon unnecessary to steal a look. They were as open as the day and quite ready to be amused by fresh company.

Thomas Erskine gave no hint of disturbance. He had come to California with his chatelaine, and no other word could fit her achieved style—a lady who could no more be imagined without a family tree than a peach or a pomegranate. Hers was the chiselled face you often see in generals' wives, and Mr. Erskine had belonged to a cavalry regiment though he would have smiled at the word "general." Being a minor member of the tribe of Erskine and Mar, he had been pruned by the severe rules that govern inheritance and had emigrated to a California ranch as the last pang of feudalism in his system, with hunting, shooting, and fishing to be light-hearted by-play. They were to rough it if necessary, to be colonials under the Stars and Stripes, and to bring up their five children in a free and open life where his good cavalry hands and his wife's courage as a manager would secure them a place in the sun that Scotland could not afford them. The Scot is a hound for emigrating. Pen him up in the bonny purple heather, and then see him streak for the horizon.

They were delightful to listen to. The matron, who extended to me a gentle warmth of friendliness, had a crystal speech in which every syllable had not merely recognition, but distinction. Those who invented glass chandeliers, asking them to reflect light and to shimmer, perhaps wished to express the incision of the diamond; Mrs. Erskine did the same for English, with a lambent and caressing style. In thought she was never keen, being perfectly conventional in this time and place, but I was content if she merely said, "Wasn't it an enchanting day? Were you in the park?"

The actual course of a family, especially when the stream of it goes from placidity to tumbling rapids, may seem more perilous than it is. For the Erskines the real peril was from leaving the English plexus without leaving the English predisposition. What they were trying to preserve, just the same, was not a mere English concatenation of aids and comforts but a definite habit of harmony. And its echoes, whether Greek or Swedish or English or Palestinian, made me wonder the more at the tenacity of origins, the magic of authenticity. These people were in the original package.

More Chicagoans

A shrewd man can always make his guess, and success is a guess made good, but Chicago at this moment was packed with shrewd men who all believed themselves to have owned the plot of ground on which Marshall Field's was erected, not counting its encroachments on city property. Miraculous prognosticators all. And why did they sell? Their wives yawned hurriedly whenever I leaned forward and inquired. "If you'll excuse me, dear. But do tell Mr. Hackett, he's so interested." And I was interested. The slippered antique would stroke his beard, pull down his woolen waistcoat, clear his throat, and fixing me with his red-rimmed gaze commence the Saga of the Loop. Everyone in Chicago at one time or another had owned everything. Only Marshall Field, apparently, had curled his fingers and held on. He was "inevitable."

All artists naturally hated him for that reason. One day at Wheaton he swung and missed his drive. Strange thing, golf, where so much that should be inevitable becomes evitable. He swung and missed again. The helpful Peter Dunne said softly to him, "Put down a silver dollar, Mr. Field. You can make that go farther than anyone in the world."

Poor Mr. Field, he died. "Poor Mr. Field," said Peter Dunne. "I trust he's in hell, measuring China silk." Hard for a dry goods merchant out of practice.

It was characteristic of Chicago that its rebels were going off at tangents. The new club, the Cliff Dwellers, was a swollen

Little Room, no less genteel and far less intimate. There was a bourgeois stuffiness since they welcomed sisters, cousins, aunts, and were cluttered with nonentities. Of course Lorado Taft was a presentable sculptor, and the architects in vogue were more reputable than isolated Louis Sullivan. But the town was uncritical. Granted that the orchestra was a redeeming institution, Theodore Thomas felt to be as renowned as oneone anywhere, the Art Institute, a magnificent receiving room, was sure to be replenished and perhaps to become consummate, yet with its millions of people and millions of dollars, this great freshwater metropolis only succeeded in being anemic and insipid. Its rebels found an easy solution. They departed.

The university had attracted a cluster of talented men—John Dewey, Charles Beard, Robert Herrick, Robert Lovett, the Schwills, Thorstein Veblen, and Lovett's collaborator, Manly. They were certainly a proof that high intelligence was commanded by President Harper. No medium existed, however, by which it could be marshalled for serious journalism. William Vaughn Moody possibly could have had a liberating influence on the genteel and a sobering influence on the farouche, but his early death left his work unfinished. The group that gathered at his house, besides, were crass worshippers, and his romanticism in *The Great Divide* left rhetoric ringing in my ears: "Done is done and lost is lost and smashed to hell is smashed to hell. You might as well try to bring down the Rocky Mountains with a rabbit's heartbeat," as something or other. Maybe it was better than "The Lion and the Mouse," but not one single book or play from that circle had vital distinction except Veblen's economics, a Norwegian snowfield that called for skis, and he was far from canny about his career. He did not last on that campus.

Among those who saw this feebleness, Harriet Monroe was yet to use her imagination by founding *Poetry*, and the work of Carl Sandburg was in the future. So was the huge contribution to the novel to be made by Dreiser and later by James Farrell, the work in the theatre that gave Floyd Dell his chance, and much more that could be cited by a cultural historian.

In the first decade of the century, however, we were closer to the pioneers, and their influence was so stifling in the realm of ideas that all the evidence of their discrimination that can be urged—the brave adventures of their soul among art dealers—fails to indicate any such real comprehension of the function of the community as John Quinn and his group were to reveal in the Armory Show in New York. A great deal of blague was avoided in Chicago by its discreet dealers in art and its refined patrons in letters, but blague was Chicago's distinguishing mark when the *Tribune* called itself "the world's greatest newspaper," when Chicago romped in the pit and bellowed in the Stockyards, cornered, crashed, and resurrected.

Henry Fuller was a strange figure in that Chicago of 1904-1911 which I knew so well. He was hovering in the wings for a long time before he came on the scene I knew, and those who spoke of him always suggested his sense at the same time they marked his sensibility. At last he appeared. He was a small, bird-like man with a little beard, who was no less apprehending than apprehensive. Miss Wyatt shook her head about him: he would not *work*. He was certainly in eclipse when I knew him. To extract anything out of him, even a book review, was impossible. He evaded that sort of pressure with something between a smile and a sigh. He ambled or shambled off the scene with the same elusiveness and went home to his private troubles, whether an invalid mother or whatever it was, as a coy bird goes to its nest circuitously. That circuitousness, of course, was the tribute of a most exquisitely discriminating and quivering set of nerves to the powers of nerve-wracking in which Chicago specialized. So, at any rate, I saw him. He should have lived, like E. M. Forster, in a community that allowed his tentacles to uncoil and to float out in the bathing fluid natural for them. But Chicago was stupendously on the make. Where Cambridge conspired in favor of an E. M. Forster, Chicago University tried to make terms with the enemy, and nothing, not Mrs. Potter Palmer or the Little Room or the *Evening Post* or anything else, could shelter this rather wistful though really incisive and highly critical being who was so starved for a beauty which could compensate his imagination for the deficiencies in his own and in Chicago's appearance. He belonged, as I saw him, to that sensitive tribe whose gayest sprite in recent years has been Lytton Strachey. But where Strachey matched his brains against Philistine England and organized his ideas with cool tenacity, Henry Fuller was too gentle and too intimidated to shoot the comic arrow. Perhaps he was too romantic, in that era of democratic romanticism when the literary Titania embraced Chicago and petted its ears.

He laughed rather like Lytton Strachey (and like John Synge), a sly laugh, and I can hear him describe Henry James as a literary cardinal. He once explained to me how the Jews are in one compartment that is rocked by any explosion, whereas the English are in a series of compartments so that an explosion is isolated. I feared the sly laugh that lurked in that little ashy beard. But no one should really have feared Henry Fuller. He was not cruel. He was very wise and, I think, anxious to share and to include. But Chicago seared him and so did the noisy literary machine that steamrolls the U.S.A. He threw up his hands and abandoned the sort of novel he so heroically broke the road for. He wrote long narratives in verse, or something like that, which I took to be an aberration. But I never read them.

Still, there he is, an implacable comment on that great grease spot of complacency that is named Chicago. Chicago failed Henry B. Fuller, and, by the same token, Henry B. Fuller failed Chicago.

Joe Patterson

At one of the large social gatherings I saw a big, shy young man who wore a shirt with a low soft collar and who occasionally jerked up his head like a horse and pulled down his collar as if it were too tight for him. He was massive and at the same time curiously loose with a queer crack in his voice. Julian Mason said he was Joe Patterson.

Joe was ingratiating. He had come out of Yale in 1901, and was about four years older than I, but the most attractive thing about him was his boyish directness. He wanted to know me and said so. I was immensely taken by him. One of the two Medill sisters who owned most of the *Chicago Tribune* was his mother, Elinor Patterson, his aunt being Katherine McCormick. They were North of Ireland people, I suppose Presbyterians, but Joe was to become a Catholic later on. That was so like him, just as it was like him to say to me not long before he died, "Tolstoy—still the greatest, isn't he?" When I met him he worshipped Tolstoy.

About Tolstoy there was the halo of genius, and this young man from Groton and Yale was humble before genius, but as an ambitious young American he didn't know how much might rub off if he kept grating himself against it. All that was unstable and lumbering in the Russian—his confused but sincere feelings about women and his honest wish to be chaste in the midst of his burning desires, his aristocratic upbringing that gave him the silken conventions to accept and his inability to accept them, his stark vision of poverty, his pitiless insight into hypocrisy, and with this his knowledge of his own clumsiness, selfishness and omnivorous envy—these were the traits that Joe could not escape from. Tolstoy held up his mirror to the Groton boy, while his mother watched with Chicago realism.

Joe was a character. The good thing about him, the thing that I felt instantly, was that he wanted to be loved, and he made a beeline for honey. But in conflict with this admirable and frequently sterilized yearning was a degree of suspicion that had its origins so far down that only a geologist could tell where and how the strata had folded. The French say that a singed cat dreads cold water, and Joe had this sort of fear in him. It was all in his face, the dimple and the scowl, and just as you had coaxed the dimple to his face, that tortured frown would assert itself and he'd begin throwing the toys out of the perambulator. Only old Mother Church could soother him into submission. He yielded to the old crooner. He was as a little child—that is to say, a little field of merit for the Jesuit fathers.

We met quite often, and always at his expense, since my $28 a week, increased to $33, could not pay for us at DeJonghe's or another restaurant high up in the Fine Arts Building was it? We had frogs' legs, and he drank a bottle of wine as I drank ginger ale. And I gave him the sort of microscopic attention for which psychiatrists charge more than the price of frogs' legs. I peered into the mysteries of Joe's interior. I was much more mature and actually absorbed in his workings, but it was four years before I heard of psychoanalysis, and I was not prepared for his eventual resistance to the doctor. It flattered me that he could consult me, and at that time it was possible for a friend to unfold himself at great length to the intense delight of his companion, who might, if luck favored him, get in a little word about his own spiritual fretwork. But usually Joe's expressive face had a wintry fatigue in it by the time we got around to my troubles, and even to myself, he conveyed their comparative insignificance. Our roles were clear in his eyes. He was the cup. I was the saucer. But he twinkled the evening he took his knife and fork at a dinner party and rapped them on the table like two sticks. We all stopped in the middle of our talk to see what was the matter.

"All listen to me!" said Joe, with a broad grin. He hadn't managed so far to attract attention. This simple method worked. He was still *enfant* but not yet *terrible*.

To the family he was *enfant terrible*, though. In the House of Representatives at Springfield he had thrown an ink bottle at someone. He was editing the *Daily Socialist*. And, as commissioner of public works, he was treading on Marshall Field's toes when they encroached without a building permit on the sidewalk. Besides this he was writing a radical novel. I read it as a friend and reviewed it as a critic which was the reverse of what Joe had hoped for.

But, for all his limitations as a son of the rich, he was by far the most exciting human specimen in my circle. He was trying to be honest, and for a son of the *Chicago Tribune* to have that target was in itself a paradox. Joe could not really write novels or plays. He was formed in a school of sensational journalism, and his palate had been ruined by the diet of syrup and pickles that he knew from the cradle. He aimed at Tolstoy and hit Arthur Brisbane, Brisbane being the corn syrup that had been sorghum juice at Brook Farm where Brisbane's father was a true rebel.

The proof that Joe was a restless and yearning soul came when he proposed that we take a cycle trip in central Illinois in the middle of summer.

He preceded me to Chillicothe, a small town on the Drainage Canal. Bertie McCormick, Joe's cousin, was a rather greasy and stuck-up young man who was younger than Joe but president of the Sanitary District and head of the Canal, and instead of meeting me with a bicycle so that we could peddle through the endless cornfields, risking sunstroke, Joe hailed me as the fellow guest of a Drainage official who lived on a river boat. It had two cabins, that river boat, with a curtain in between. The official was a pleasant young man with a shy wife. They bunked on one side of the curtain, we on the other. They fed us on the best and in huge quantity, but even a swim in the Illinois River could not enable me to digest the little yellow bullets that grow on sweet corn. I was persecuted by indigestion. Joe swam like a grampus, with fierce disregard of the Illinois River's earnest haste to carry off the waters of the Drainage Canal. I plopped after him in despair of my feebleness, while he clouted his way down the wrinkled lane of waters. He enjoyed his prowess, while I, knobbed inside by pellets of sweet corn, struggled back to the house boat.

Up till this moment we had been disentangling our confused literary judgments, by that process of assertion and counter-assertion which only seems to tug the skein of opinion into black knots of a fatal tightness. Joe would say, "Henry James! How can you read him? He's got immense verbal felicity, I grant you. What does he know of life?" My brow beaded with perspiration, I defended Henry James with the sad knowledge that *The Ambassadors* had baffled me so completely that I had put it aside until I had a whole fortnight at sea in which I could stalk it to its lair and discover what exactly was cooking in it.

After futile splutters in defense of the uncomprehended, I said, "Well, Joe, let's go on. Where do you stand on Meredith?"

Perhaps I had been supercilious about Henry James, because I remember Joe's sticking out his jaw with a formidable glare in his eyes. He was sitting in a posture I always envied but could never imitate—one knee bent and the leg crossed at right angles. Leaning down and tapping the broad sole of his shoe, Joe stated in a loud voice that resounded through the show boat, "I stand right there on Meredith!" It was worthy of Patrick Henry and I knew I could not rock him.

We went to Peoria together to visit a distillery. I remember colorless alcohol twisting in a long rope of fluid out of a container of some sort, probably a vat. Joe asked questions.

Then I checked the bicycle that had been given me by Uncle Ed, and Joe waved to me from the platform. I saw him in Chicago, his smile restored to its amazing sweetness, and we discussed the new typewriter I had bought, a Blickensderfer. It had a different system from other machines. It had a drum in the center that revolved when you hit a key, and if you hit the right key the drum stopped at the right letter. The alphabet on this keyboard did not correspond to the Remington alphabet.

"Did you know that when you bought it?"

"Yes, Joe. I can learn a new alphabet."

"Well," he said, "that settles it. Now I know you're a genius."

One evening Joe asked me to dine with him, and we went again to DeJonghe's, where the people all had their noses. Joe and I in fact put our noses together over a small table in a nooky corner.

"My mother has put it up to me," he said.

"What does she say, Joe?"

"She said, 'Joe, five percent of what you spend comes from the *Daily Socialist* and ninety-five percent comes from the *Chicago Tribune*. Do you think that's fair?'"

"And you said?"

With that boyish crack in his voice Joe said, "No, mother, I don't think that's fair." He looked at me, "And I'm damned if I do, Francis. What do you think?"

I thought his mother had made a point. But would it leave Joe frustrated? Once we had talked of "The Statue and the Bust," written before Freud had patented the word frustrated.

> *And the sin I impute to the frustrate ghost*
> *Is, the unlit lamp and the ungirt loin,*
> *Though the end in view was a vice, I say.*

Here he was, with one side of him, the rudimentary side, yearning for an understanding of people and a response from them, and the other side, much more developed in the family as a whole, suspicious of everything that might injure the source of 95 percent of the income. How to love people and sell them a mountain of newspapers? You couldn't do it with the *Daily Socialist*, and yet Joe's revolt from genteel Chicago was almost a physical revulsion. He was antigenteel, antirational, and antiaesthetic. He craved ultimate achievement, either above or under the levels of respectable Chicago.

Murry Nelson, who was a broker but who wrote plays and acted Synge's plays in Lake Forest, was laughing one day when I met him in the Northwestern station. I asked him to tell me the joke.

"There isn't any joke. I just saw Joe Patterson hurrying to the train with the polo saddle. You know the great three symbols of the useless life? A polo saddle, a champagne cooler, and a yacht cannon."

It was Murry Nelson, too, who put me right when Chicago was shocked at Isadora Duncan, and I said to him, "But if A lives in sin and B lives in sin, and C lives in sin . . . " Murry answered, "But for businessmen a girl is necessary. They can't tell their wives what's going on in business. Their wives would tell other wives. They can't talk about it at dinner parties. The people they want to talk about are at the dinner parties. So they have to have a girl. The girl may not care or understand, but the man can babble on. He has to talk to somebody."

Not long after this Joe's sister arrived back from Poland, having kidnapped her own child from a Count she was going to divorce. She was a slim, red-haired Circe, extremely continental, but with the sort of face that could irreverently be called an Irish mug. One of her first conquests was Joe, but I do not think her weight would have been thrown on the side of the *Daily Socialist*. The twenty-six servants in her Polish home were not the only thing to make feudalism seem close to her. She returned to Chicago as if to baby's milk after fire and sword, and she looked on me as milk-and-water. I thought of her as playing Lucrezia to Joe's Cesare Borgia, and said so at dinner one night.

Next morning I was called on the telephone. "Good morning. What's this I hear? You compare us to the Borgias?"

"I? Never!"

"Oh, don't disappoint me. I am delighted."

She meant it, but I hadn't. I only thought she might have a bad influence on Joe Patterson.

There was a real quality in Joe, but it was almost indefinable. The fact that he was a rebel was exhilarating, but was one to defer to a rebel as such? When a man of heroic creative vitality like Tolstoy went on to smash European literary tradition in *What is Art?* and to argue for an attitude of pure innocence and simplicity, there was something forced in it, even perverse, as if the artistic aspirations he belabored were a reproach to himself. And on that account induced in him a touch of megalomania, leading him to drive his predecessors from the temple. But sweeping denunciation from a man of genius is one thing. He has earned the right to be radical. He has served his apprenticeship.

Joe hadn't. He was a rich woman's whelp. His literary perceptions were blunt. He had been given local opportunity because of his family and had floundered into trouble as commissioner of public works, only to resign and retreat under fire. He was still an amateur. Yale and Harvard had turned out many like him before and would do it again. Wealth gave them prestige, as if they were hereditary nobility, and they usually cut their eyeteeth as their predecessors' critics. My feeling for this man was not uncritical, and he could sniff it. But in spite of his submission to his mother, which would mean an uneasy compromise, and in spite of his consequent toughness and cynicism, plus his heavy drinking, he had in him what Carlyle called "fire in his belly," and this native force, unless utterly defiled, can be persistently attractive. When you have good people with low vitality and bad people with high vitality, the luster of these Lucifers tends to dim the mousy people. The tigers and the lions keep the zoo exciting. Even complete scoundrels like

Goering seemed to have power to attract discriminating observers. I liked Mussolini when I talked with him. A conversation with a well-disposed tiger would be extremely enlivening. I don't say Joe Patterson was a tiger. He was a bear, but bears love honey, and I loved that side of him, even while I watched his claws and estimated their sharpness, because as he grew older he became cross-grained and formidable. He came to edit a newspaper that stressed pride, covetousness, lust, anger, gluttony, envy, sloth. It was a perpetual fable of the seven deadly sins for people whose lives go at a municipal dog trot. Every morning he showed them the zoo, and he rolled up enormous circulation, as a bear rolling a barrel. It was life as a circus, paper hoops for playboys, the high kick as a substitute for rebellion, and politics music from a band wagon.

The ultimate objection to Joe's toughness and levity, I felt, was its servile concern with any and every kind of prowess. It makes life a jungle. And America, as I see it, is waste if we accept life as a jungle. The worship of force negates America. It only becomes significant at the point where fire in the belly leads to a lighting system. Joe dwelt, and preferred to dwell, in the heart of darkness.

Tiffany Blake was threatened with tuberculosis. He went to Cuernavaca in Mexico, and when he was sound again, soon after returning to our editorial room, he took himself to the *Chicago Tribune.* This was leaving an insignificant paper for the most powerful in the Midwest which was making him chief editorial writer.

He knew what the *Tribune* was. The only thing he had yet to learn was what it would be like when Joe Patterson and Bertie McCormick agreed to take the paper on alternate months. Joe's policy being roustabout and cynical in January, March, May, July, September, November, and on the first of every other month becoming pompous, loudmouthed, and ducal with

Bertie. Tiffany told me, not long before he died, that this was not so funny. I thought it a shameless arrangement to impose on a sensitive and self-aware man. They paid him well and used him like putty, until Joe Patterson went to New York, where he discovered an editorial writer that beat Tiffany all hollow, taking the word literally. This was a man whose head had a sponge in it. He could soak up any given idea, pompous or roustabout, ducal or taproom, and he operated for Joe and for Bertie like an automat. All he needed was the nickel and someone to turn the spigot. Out jerked or flowed from the front or the corner precisely the dope as ordered. If only he could have been patented! He could talk in two voices and wag at both ends. His was a mastery of gyration. And he didn't even have a headache while Tiffany was, or seemed, crucified.

Once Tiffany was gone from the *Post*, I wanted to have nothing more to do with writing editorials. Then our managing editor, Leigh Reilly, said to me that I ought to think about editing a special book section, rather like the supplement that the *Times* published on Saturdays, but with a leading review by myself on the front page every week, perhaps calling it the Friday Literary Review. And I could run it myself, have sole responsibility for it. I was to mull it over.

Well, it was 1909. I was twenty-six. I had been on the *Post* for four years. It was about time I did something. I stood on the bank, looking long before I could plunge. Was I to make a fool of myself?

One of the best things in life is a commanding officer who has faith. So long as Tiffany Blake was on the paper, I felt that extraordinary generosity of spirit which you call brotherly. He could be tart. When Dorothy Dudley, a girl with amazing good looks and with a voice that had not yet decided as between the high road and the low road, came to him for books to review, he listened to her patiently, no doubt drinking in her looks as well as her halting words. As she stood up her nervousness made her drop the clutched carfare. Tiffany stooped for it. "Little girls should not drop pennies," he murmured.

Admonition was sometimes painful. "Look at this," he said to me. "An editorial on the Art Institute. My God! Chicago 'a stamping ground for art!' Isn't it perfect Joe Sheehan!" I blushed. "I wrote that, Tiffany." "Gosh! Am I to believe that?" And I had quite liked it.

An entirely casual remark of his, however, cheered me for years. We had been playing tennis or taking some sort of exercise and were changing at Ned Yeomans' house in Winnetka, using the same bathroom, and as I was slipping into dry clothes he said, "My, you have a good body!" "Potbellied, Tiffany."

"Why do you say that?" "It's a national trait. From long generations of eating potatoes." He was amused. His outspoken comment, however, was one of those affectionate words which, from a reserved and honest man, lie gently on the heart and yet root in memory. My body was issued to me from general stores, and I took it with misgiving. He was the first ever to commend it.

Once, as Learned Hand was dancing naked under a waterfall with vine leaves in his hair, I stood watching him with delight. All he lacked was horns to make him a perfect statue for the Vatican. And yet I cannot remember telling him so. Others, I do not doubt, had long before cheered him.

But Tiffany's departure, sundering the editorial tie as well as the personal, left me in the worst despond of youth. How could he do it? I had not the civilized English art of compromise in my veins.

The Rebel

When people said to me later on, "Did Floyd Dell precede you on the *Post*, or did you precede him?" it brought home the difficulty of self-importance. The supplement that I had hatched out became Floyd Dell's, and for a lot of its readers he was the starting point, while I belonged to another party, another administration. To the friends of Charles II, Charles I must have seemed a dim number.

Floyd came from Davenport, Iowa. Charlie Hallinan was his buddy on the *Post*. The literary adventure for Floyd Dell, four years my junior, was qualified by early poverty. In appearance he was touchingly young, with a long pre-Raphaelite face, a pair of big melancholy eyes, and a mane of poetic hair. He looked, if not tubercular, at least on the edge of it. But if you have noticed the teeth of a young fawn, they can bite through barbed wire. Floyd Dell was belligerent, with a mixture of suspicion and hostility. He had fed ravenously on Marx. The works of Lewis Morgan, or his book on *Ancient Society*, had done for him what ethnology was to do for many before and since—serve as lye to eat away the Victorian wallpaper. It left him naked of easy sentiment, a materialistic monist in his pelt, and curling his sensuous lip at the deluded bourgeosie.

This appealing and exasperating young man would tilt his head superciliously and utter pitying comments on poor devils who did not happen to be materialistic monists. But his possession of the True Faith did not keep him from literary aristocracy. At some period or other he had been a candy puller, perhaps in a Davenport factory, but other poets have spat on galley oars. When, however, he saw a cut-heading I used on the *Post*, "Poets Minor and Minus," its cruelty made him wince, and, much as I resisted any crashing self-assertion, I agreed to cancel it. The morning he came down with a little brown handmade book, however, and handed it to me, saying with a tentative smile, "Here is all that is worth preserving of *Paradise Lost*," then I had to laugh. He could carve steaks out of a live Milton.

Robin Redbreast in a cage! America had made him a rebel, and he had something to rebel with. I never knew what it was to have a collaborator before, but here was a tireless worker, wholehearted and resolute, ready to take on any task assigned to him, to do it vigorously and vivaciously, and go deep on occasion. The pains that an editor suffers from slovenly or even worse, from dry and impenetrable reviewers, can hardly be measured. Not many outside the academic field are able or willing to give themselves in a book review. They may not be smug, but they are so shallow that only gutted farmlands of the Dust Bowl itself can suggest how disastrous they are in another type of husbandry. They will tackle anything, although botches and frauds, and yet pay no price to master their art. And when, being academic, they do know the cost of application, they are in general so wary and juiceless that you feel they have no more to give than sour customs inspectors.

Floyd Dell, creative by endowment, had all the application that a scholar commands and all the response that a published book challenges. Give an American a chance to be a prima donna and he may exert himself, but Floyd Dell did it as an assistant editor and then as an associate. He did it because he was a scrupulous workman and a fine one. At 21, self-educated, aggressively radical, he was equipping himself for his career on the *Masses*.

That this was to be frankly Socialist I thought was excellent. That it was to be revolutionary seemed unreal to me. If Chicago snobs imported tandems to distinguish themselves from a horse-

and-buggy public, it was equally snobbish for radicals to import palpable economic falsity in regard to the American situation. A revolutionary dictatorship of the proletariat, on the assumption that economic conditions must unavoidably go from bad to worse, was not a good premise in a democratic republic. Ernst Cassirer quotes a phrase from Heraclitus: "Men do not understand how that which is torn in different directions comes into accord with itself—harmony in contrariety, as in the case of the bow and the lyre." I welcomed Floyd Dell's contrariety, but I kept waiting for the music in American terms, a contrariety not so rasping as to refuse a harmony. It was for that reason that the Chicago bourgeoisie, stifling though it might be, could not be excluded out of a theory. Floyd had much intolerant theory in his cosmos and partly out of awkwardness. The anguish of apprenticeship is bad in journalism. "I have gone home ill," he said in a note left on my desk. A repeated misprint of the word "egoism" in a review of his had sickened him.

Life among the bourgeoisie required a not less hazardous apprenticeship, but he preferred to look down on it, as the young T.S. Eliot, unable to drive a car, preferred to be bitter about motorists. Incompetence resorts to disdain, but as Floyd Dell was to continue creatively, he needed other strings to his lyre than the class struggle. He needed "Joan of Arc" as well as "Widowers' Houses." In short, given America as it was, he needed lenience, or else, like Jack Reed, a ticket to Russia to discover whether the grapes of wrath were actually as represented or simply sour grapes in the novice period.

But this inelasticity of theory did not impair living criticism. He eagerly took over the Review when I said goodbye to it, giving him the wheel and my charts and my blessing. He started off with gleaming eyes, as proud as any young pilot on the Mississippi.

I never learned how Dave Towne and John C. Shaffer like it when Floyd pressed his nozzle against the Banks and the rest of the Capitalist system. It is improbable that they read the book supplement.

"Dear"

A deep difficulty had early been so apparent in my Chicago life that it became noticeable even to friends, and they behaved about it as family councils in France do. They attacked me about it one evening after dinner.

It appeared to these friends that I ought to provide myself, in some way or other, with a woman.

Three of these friends are now dead, Percy Hammond, Florence Hammond, his wife, and Tiffany Blake. And, of course, it was out of sheer affection and in the kindness of their hearts that they intruded on my obviously celibate existence. They disagreed about the type of woman I needed. Percy said it should be a chorus girl. Tiffany shook his head. He thought it ought to be one of my friends on the North side—some woman who needed a lover. Florence Hammond kept saying, "Isn't it terrible? Leave him alone." But she laughed at this outspoken conclave which was inoffensive to me because Percy and Tiffany were in a way like elder brothers, and the "I" they were discussing was a matter of interest, and indeed of wonder, to its proprietor.

My Catholic training, was it ineradicable? It was based on the corruption of human nature, and on a concept of purity that excluded my having a woman unless I married her. But married on what, on $18 a week? That was a weird prospect for any young woman, unless she brought me financial help, and I did not want to solve it in that fashion.

But if I married a Catholic girl, it would mean children. I had seen what that meant in my own family, and it was irksome for the father, slavery for the mother, and a mad scramble for the children. Instead of writing independently, I should have to earn more money and fit into the market, perhaps by mastering the art of murder and mystery stories, a form of literary perversion that was beyond me. Or we could dodge having children by means I was not familiar with, and not known to Irish families in my father's time.

Marriage was impossible. It would be settling down, and I was not in the least ready to settle down. I had no roots in Chicago and no plans to remain there indefinitely. All I owned was in suitcases and trunks. I didn't possess a stick of furniture. I had no capital beyond what I could jingle in my pocket. I lived from one $18 to another $18, and on Tuesdays not enough was left to buy lunch with. When it came to the advance for two weeks' vacation, I felt prosperous. But you can't marry on $36 in lieu of vacation.

An affair did start, however. Begun in frivolity it developed into happy and painful sincerity. And yet, in the midst of it, another affair blossomed briefly, a flower from a slowly germinated seed.

Every year I went to see the publishers in Boston and New York about forthcoming books. This time the train from Boston came in early. I got off at 125th Street to go to her address. It was a big modern complex of rather small apartments, and as it was Sunday morning the milk and cream and newspapers were on the mat. As I rang, I felt sure I was too early; everything was so quiet and the morning sun had sleeping New York all to itself.

My friend opened the door. She wore a light dressing gown, and made a sign to show no one else was awake. Then she put her hands on my shoulders to look at me. We stood in this way for a little while, the warmth of her hands running through me, as we gazed straight into each other's eyes. She closed the door; we stood in the dark hall, and without a sound she gave me her lips. I had never touched her before. She led me into the front room, which was curtained and shaded; it was a smallish room that was cozy, thickly carpeted, with a couch to the right. I took her in my arms, her body warm from the bed, and desire for her, whom I had known for years and never as a lover, was flaming through me. I kissed her with my whole heart.

This was our perfect moment, or I should say our perfect hour. She was born Catholic, and we had come together as comrades in New York, as lucid and candid friends six years before. We were both young exiles, consumed by our literary interests, and both hindered from making love by more than our upbringing. An extraordinary reserve dwelt in her, as if she had been grievously hurt, but as a grave, studious, somewhat rigid and overcast girl, whose melancholy was visible in her large dark eyes and sunken cheeks, I could share her presence without sharing her confidence. She was cordial with me, and brunette as she was, her skin dark with vivid color, her bones strong, her tresses black, it was in my power to take her out of herself. Our talks were often highly animated, even if she could be quiet and reasoning to being with; without being coquettish she would rally me as a sister might rally a brother, troubled by my not believing in myself and refusing to let me deprecate whatever gifts I had. We both had to earn our living to make our way and keep from succumbing to the Enemy. She did her best to have me meet people, with a sound worldly sense, because she came from sturdy stock. When I went West I took my fate with me and cut myself off from New York, but occasional short letters kept us in touch, and this reunion we had promised ourselves, our bond a real one.

What was happening was as if we had long desired it, and had I returned from a war, whole or scarred, she could not have loved me more. A nest could not be more favoring than this embrasure we sank into. The place was our own. Only our young hostess who was my friend's devoted slave was living there, soundly asleep. We had it all to ourselves; I was to stay there, to be with her for my whole stay. The dark, melancholy stream that had held us separate, moving clear and deep without a ripple, was now bridged by her loving body, which she gave into my arms. She was supple, strong, and firm, and we said little beyond blessing this moment. She did not hold herself back from my desire, as I opened her light gown and kissed her ardently. Her self-possession was melting into defenseless desire as we were transported by a love we had not foreseen.

This miracle, so unpremeditated, shut out from my conscience that in a few days I would be going back to Chicago, and in Chicago my heart had been committed without reserve.

The miracle of love transmutes humble metal into gold. It is nothing but that. This alchemy was now about to perfect itself. During the years we had been living apart, my reticent companion had come out of the dark wood, and she had new friends, was no longer dependent on exacting work, and had in some manner escaped from the toils so familiar to us. After all that could have estranged us or sent us on divergent roads, she could release herself to me as to one she had always yearned for, and her murmurs of ecstasy sent piercing joy into me—the erotic moment so beautifully offered and so propitious. Love and the erotic are not the same, though they strive to be. We were not flirting with one another; we were drawn by a pent-up feeling that her generosity of spirit had fostered in me. It was this I embraced in her and caressed with a full heart. In her surrender she filled it to overflowing, and my carnal desire, now transmuted from voluptuousness into the happy surge of magnanimity that centers in the heart, gathered into the fusion of soul and body which merges a man with a woman. We were so close I could feel her self-possession yield to my approach, and then in a voice that moaned rather than spoke she murmured a name that was not mine.

I had a wild hope, a desperate wish, that it might be a slip of the tongue. She was oblivious that she had uttered his name, and I did not flinch or shrink from her. She never knew she had spoken, but ten minutes later, when she opened her eyes, shook herself, stroked my hair, and laughed, "We left the things outside, didn't we?" I answered as naturally as I could.

I sat on the edge of the couch, my head in my hands. I knew that name, not the man himself. It was distinguished, as though one might say a generation later, "Aldous" or "Sachy" or a generation earlier "Algernon" or "Walt." He was a love poet; I could understand her being enamored of him, not with the sweet indulgence she might give to me, but with a peculiar abandon that would lead her to him naked, unashamed. Her love of him ran in her blood, and in her being, and I was in place of it. As her laugh and her peculiarly harmonious voice carried from the other end of the flat, I stayed physically immobile but inwardly in turmoil. The erotic watchdog is so single-minded that at the slightest flutter of a strange presence it bares its fangs, mine so sharpened by an earlier whetting that only one thing, the knowledge of my lover in Chicago, kept me from fury. The impulse that had been born in me when she opened the door and looked in my eyes made me possessive of her, but I did not hide from myself that I was possessed. Chastity meant nothing to me, but loyalty everything—the woman's sole right, to have and to hold. And this now asserted itself. But I had to borrow a brush to make myself look less tossed and tangled.

Josephine, the hostess, was a dimpled, tiny darling, and I was her friend's beau; her house was mine. My scruples melted, but so did my clothes and I had checked my bag to Grand Central. What was I to wear? My friend laughed. "You must have one of my nightgowns." And this dainty garment was presented. Not being perverse, I took it as one takes a paper cap at a New Year's party, and my humor was softened by this idiocy; we had a lively breakfast as they laughed at me. We were enraptured to be together.

But my brunette was more parsimonious than I had expected. She may have felt, for all her loving kindness, that the poetry which led her naked, unashamed, to her Algernon was not in me to transmute and consummate her passion, so in bed she wore a perplexing garment, all in one piece, that could only be torn off if I were to have her naked. Had I not overheard her unconscious, I might have fought with her, but whatever I had touched in her was numbed in both of us by this high priest of love.

At the end I left her, nursing disappointment, yet going back to another woman, a generous lover, and as I was smarting from erotic humiliation, I said to her I had not loved. This angered her. She said it was wounding to say such a thing to a woman, and so it was. But I resented her. "Was it not wounding," I said to myself, "to lie in my arms and murmur that name?" Yet we could not injure the attraction between us. I would now ask her, if she were living, if she had been nakedly his. I fear she had. But I was not myself free to come to her, and where the heart is already engaged it is useless to evoke the erotic. Neither of us could make love our pastime; we were too near to attachment, though those poems, really, should never have seduced her. Sweet, aphrodisiac poems! I never could read them.

❦

Kitty was colorful, abounding in curiosity, voluble, and romantic. She loved to entertain, often sweeping her glance—she had rather prominent pheasant eyes—over ponderous guests to whom she would gladly give a nip of nitroglycerine. The profusion of her temperament must have been what captured her husband, Jim, but it had come to rub him raw and stroke him with alum. He was a man schooled in his decorum, tight, considerate in details, rasped on exposed nerves by his wife's bravura. He could readily forgive dullness, even provide it, but from extravagance of nature he shrank audibly. I, poor fool, was equally at home with both of them.

And in any case, apart from her excellent dinners, Kitty had an Irishness that was to my liking. Her father had tried to corner real estate in the Loop. It was the nuns who prepared Kitty for that species of real estate known as a husband. They issued her with a relatively unkempt mind, to which the Yankees are as little accustomed as to a disheveled head of hair, but this natural imprecision never implied what it would with a Yankee. It meant no more than the wind-blown dishevelment of those passengers who first ventured forth in open cars. Kitty was avidly interested in books, eager about people, vehemently concerned about Ireland, and prompt to express herself. In a society that occupied itself chiefly with tangible values, discarding the interests that take men and women far afield, I was naturally drawn to a person who instead of measuring approbation out with a medicine glass opened her door in unconstrained hospitality. Were an American of Puritan stock to do this at that time, it might have implied impetuosity and even looseness, which the Chicagoans then took enormous pains to avoid. But the convent-bred Irish-American girl was often more Puritan than the American, perhaps because of her Catholic accounting system, so literal and so explicit. And in addition she could be noisily expansive where an American was discreet out of poker-face individualism.

I had seen enough of her to have reservations about her lack of critical sense and social fineness. She had a profuse nature, and she could dash into enthusiasms like a child clapping its hands at a fire. But if there is one thing certain about people, it is the difference there is between a cold-blooded estimate and the warm recognitions that come from intimacy. Once I was admitted behind my friend's rather florid and even ostentatious exterior, with observable avidity and forwardness—the traits that might make the long winter evenings that much longer—I discovered an entirely different mood, a mood of many reserves, of reflection, and of dignity, and I could, without any of the antagonism which is stirred by deception, see that her contemplated marriage to another man was not only right but could be entirely candid between us.

But when I retreated, with no vicious deception on either side and no food for rancor, the throes of absorption did not cease. Once permitted it has an eagerness to devour. There was nothing I could do. For the first time in my life I had invited it, and now I was caught in an impulse beyond my control. It was not a frenzied impulse; for no matter how much it tore me, I could not obey it. The insincerity that infected its origin was one reason for this, but her commitment to the other marriage was right for her. My punishment was to have allowed the enemy to slip into the citadel, and then to be forced to dislodge it. You can be gnawed inside by the unkindness of love.

I went on a Northern vacation, and I came back from it with a new feeling about life. Common sense is all on the side of mankind when he digs for iron ore or hacks down forests for comic strips, even if he has to befoul nature to do it. But he cannot intrude on nature in its wild setting in the North without maiming or slaying a presence that pervades these regions and moreover revives ancestral emotions to their depths. The Northern forests were pre-national and they stretched in space as they did in time. One has forgotten or never personally known what a forest is in its undisturbed existence. But on this north shore of Lake Superior, stretching as they liked to say from the water's edge to the Arctic Circle, lay a domain of uncontaminated solitude, which was free of human beings except for tiny outposts and the retreats of a few Indians, but with a life of its own, a million forms, a range of every color, and a compass of every sound. It had an estranging severity to begin with. It frightened me. But it was a well-spring of such poignant beauty that it filled the heart. The mountains affect one, and the sea, but this was a proud loneliness, with the solace that is offered by reunion with a state of being natural to us many centuries ago. We could not enter into it. But on its fringes, by our comforting fire—I was with friends—with the lake insinuatingly present and the night unfurled above, we could hear and feel and see and smell the nearness of this immensity, the mother that cradled us, the Old Man who broke us in. It wrapt the dark around itself, and still we were aware of it. I envied the letter-carrier who followed his trail on foot covering thirty miles a day. He lived with the forest. Cities, buildings, streets, yapping motors, grim pedestrians, factories, theatres, cemeteries—they were forgotten by a laconic man who would live with the trees and die like one of them. He was well out of it.

At times up there I was half demented. If I am to credit nature with a mother's disposition, she was spanking me. She was telling me I was one of those unfortunate devils who had played with fire—begun an affair for amusement, not thinking it would be taken seriously or be serious, and come away burned! Near us in the forest was a "brulé," a patch eaten out of the living tissue and left a black smudge of charcoal on the bare rock and earth. I had been brulé as well.

Gradually the turmoil quieted. I knew it when we stopped in an inn at the Soo, where the odor of burning wood was delicious in a big room lined with dark timber. I caught a few words from a soft voice, and a little while later, as Louise Burling glanced from the deck of our steamer on a French couple in a rowboat, with a guide at the oars, she was so offended by the man's amorousness—he was certainly smitten—that she exclaimed, "How disgusting!," while I thought, "How public, and how private!" His hollow, white face, with eyes sunk in his head, yet rivetted on his beloved, remained forever in my memory. They were consumed in one another, while the man at the oars pulled them out of our wake like so much freight.

Getting Away

Toward the end of the summer in 1911 I resigned from the *Post*, and I gave the usual reason that I was going to write a novel. But the real reason I could not put in words. Even now I find it hard. I think I was dying of a disease called Chicago.

You sometimes see in the papers a joke about an elderly lady in Oklahoma who is having a well sunk for water. The drillers rush in to her and shout, "We've struck oil, oil!" And she answers, "You must cut it off. I don't want oil. I want water."

All around me, even on the *Chicago Evening Post*, were colleagues who were striking oil. Fontaine Fox had invented a comic strip called the Toonerville Trolley. He soon began to syndicate it, and he is still syndicating it forty years later. The poor devil struck oil, and he has been tied to it ever since.

Charlie Frey was a ball of energy, and he charged at life as if it were a football match. He was our art editor. But "art" was for Charlie a means to an end, and the end was an advertising agency. I am certain he struck oil. Both he and Fontaine Fox were thoroughly companionable. Fox was from the South, and under his dry, shrewd, and almost withered blondness there was a whimsical understanding of reality. There was a sliver of a smile as he recalled one of his kin on a Mississippi river boat. This man got into a quarrel and he and his antagonist agreed to fight it out. They went into a pitch-black cabin and drew out their knives. Fontaine Fox could well imagine this horror.

Chicago, as Frey and Fox were to demonstrate, could gush

wealth if you knew where to drill for it. But the insupportable thing in Chicago was to say: "I don't want oil, I want water." Who could drill better than Peter Dunne and George Ade? In any civilized community they would have been artists. But no Chicagoan wanted them to be artists.

It was dimly evident to me before I told Leigh Reilly that I was going to resign from the *Post*, that he might take it to heart. But, after all, it was I who had edited the supplement and put myself into it, and I had the right to give it up. So I faced him in his office, telling him definitely I was resigning. He had a bunch of proofs in his hand as he stood listening to me, looking down. Then he lifted his eyes. He flushed with anger.

"You're selfish, ungrateful, and irresponsible," he said, and walked out of his office to the pressroom.

The words stung. All he had asked of me, after all, was to do the best work I could. I felt I had done it.

But the supplement, as I failed to see, was just as much Leigh Reilly's business as mine. When I began it, deliberately using it for free opinion, I at once put him on his mettle. It was not that either he or I were adopting shock tactics, taking book criticism as a convenient means of stirring the bourgeois in his lair on moot questions of sex, religion, economics, politics, and all that. Leigh Reilly was perfectly aware, I think, that the "transvaluation of values" was a necessary sequel to the fact that, on the one hand, clergymen had become fossils, and, on the other, business had become ruthless. But if the *Post* was not the medium for iconoclasm, how far could it go in breaking the entente with "the family trade"? The minute our book criticism dealt with reality on sober terms, then the paper's publisher and the business office would surely take it up with the managing editor, since it might affect advertising or circulation. And why "take a loss" if sharpshooting was not the attraction we were offering? The right reviewer on a paper of big circulation should share the current estimate of wholesomeness, should purr or claw by instinct, and should never offend "the damned old ladies" who read the paper to be soothed. Why put obstacles in the way of circulation when to lather mediocre books with praise and deprecate irregularity was the first rule in the family trade?

But Leigh Reilly took the brunt of whatever objections the business office or the paper's publisher made. He gave me my head. He knew I was not adopting shock tactics for the fun of it. He was not considering moot questions to be used as topics to be subordinated to showmanship. He put me on my mettle to deal with them, and to the business office he said, "Hands off!" As a result there was not a publishing house in New York that had not some man in it that welcomed the *Post*. The Friday circulation went up considerably, perhaps by 25 percent. But having initiated and protected this experiment, Leigh Reilly was naturally eager to have it strengthened as a feature of the paper. It takes time to do such things. And he saw my decision to resign as a shocking disloyalty. Was it for this he had fought our battles?

On the last page of his *Essay on Man*, Ernst Cassirer concludes that "human culture as a whole may be described as the process of man's progressive self-liberation." It was really this that made me leave the *Post*. And I took a simple method for self-liberation. I put an advertisement in a newspaper published in Madison, Wisconsin, saying I wanted to live on a farm, and would pay $10 a week for board and lodging.

My savings were very small, but I thought they would cover the period in which I would write a novel. When word of this novel had reached New York publishers, fourteen of them wrote to me for a chance to look at it. At the time I did not know enough to ask one of them for an advance; I did not know what a publisher's advance was.

Some of my Chicago friends thought me foolish to leave the *Post*. I was only 28 and they felt that I had begun to make the

Review count for something. It was in fact a serious step, since it meant cutting my economic lifeline. If I lost my gamble I would have to go back on a payroll.

But misery is one way of living so intensely in the present that the future is wiped out, and apart from the *Post* I was an unhappy human being. In such a state who cares about his economic lifeline? I had reached a terminal, and at the end of this line I saw nothing clearly ahead. I was forced to retreat and collect myself.

But it might be well to define the feelings of a literary journalist in any event. A good critic who writes regularly for a daily or a weekly has the job of reading current books and telling a discriminating public what it should read. He stands in a judicial relation to the various men and women that this involves, to the firm that publishes a book and advertises it, to his own paper, to the author, and to the public. But when all is said, literary discrimination is his real task, as it relates to current books and current readers. He is, in a manner of speaking, not a specialist or a worker in the laboratory. He is, in a broad sense, a general practitioner.

Many specialists delimit the general practitioner, feeling he should regard himself as a clerk at an information desk, a hyphen between the patient and the specialist. In literature as in medicine, beyond question, the popular field cannot include the finest appraisals, and on the lowest popular level you are down to the effrontery of patent medicines. But as between such rough and ready commerce and the ultimate verdict of a specialist, the newspaper critic can be an extremely important guide to the public, provided he can judge for himself and convey the grounds on which he judges. If he conceals his norms of judgment, being, let us say a fanatic communist, a fascist, an atheist, a Catholic, or a psychoanalyst, he misleads those readers who do not take his master key into account, and his partisanship may even warp him. But in general his worst defect is an inclination to give the public what the publishers want and commend it without any feeling for the scope of literature outside the immediate fashion or season. Since fortunes are made in bookselling by turning the public into a mob and making it buy books like hot cakes, the critic is particularly in danger of contagion from the authors who play on the public, the publishers who abet them, and his own business office that is looking for advertising. To write for the public at all, in a daily or weekly, he must have some journalism in him, some capacity for contagion, and some preoccupation with the here and now. But unless he is a cultivated man, he cannot discriminate. And if he is able to discriminate, he will very likely want to escape from the trammels of journalism. The delicate task of good judgment is so exacting that unless the public really values it, and pays for its support, the critic is deprived of the means by which his faculty can be cultivated. Either he has to sell his discrimination to publishers who can turn it into money, or he has to join the subsidized—teachers, clergymen, and research workers—or he has to diversify his criticism with all the seductions and attractions of which he is capable.

Of course he can fascinate a select public by disclosing how he, as an artist, would have surmounted all the limitations of the work in hand. Bernard Shaw, a creator rather than a critic, made the most excellent newspaper copy. His motto was *l'audace*, and, disregarding the author's creative intention, which he was formally supposed to elicit, he made it clear what his own intention would have been, thus energizing his readers and diverting them to Shaw. The ultimate bearing of a work of art was not necessarily its bearing on Shaw, but he somehow brought everything to this measuring stick—Ibsen, Wagner, Shakespeare, Jones, Wilde, and Pinero—and more exciting or bracing shoptalk could not be imagined. It ranks as *obiter dicta*, not as judicial. Even Macaulay, the foremost in his era and perhaps the most magnificent in his endowment, was not less abounding in his own sense. He slanted all his criticism and made his mark by doing it. Only the French critics, so far as I know, could be sufficiently sure of a public to weigh judgment for it as a function of contemporary French literature and in this way having an immeasurable significance as a factor in French self-liberation.

But the plight of a young critic in America, discriminating about other people's work while economically unprepared to undertake his own, was all the more difficult because he did not at that time have a loyal Princeton, a Harvard, a Sewanee to reverberate his words and discern his emphasis. The very fact that he took America, not primarily as subject matter for his ambition but as an experience in which he thoroughly participated, could only divide him from the literary cliques and claques that base themselves on shared ambition. To go it alone was his evident necessity, even if it took him to Japan, as it did that remarkable fugitive from the undiscriminating, Lafcadio Hearn, who could have been an invaluable American critic.

The criticism of society, American capitalist society, was one obvious approach to self-liberation, but for my part I could not espouse the idea of a society in which the state was to prescribe the norms of judgment. Unless individuals were extremely wary about state servants who concentrated power, unless these servants could be scrutinized before appointment, and recalled or dismissed, it was my conviction that we'd have Bismarcks to deal with and all the bureaucrats through whom a Bismarck operates.

Insecurity gnaws one's nerves, and I regretted to have no income—just a few hundred dollars to nibble into. But no one owed me a living. I had been given an education. Till I was seventeen I didn't have to fend for myself. If I were to avoid the usual fate of a man without capital, being compelled to drudge for the benefit of someone else who preferred my services to my development, I must use some initiative. On the *Post* I had done this. I had lavished my strength on the *Review* to the point of exhaustion. But since journalism in Chicago came down to freedom and little money, or money and little freedom, I preferred to get out. I wanted both money and freedom, if it were humanly possible. And that, it seemed to me, is exactly what a capitalist society can give a writer of books, provided he is nimble—like, let us say, Harold J. Laski who was a highly successful author who was completely free to express himself. It is the reward of an author's first requirement, initiative.

I got one answer to my advertisement in the Madison newspaper for board and lodging on a farm. It was from a man named Latham, so I took the train to Madison.

I got off en route at a small town; life on the train had been crowded, and this was a chance to be alone, to get away from people. I hurried away from the settlement, and soon I had left it behind. The sun was still high, that late afternoon sun which was beginning to take the downward slope, and the plateau to which I had gradually mounted met the vastness of the sky with a bold and simple serenity of its own. There were no trees in the landscape, and no trace of man. The wind from the south combed the contours of the ground and bent the short grass that trembled and vibrated under its pressure with the glisten of the sun and the whistle of the wind in it.

I sat on the bare ground and gazed to the horizon. I had never before had such a sense of space. The light from the sky was as steady and relentless as the wind. And apart from these two presences, and the folding of the earth's undulating surfaces, I felt remoteness from my familiar world and the nearness of a great land that was as untouched as the future. It was neither empty nor bleak. It was new. But this was the newness of a sparse and unrelenting expanse, as clear as a sword, that swept as far as the eye could follow and offered itself to the unflinching.

Its peace was immeasurable, and after the fever of these last days I could welcome it. As the light of the sky more amber, however, the cool of the wind penetrated my marrow, and I stood up to begin walking again. A single bird flew down at some distance from me, and this was the only sign of life I saw. We shared the immensity between us. It was beyond my power to match myself against it, but by submitting to it, I kept it from overwhelming me. It had a force of its own, like the force of a supreme innocence that one must share if one is to absorb it. The earth seemed to roll under a seeing sky, and the wind streamed between them, keen and unceasing. I was but a leaf that fluttered in it. It was as if I had opened a door on the edge of my existence and gazed on a sphere beyond my ken—a virgin world that neither excluded nor invited me. It was aloof and beautiful.

Few moments are imperishable. This was one. I can see the light on those blades of grass and feel the tongue of the wind. It was a new world to me.

My farmer, Cuthbert Latham, was an English gentleman. He too had seen an advertisement in a paper, in the *Times* of London. "Estate in Wisconsin: hunting, shooting, fishing," so he and his English bride came to Wisconsin to live like gentry on a seventy acre farm.

I came in October, but the winter of 1911 was a snorter. It was 25 degrees below zero for three weeks. So cold was it in the upstairs bedroom that the water in the pitcher froze nearly solid. The morning fire in the stove was just a rosebud in a vase of creamy ashes. Outside, perched in a cottonwood tree, there would be a hen, frozen stiff. Actually so cold was it that a calf in the stall lost all four hooves.

"Oh, Cuthbert," said Mrs. Latham, "how could you?" That was the day he announced he had killed the calf.

"You would do it yourself," he answered mournfully. "The poor beast's hooves were gone."

The farmhouse had gentility inside. I remember when Janet Fairban Chicago swept out in a motor one afternoon to look me up; the farmhouse seemed actually to shrink. But it housed a family of gentle and charming natures; none could rival them. Cuthbert was from Oldham, as I recollect. He was thin, slow-spoken, upright—and uprooted. His wife was a brisk, matronly, black-eyed little woman with red cheeks and a short, upturned upper lip and coal-black hair. She was like a black cherry, and she was a mine of amazingly Victorian sentiments and a gushing flow of exclamation. Cuthbert had the obstinacy of an overworked farmer who would not be beaten by the game. Up at five every morning, he was woe-begone with fatigue by nightfall. But on Saturday nights we'd gather around the piano—the father, the mother, and the three young daughters—and we'd go through a sheaf of songs. The eldest, Gladys, taught school but was engaged to marry. The youngest, Gwen, was to go to the university. She was attending high school with the third of the sisters whose name was Nellie.

It was undulating dairy country but with wooded lots that gave it poetry. I enjoyed being alone and avoided trampled corn stalks and hungry cattle. I went for long walks, or chopped wood, or did something strenuous to counteract the superb meals provided by Mrs. Latham. She was a hostess who could not do enough for her boarder. And the boarder, bloated like an alderman, would sit down at his work table and vainly try to concoct a novel. I still have three chapters of it somewhere. It had the bloom of literary innocence. Framework, work in the tobacco shed, work with the pigs or the 18 cattle—no, I did not attempt it. I doubt if it would have been permitted.

We used to have the devil's own arguments about politics, Mr. Latham and I. Though tobacco had fallen from six cents to about two, he was still a conservative. I was all for LaFollette. I went in to have a look at the red brick university with its candid atmosphere under Mr. Charles Van Hise, and I seem to recall some words of wisdom by Professor E.A. Ross. I had a grand free talk with Charles McCarthy in an airy library room. I knew a little about the Irish cooperatives, and I can still feel the breeze and realism of his personality and the high liveliness in his voice. Horace Plunkett, ten years later, proposed (in vain) that the Rockefeller Fund give me the chance to write his life. But at that time I was a loafer. I absorbed the dignity of the Capitol, the good proportions of the placid square about it, and the serenity and sparkle of Madison that always gave a lift to my spirits. And I stopped at a new hotel that was as expressionless as an egg.

One night Mr. Latham and I went by sleigh into Madison to hear an address by a presidential aspirant named Woodrow Wilson. Even Mr. Latham had to admit that it was powerful and persuasive. We were much moved by it. I was reading a little tome at that time called *Creative Evolution* by Bergson, and I kind of thought Woodrow Wilson in some ways was in need of my intellectual help, but apart from this I was for him. And until our horse bolted at Syene station on our way home, spilling us into the soft snowdrifts, we enjoyed the clean air we had brought from Woodrow Wilson, as much as the crisp beauty of the night.

In that farmhouse on the lane, I had every comfort. I had brought with me a marvelous folding tub. Mrs. Latham would melt down snow and heat it. I'd carry it up in buckets. Then I'd have a long bath in warm snow water, nothing more velvety. And then, with many dippings of the bucket, I'd empty it out of the window. I left that tub, with a complete *Century Dictionary*, when I departed from the farm. My bump of private property was not yet fully developed.

It was sad to leave in the spring, but I had word that my father was gravely ill, and I wanted to be with him in Ireland. When I was back in America, I visited Milwaukee in 1915 to see Victor Berger and to interview Leo Stern. I returned to Madison to look up my old friends and, to my astonishment, I found the Lathams no longer on the farm. They had moved into Madison, and when I at last got to their house, only Mrs. Latham was at home. It was perhaps the most shocking visit I ever paid. These people had been bludgeoned by fate with unbelievable cruelty. The great tobacco shed had been blown down by a hurricane. The farm had had to be sold. Nellie had died of cancer at the age of twenty. Gladys had had an accident with an iron heated by oil and burned to death. All this, and more, was narrated to me by Mrs. Latham, her eyes big with sorrow and reproach. What had they done? It was a question Job might have asked. And so I left the Lathams.

Yet that winter under their roof, in the light bright room above, in the shadowed rooms below, at the long table with the Englishwoman cooking such ham, such eggs, such slabs of buttered toast, with rich cream for the coffee, grapefruit, and all the rest while the straw-haired Gwen or the fawn-eyed Gladys listened, and Mr. Latham waited to light his pipe, so enamored of his daughters, so baffled by his estate—it lingers in memory like a crystal day. We had many a laugh and many a dispute. Just one family in Wisconsin and a boarder at $10 a week.

Politics

In the spring of 1912 I had gone home to Kilkenny to be with my father who was gravely ill with cancer. When he seemed to be recovering I returned to America, where my friend John Quinn had invited me to go with him as his secretary to the Baltimore Convention of the Democratic Party.

I did not particularly want to go to Baltimore, being still in an emotional uproar which I had in vain tried to soothe into a novel. I was too close to it. So I thought it might distract me to join Quinn. It was not for profit. He was only going to pay my room rent.

It was a sizzling afternoon when I arrived. The streets were surging with newcomers who stepped off the sidewalks into the baking sun and looped under the noses of bonneted horses and around fuming cars. Under their straw hats or fedoras many of these strangers had hung handkerchiefs to ward off the sun; some of them slung their coats on their arms and walked in boldly striped shirts; fat, dissolving men carried big palm fans. Streaming in contrary directions with the minimum of agreement, the crowds swarmed with a joyous disregard of order; motor horns and the grind of wheels and the shouts of drivers were punctuated by the insanely vehement clang of impeded street cars.

It was Thomas Fortune Ryan, Quinn's star client, who had got him a place on the New York State delegation. I was glad to spy him in the crowded lobby of the hotel, but I had hardly checked in before he ordered me to go and find a Major Paddock from Maryland.

"Where'll I find him?"

"Christ, I don't know. *Find* him, Hackett, that's all. He's in Baltimore somewhere, that's all we know. Bring him with you and keep him till I come. See you later." And with a bang of the outer door he left me.

For an hour and a quarter I went the round of hotels, but I had to return empty-handed. I found Quinn confabbing with a thin, lugubrious, secretive-looking statesman, Major Paddock of Maryland.

"Found him myself, Hackett," Quinn waved from his chair. "Now get Washington for me on the wire, I want to speak to Senator Waterman, at his home. Meet Mr. Hackett, Major Paddock."

The Major gave me the most mournful of glances and extended the limpest of hands.

"Order a couple of highballs and some Corona Coronas," gestured Quinn. "Bring a highball for yourself—excuse me, Major, look here, Hackett." He came over and put his arm around my shoulder. "Talk low, don't let this son of a bitch know a thing, get hold of Iowa for me and Ohio. Puhlman and McIntire. Put 'em in 823. All right, Hackett," in a firm loud tone, "that's fine. Good luck to you," and he gallantly opened the door.

"Highballs, highballs, highballs," I muttered to myself, churning rebelliously at this humble mission as I walked down from the eighth floor, the elevators being overcrowded. Highballs, Waterman, Puhlman, McIntire—this chain of words kept me going till I reached the bar. In the bar I ran up against solid wedges of thirsty humanity, drinks travelling overhead from the counter to distant corners where wagged a recipient hand. In the roar of this drought, I tried in vain to order highballs. Men laughed at me out of their blistering lips.

I could not get Corona Coronas. I had to be content with

Lillian Russells. Then I wove my way to the telephone desk where a troop of hot human beings surrounded a wild-haired Southern belle. In the frenzy of their demands, she had lost her canebelt drawl, her languorous glances, her clinging femininity, her coiffure. She humped her back and screamed at Central like a blue jay. I fled. Then I heard someone say, "Hello, Mr. Hackett." I turned; it was Tim, one of my Irish office-boy friends. I seized his hand. "Tim, you know everything. Where can I get hold of Colonel Puhlman and Judge McIntire?"

"Hotel Rolly, 208 and 345," replied Tim offhandedly. "D'you want them? I was talking to McIntire meself fifteen minutes ago."

"Yes, we want them, Mr. Quinn and myself, room . . ."

"828, I'll do that for you."

"And where can I phone Senator Waterman?"

"You want to call up Washington. Aw, you tried the switchboard. The girl's bughouse. Go round to the Rolly, it's nice and quiet. They have a man operator."

"Look, Tim," I said, trying to make it sound as if I were sharing a privilege with him, "where can I get a few highballs?"

"Say, Mr. Quinn must be getting shorthanded. I'll be getting McIntire and that other guy, and then I'll bring the highballs. That's all right."

Tim pulled his cap even lower on his thin white face and mooched away.

It was not until after dinner that I had my introduction to the convention. It was in an "armory" or drill hall and into this were packed the delegates from all the states, the delegates' alternates, the leaders, the Press, the police, and the public. It was an enormous crowd and a hot crowd, so hot that it almost melted. This evening's session was to be taken up with balloting, and Quinn had told me to be on hand "on the floor of the convention."

I was plaintive. "How am I to get in?"

"Get in? Haven't you got two feet? Walk in!"

"But I'm not a delegate, I haven't a ticket."

"Where's your nerve? Be on the floor of the convention at seven-thirty."

As I approached the delegates' entrance in the golden evening light, it seemed to me I was like a foot passenger looking for a seat in a stream of brutal motors that were already under way. In the dust, the noise, the speed, and the smell, my head was already spinning. I feared the doorman I'd have to face; soon he'd catch on, I told myself, if I weren't too deafened and baffled.

"Where's your ticket?"

I mumbled something unintelligibly. Luck came to my aid. "Hey, move in, move in, can't you, don't block the passage!" Someone pushed me into the hall. In a haze I went up the center aisle, among the totem poles of the delegations, stopping at the one labelled New York. Here I was. I felt I was rather smart after all.

Nearly everyone around me in the big hall was noise-drunk. Great blobs of illumination fell on me from the roof, papers fluttered in the air, and men in red firemen's shirts yelled distractedly in the galleries. It was like the inside of a frenzied kettledrum. I sat down on a varnished kitchen chair in the row directly behind the head of the delegation. No one paid any attention to me; the chairs were not half-filled.

In a little while the delegates pushed in. They were red in the face, hoarse from having cheered their candidate, and full of beefsteak, asparagus, whiskey, beer, Maryland strawberries, coffee, and cigars. They were astonishingly hearty and good-natured, the drill sergeants and the stable sergeants of New York politics. They were enjoying the mighty hullabaloo, glad to be away from work and away from home.

In order to increase the excitement, hired noisemakers jammed the galleries ready to begin a stampede at the right moment. They had brought whistles with them, and clakers, and all sorts of noise producers, if their throats and their heels could not make noise enough. To rival them, the volunteers and professionals on the progressive side were ready to demonstrate. They stopped occasionally, when a statesman took the platform to say something, but even then their noise came through his oration like a strong light through a worn blind.

Quinn tapped me on the shoulder. He spoke almost kindly. "Come here." In the aisle he said, "Glad you got in. This balloting means nothing; we have to keep on balloting to employ the suckers while we try to get together on our Man. Our man has an irreducible minimum, remember that. But I'll explain in the morning. Come out in the lobby now; I want to tell you something."

Down the aisle, his chin in the air, his white coattails flying, Quinn led the way. He loved it, and his figure was curiously racy and spirited. He was working for an outsider; Waterman mightn't win, but there was a big chance against the opinionated popular favorite, and then who would be attorney general? Already his chest was slightly inflated. He might even be in the cabinet.

In the hall, however, he swerved and his face darkened.

"They're double-crossing us," he told me in a sensational whisper. "You see in there, the telephone booths? I have a man you don't know in the booth next to the Wilson man. He's tapping the wire, and I know. We're being double-crossed." He looked at me with marvelous Machiavellian eyes. "Now, keep your mouth shut, watch everything you say when you get Waterman on the wire. Refer to me as 'Your man.' Say, 'Your man told me to tell you'—understand?"

"Blah, blah, blah-h-h," came the noise from the convention hall into the brown empty little entrance hall where they were talking. A tiny man with twinkling eyes and a face like Punch had come out of the convention, just as if he had stepped from behind the cash register without his customary apron, and was about to ask politely, "what's yours, ma'am?"

"Close the door, for God's sake, we can't hear a word," Quinn snapped. Then he identified the newcomer. It was the Boston boss. "Why, hello," and he went to him with outstretched hand.

The two Democratic captains conferred, as I stood apart. I could hear, "Sure! Yeh, that's right. That's a fact. Oh, indeed." But no kernel.

"Blah, blah, blahhhh," again the big door was opened. A sallow man, eyes on the ground, was leaving the hall, deeply preoccupied. He was another political captain, acid-bitten with ambition.

"Hello, McMurdie," cried Quinn. "Do you throw in the sponge?"

McMurdie parried with a sarcastic smile.

"Blaaaaaaah," the sound escaped from the arena. A wild young man rushed out, brushing the door wide open. "Bryan is speaking, Bryan is on the platform!"

Quinn turned to me abruptly. "Go on in, Hackett, and hear what the big wind has to say," and he went back to his talk with the pocket boss.

I reentered the hall which had fallen almost still. Every pink face in sight was fronting to the platform. A baldish man was speaking, an elderly, square-cut, semi-ecclesiastical man, with a black string-tie and a wide histrionic mouth. He was orating proudly with perspiration on his brow. I was in the aisle; I could not disturb the New York delegation. They were listening as if sitting for their photographs, a strained solemnity filming their faces. But something in the performance was lacking. The man on the platform drew up oratory from his depths, but it was a stale oratory; it had no inspiration. He lashed himself, conscious of it, he flourished in the old manner, he exhibited his muscle, he repeated his classic blows, but he was like an antiquated prize fighter whose fire is dead. A ripple of relief ran through the Tammany men; one by one they relaxed, and a smile flickered from one sharp eye to another. For fear of some accident they dared not laugh outright, but they were comforted. Soon the Lion of Judah would be a hearth rug.

Quinn was still in the hall, cornered by a tallowy young man who was a son of the star client. Quinn was withdrawing inch by inch, at last escaping. "My God!" he exclaimed to me in a tone enormously aggrieved, "he has tuberculosis, and he was breathing on me!"

"He has tuberculosis?" I was shocked. The poor fellow.

"Sure, he has it, but that's all the more reason he oughtn't to breathe right in my face. My God, some people have no *feeling*!" A kind of panic, a fear of disease, ran over Quinn's thin face. In a moment the spasm exhausted itself. "Come on," he said quite cheerfully, "there's going to be a conference in a minute."

We walked towards the directors' rooms. A group of men was gathering, the bosses of the party, to make a deal. I was surprised to see how deferentially Quinn was greeting them. There were Catholic Irish from the big immigrant cities of Chicago, Boston, and New York; Protestant Irish and stoutly Orange from Indiana and West Virginia. The green and the orange were here to do business, as was their habit, behind closed doors.

It was a gathering of energized men. The Chicago leader, Garrett Burke, was a stumpy man whose heavy head lurched forward and who, out of a hot, genial face, peered with crafty eyes. The Boston man, of impish intelligence, looked oddly perky beside him. The New York boss was plumpish, with a face the color and texture of a Frankfurter sausage. His mouth was tightened into a pained smile by an invisible drawstring, and he had a suspicious blue eye. He wore an ill-fitting, expensive straw hat.

These were the heads of the wholesale vote business, the men who delivered immigrant votes in quantity. Experienced in municipal politics and in private political war, they were so new in the great game of imposing on the convention a candidate of their own making that they had the air of being a little baffled. They were handicapped by local points of view.

Quinn followed them, while I cooled myself in the hall. After a while he came back and announced that he had to have a talk with Thomas Fortune Ryan and invited me to come along. We went on foot. It was a strange contrast, the city beyond the convention hall. It was like stepping into human reassurance after hours in a bearpit. And they would be there all night. Here the air was warm but bland. A young sailor went by with saucily cocked hat, a girl on his arm. The rattle of the traffic was no longer feverish; it was the ordinary light-wagon traffic of a Southern city. In spite of the noise in the armory, the city persisted in its regular existence. The sailor, the colored elegants chaffing and hopping on the corner, even the wagon drivers would have different fates because of the convention, but it was as remote from them as the obliterated sky.

Quinn did not see the town. He carried the convention with him as he and I flicked hurriedly to the discreet side street where Thomas Fortune Ryan was housing himself for the convention in the company of his editor, Leigh Merritt.

What had they been discussing before we dropped in? I can imagine it; in fact, I have done so. Here it is: They had dined late and well and alone. Comfortable in their white linen and dinner coats, they were deep in armchairs that faced the garden. They were smoking and occasionally they talked a little. The elderly financier, taciturn yet plaintively simple, was inclined to defend his candidates for the presidency. He had two of them. Garland, the first of them, had foundered, but he contended that the second, Waterman, was a long-winded creature and still in the running. Leigh Merritt, high-colored with tossed grey hair, a singular man who had made a career out of being a corporation editor rather than a corporation lawyer, did not hesitate to tell Ryan that he didn't know what he was talking about. Slow-spoken, acrid, biting, Merritt made no disguise of his opinion.

"You are on the wrong track, Tom," he had been saying, flicking his cigar and pouting his wet underlip. "As sure as I am well lubricated at this moment, Woodrow Wilson can be president and no one else. I'll explain why. Teddy is counting on the Democrats to elect him, to make him Theodore the First, Emperor of all the Americas, by the grace of Monroe. You laugh, Tom, but it's good sense. He has made 'progressivism' and 'the new Nationalism' the issue, whatever they are, and he is sure that you and I and the rest of us will be so panic-stricken by his wow-wows, we'll nominate any dummy whom we can control. Well, you're playing his hand for him. You have groomed two amiable nonentities, Garland and Waterman, and the boys at the armory are sweating to put them over, but it's a capital error. One second. Teddy had a long time to think it over in Africa, and he's shown a lot of head. He came back hungry. He's got most of his party away from his beloved Taft. All he needs is a little help from outside, and that means ourselves. If we put up a puddinghead we are beaten. We'll drive all our restless young illiterates into Teddy's voting booth, and he begins as First Consul in the third degree. Then the European war breaks; he saves the country, and he founds a dynasty. He proves he's the real thing, according to the Bible and Plutarch's *Lives*. There's no use sending him to Elba; he swims like a spaniel. Very well. We'll have Theodore the First, Theodore the Second, the Princess Alice, Prince Consort Nicholas of Cincinnati, and God knows what. That's the plot, and there's only one way of smashing it.

"We have in the wings a spotless progressive of our own, a Democrat whose fleece is white as snow. Our only hope is the blushing Woodrow, and the Democrats are characteristically asinine if they don't turn this convention into one of the prettiest annunciations you ever saw. I don't like this long-toothed schoolma'am. Neither do you. But we have no choice."

It was at this moment, I believe, that Quinn and I were brought in. Leigh Merritt dropped his wet underlip, a little sulky at being interrupted. But Ryan in his subdued Southern way had courtesy. He hailed us pleasantly. I'm sure he looked on Quinn with the amused affection of an old hunter who has a spirited dog—a dog that is too anxious, too impetuous, and too game. As a rule Ryan neither perceived nor commented on his fellow creatures, except to chafe at them, but "a wild man" he smiled to Merritt after Quinn and I departed.

We returned to the convention. About three in the morning Quinn demanded that I should spy on two of the delegates. I was to follow them and peer through a window and see whom they were following. One of them was his own employer, Thomas Fortune Ryan. I refused; in fact, I threatened to leave, and I did pack my suitcase, but he realized that the gruelling process had been going too far, and he won me back.

The convention had adjourned at seven in the morning. The weary statesmen, saturated with tobacco smoke, rough with half-dried sweat, dirty of hand and face and body, semi-delirious with stimulants and fatigue, staggered back to their hotels and lodgings to wash up and perhaps have an hour or two sleep before, at two o'clock, the solemn task of balloting for presidential candidate should be renewed.

The next day Quinn blazed into my room. "We're sold," he said. "I've just had it out. You know Garrett Burke. The heavy-jowled, yellow-eyed fellow. He's sold us. Today he refused to do business as long as I was in the room, and he called me a 'hired lawyer.' I'm not a hired lawyer; I've told you what I am. I'm a hired gladiator. I came here for the same reason he came here, to *fight*. The law, hell. Politics, hell. It's *warfare*. This convention is warfare. The whole game of life is warfare. Sex is warfare. Business is warfare. A lot of schoolboys and insurgents and progressives and old women want that canting, long-jawed, Presbyterian hypocrite elected president. I have *his* number. He's lily-livered. Garrett Burke wants him to be president so he can carry his own state. To hell with them. Before this convention's over, I'll smash Burke's face. You hear what I say. I'll smash his face. I'll take no man's insult. I'll let no man bawl me out in front of everybody. God damn his soul."

For once Quinn allowed me to see him quiver with pain, with anguish. But he recovered in an instant. His drawn face crept into a haggard grin. "You think I'm right, eh, Hackett? He needs a good punch in the jaw."

An hour later, when Quinn slipped into his place in the New York delegation, he spoke to me behind his hand. "Did that Illinois fellow talk to the chief here?"

I nodded. "What did he say?" asked Quinn.

I'd listened carefully. "I think he said he was going over to Wilson for just two complimentary ballots. He would vote for him twice, but it wouldn't mean a thing."

"That settles it." Quinn folded his arms and ran his tongue ungracefully around inside his mouth. "Look," he said suddenly, "he's trapped us. Just the same, you go up now to Senator Bankhead and pass the word to him it is a complimentary vote, means nothing, just for two ballots. Then they'll go to Wilson on a third ballot, and the jig is up. All our people will go panicky. They'll break. They'll cave. Wait till you see."

I did go up to Senator Bankhead—as I had done several times before—and gave him the message. He was so deaf I had to take hold of his large hairy ear and shout into it. He shook me off. This was after the second complimentary ballot. He gathered up his weary body, this old man who was the head of a staunch Southern delegation, with a body that had never been so tired since the Civil War, and he climbed laboriously onto the platform. There in a few words he withdrew his candidate and threw his strength to the victor, Woodrow Wilson.

"All over. It's all over." Quinn locked his mouth.

That morning, near cockcrow, Quinn and I were privileged to sit at the same table with the chief of the New York delegation, to have a bottle of champagne.

The great boss sat mum at the white-clothed table, after I'd been introduced to him.

"What do you want, Chief?"

The little slit of a mouth opened piteously. "I asked for a cigar. Nobody gives me a cigar."

"Can't you get the Chief a cigar?" Quinn glared at me.

"Nobody gives a damn whether *I* have a smoke or not," mumbled the great politician, "and all the rest of them with cigars."

Two or three commissioners with wooden faces, seated mute around the table, removed their cigars guiltily. The Chief was mad.

As I hurried up with three cigars, Quinn took them and handed all three to the head of the Wigwam.

The Chief eyed them.

"Is anything the matter with them?" Quinn asked with a touch of alarm.

The Chief gloomily struck a match. "I'll make them do," he said grudgingly. He inserted a cigar in his tight mouth.

"Well, we have a candidate," remarked Quinn guardedly, coughing a little. "We have a candidate."

The Chief laid his doubled fist on the white tablecloth. The wooden-faced commissioners turned to look at him simultaneously. He cleared his throat and blinked his white eyelashes. "I think we all ought to be very well satisfied." He was a man of few words, most of them grammatical. The commissioners jerked their heads in assent. "Aw, here's Garrett Burke." The Chief got up heavily, smiling as he went to greet Garrett Burke, his Chicago peer.

Burke went around the table, greeting the bodyguard. My heart almost missed a beat, this was the man whose jaw John Quinn was going to smash.

"How are you?" Quinn was saying. "Well, we ought to be

very well satisfied with the result, Mr. Burke," and he returned Mr. Burke's hearty handshake.

"Fust class," said Mr. Burke, "fust class."

The New Republic

One evening in Chicago, back in 1910, when all the material was ready for my *Friday Literary Review*, I picked out a book for the front page. There was nothing more to do that week, nothing except to read the book, write a full page about it, and have it at the office by 8:00 A.M. Tug Wilson, Joe Hurley, and Lou Webb were used to me in the composing room, and they bore with little delinquencies, but the foreman, whose name also was Wilson, was made of sterner stuff. He wanted the copy in early and did not want changes at the last minute. So it was my job, after I had read the book, to think about it hard, to take a little snooze, and to get down three thousand words or so in final form, so that I could walk down the Lake Shore Drive, have breakfast in the Loop, and arrive on time at the office.

On February 18 the review was published. It was of a book called *The Promise of American Life* by one Herbert Croly. We had no photograph of him, so I had to print the portrait of Richard Brinsley Sheridan that pertained to another review, but I filled the rest of the front page with the Croly review, saying right off that he was unknown, but that, "In the long list of political books his stands out for breadth of vision, sanity of judgment, and inspiration." I was so aware of my own incompetence to pronounce on a work so grounded on intimacy with American political thinking that I did not have the courage to sign the review.

Naturally I'd long forgotten that when I stood without a job after the 1912 Democratic convention. It was then, in 1913 that I was asked by this Herbert Croly if I would join the staff of a weekly he was going to start. He had conceived the idea of a journal of opinion, more or less on the model of Massingham's *Nation* in England and Godkin's *Nation* in the United States. He had found out who wrote that review of his book, had gone out to Chicago to see if I would "do," and, though I was not there, he found I knew scores of people who could say I'd be companionable in the group he had in his mind's eye. Croly set great store on the personal association, the daily contact at the lunch table, the pleasantness and the amenity of our social gatherings. I still have the letters from Croly about my joining the staff. I named my own salary, $60 a week. The same as Walter Lippmann's, to start with. Lippmann became engaged and asked for $80, unknown to me. I was not sure of the paper's policy and wanted to be under as little obligation as possible.

Besides myself, the editorial staff consisted of Croly, Lippmann, Walter Weyl, and Philip Littell, along with Charlotte Rudyard. Herbert Croly conceived the idea, asked Lippmann to go in with him, and then the rest of us were approached in the year 1913. We met many times to work out plans in the year before it started, and then we formed an editorial board.

We began planning it a year before the 1914 war was generally dreamt of. As for money, it did not trouble us. Herbert Croly's ideas for a journal were mentioned casually to two people with a desire to do good with their money. One of them, the husband, Willard Straight, was the son of a missionary in China; he worked for J. P. Morgan & Co., but it was his wife, Dorothy Straight, who was the great heiress.

Her father, William C. Whitney, was a Yankee from the same small town in Massachusetts as Marshall Field, who rolled up a hundred million dollars more or less. Mr. Whitney rolled up many millions himself, mainly by securing the rights to run streetcars in New York, and his daughter was endowing the weekly because she believed in Mr. Croly's high-minded and broad-minded ideas. She was acting out of native goodness with motives that were limpid and beyond reproach. She reposed confidence in Croly, who did in fact inspire it. Croly's father had been on the New York *World* as an editor, and his mother under the name "Jenny June" had written soulful articles and founded Sorosis Clubs. But Herbert was a bit of a Herbert Spencer in his way. He would have been perfectly at home in the England of George Eliot and Herbert Spencer, and his grandfather was a Chartist, I believe. Socially Herbert Croly could be benign and cordial, though something of a sunflower, turning instinctively to prime sources of heat and light, but politically he was a convinced liberal and democrat. He sidled towards idealism, prudent but troubled.

He was far more of a pragmatist than Woodrow Wilson, who had a lot of the Covenanter in him. And the grand thing about pragmatism is its invitation to trial marriages. The pragmatist is not the heir of the ages, the anxious carrier of moral and intellectual primogeniture. He is the inheritor of a frontier, sometimes high and always wide and handsome, and he stakes his claim in virgin territory. He does not submit to history; he makes it, and this simply means that he trusts to his quick reactions, to his felicity, and his sure foot to improve on the traditions that he, like everyone else, had imbibed and absorbed as a matter of course, but itches to shelve so he can go one better. In the region of business enterprise, the pragmatist is one jump ahead of his competitors. In the region of the intellect, or of politics that can put intellect to work, he is one jump ahead of Reynard the Fox which qualifies him as an intellectual. If he is ten jumps ahead, he is not an intellectual. He is a pauper.

During the year we were hatching and hatching *The New Republic* weekly, the group got acquainted. Walter Lippmann had been secretary to the Socialist mayor of Schenectady, and Walter had studied with Graham Wallas, who was a sociological wizard with a long alimentary canal that could convert Marxism into good liberal chow which would be easy to absorb into the bloodstream of democracy. Graham Wallas had been Walter Lippmann's nanny, and Walter glowed with that peculiar, rather attractive heat which passed through the coils of his intelligence before it raised the temperature whenever he spoke of Graham Wallas. From Wallas he had learned how to stand away from current prejudices and presumptions. Since Walter knew next to nothing of human circumstances, except in their political bearing, it was perfectly easy for him to treat abstractions as realities and to shift from one set to another, according to the suitcase he was packing them into. Where Georges Sorel as an advocate of revolution seemed to me a monster of recklessness, to Walter he was no more abhorrent than a painter who uses mustard yellow. A little more Sorel might make a better picture. Walter was delighted to utilize Sorel for that purpose, just as an ingredient. He was himself detached, evasive, nimble, and completely irresponsible. Politics was a competition in abstractions, and his career was to be a career of selecting and recommending the best abstractions for Spring, Summer, Autumn, and Winter, for Long Island, for Washington, for Florida.

In the prenatal period there was one figure who stood out for me. This was Judge Learned B. Hand. Like Herbert Croly and Walter Lippmann and Philip Littell, he was a Harvard man, which gave him a certain homogeneity with *The New Republic* group. But Learned Hand was by no means a member of a group, let alone a herd. Without actually being a rebel, he carried the capacity for dissent to a degree that flustered the anxious round-up man in Herbert Croly, and this gift for dissent sprang from an awareness of his own processes which, to my delight, sought occasional relief in words. It had been Herbert's intention to make "B." Hand a "trustee," though God knows what that was supposed to mean—a copilot of some sort, who was expected to keep his hands off the controls. But after a short acquaintanceship with the Judge's need for disintegrating the pieties, Herbert saved himself and his magic carpet by dropping the Judge overboard. We had to integrate, not disintegrate, *The New Republic*, and B. Hand was incapable of subordinating himself to the rules of an oblique political game. Herbert Croly, after all, had been able to write two such contrasting books as *The Promise of American Life* and an official life of Mark Hanna.

One glance at Croly's rubber features was enough to show why a craggy visage like B. Hand's could not be brought into the same focus. Under black eyebrows that jutted from a ledge of forehead, B. Hand looked at his interlocutor with steady, considering, mournful eyes, and when a statement had been made to him he often began, formidably: "I should have thought . . ."

The mouth he then pushed forward was a gash in his granite face—a lugubrious, elastic feature that had in it the most melancholy of smiles and the most sudden of grins. Below this mouth, what a jaw! Great bones of cheek, grim as capital punishment, had grooves for commiseration. The deep-socketed eyes, the sulphurous skin, the tragic mouth, the bastion brow—no nobler window ever opened on a thronging interior in which temperament wrestled with intellect for honesty's sake. B. Hand had leonine magnificence in the enormous head, the lean flanks, the generous, warming disposition. He was the true American introvert, frowning on moral quackery like a furrowed sunset—and yet with a clown in him.

There was a young man in the publishing business by the name of Fred Hoppin, who was at home in it at a time when the dilettante could give it his manicured hand. Once when I mentioned Learned Hand to him he laughed incredulously. "No one could possibly live up to that facade." But the facade, rusticated through it was, was by no means adequate to express the man behind it. Had some devotee done for B. Hand what Felix

Frankfurter was to do for Justice Holmes, then might Hand's self-depreciation have been sufficiently benumbed to give his intellect and his taste free way.

As a man B. Hand was right out of Shakespeare—warmth in his veins, blandishment in his mood, caprice and gay truancy in his spirit. I don't know why he flirted with Fame without seeming to possess the Floosie, but perhaps he has nailed her down in his opinions. He was always of original mind and inexorable honesty.

I remember a dinner at the Players, a sort of christening party, where Walter Lippmann and I debated as to which of us should say something "real." Walter was tense about it. "We don't want to sit with our knees under the mahogany and pretend to agree when we don't. Why don't you, Francis, say something 'real?' " Walter was much younger than I. He was up bright and early like the sun in the South—really brilliant and wide-awake at the age of twenty-four—while I was still with faculties half-mobilized in an Irish haze at the advanced age of thirty, but the gathering was small and private and we were all in *The New Republic* family, so I took it as a possibility. "Why don't you? Go ahead."

My knees under the mahogany were not very firm when I stood up. I was no practiced figure skater on this ice arena, and what I wished to say was difficult, but someone had to say it. Learned Hand was on one side of me, Walter on the other, and they gave me courage, but I did wish I knew how to skate.

Had I known, before I opened my mouth to put my foot in it, that Elihu Root had always been William C. Whitney's attorney, I do not think I would have mentioned him, as it was Whitney's daughter who was endowing us with the purest of motives out of native nobility and goodness. But the America I loved, the America that was "real" for me since I had landed in 1901, was not the America of a Wall Street lawyer like Elihu

Root, and I wished to say so. I wished to contrast him with a figure that made intellectuals wrinkle their noses, William Jennings Bryan. I tried to say that as between the two, the man whose brain told him that "the invisible government" of the U.S.A. was its curse, but who was himself one of the architects, and the man whose brain told him next to nothing, but whose hazel-twig made him a water-finder in the desert, I should always be for a William Jennings Bryan. As for Mr. Root's America, it reminded me of a farm in Wisconsin where I saw pigs going wild chasing hens and killing them while other pigs got into the trough, and a farmer had turned to me with a twisted smile, "The quiet hogs get most of the grub!" Mr. Root seemed to me to symbolize this quiet America, and I hoped our *New Republic* would never lose sight of it.